Women in Agriculture Worldwide

Over the past two decades, existing documentation of women in the agricultural sector has surveyed topics such as agricultural restructuring and land reform, international trade agreements and food trade, land ownership and rural development and rural feminisms. Many studies have focused on either the high-income countries of the global North or the low-income countries of the global South. This separation suggests that the North has little to learn from the South, or that there is little shared commonality across the global dividing line.

Fletcher and Kubik cross this political, economic, and ideological division by drawing together authors from 5 continents. They discuss the situation for women in agriculture in 13 countries worldwide, with two chapters that cover international contexts. The authors blur the boundaries between academic and organizational authors and their contributors include university-based researchers, gender experts, development consultants, and staff of agricultural research centers and international organizations (i.e., Oxfam, the United Nations World Food Program). The common thread connecting these diverse authors is an emphasis on practical and concrete solutions to address the challenges, such as lack of access to resources and infrastructure, lack of household decision-making power, and gender biases in policymaking and leadership, still faced by women in agriculture around the world. Ongoing issues in climate change will exasperate many of these issues and several chapters also address environment and sustainability.

This book is of great interest to readers in the areas of gender studies, agriculture, policy studies, environmental studies, development and international studies.

Amber J. Fletcher is Assistant Professor in the Department of Sociology and Social Studies, University of Regina, Canada.

Wendee Kubik is Associate Professor, Centre for Women's and Gender Studies, Brock University, Canada.

Women and Sustainable Business

1. Women in Agriculture Worldwide
Key issues and practical approaches
Edited by Amber J. Fletcher and Wendee Kubik

Women in Agriculture Worldwide

Worldwide

Key issues and practical approaches

Edited by
Amber J. Fletcher and
Wendee Kubik

Routledge
Taylor & Francis Group

LONDON AND NEW YORK

First published 2017
by Routledge

2 Park Square, Milton Park, Abingdon, Oxfordshire OX14 4RN
52 Vanderbilt Avenue, New York, NY 10017

Routledge is an imprint of the Taylor & Francis Group, an informa business

First issued in paperback 2020

British Library Cataloguing in Publication Data
A catalogue record for this book is available from the British Library

Library of Congress Cataloguing in Publication Data
Names: Fletcher, Amber, editor. | Kubik, Wendee, 1951– editor.
Title: Women in agriculture worldwide : key issues and practical
approaches / edited by Amber J. Fletcher and Wendee Kubik.
Description: Abingdon, Oxon; New York, NY : Routledge, 2016.
Identifiers: LCCN 2016006565 | ISBN 9781472473080 (hardback) |
ISBN 9781315546780 (ebook)
Subjects: LCSH: Women in agriculture.
Classification: LCC HD6077.W664 2016 | DDC 338.1082–dc23
LC record available at http://lccn.loc.gov/2016006565

ISBN: 978-1-4724-7308-0 (hbk)
ISBN: 978-0-367-60531-5 (pbk)

Typeset in Times New Roman
by Out of House Publishing

Contents

Figures

Tables

Contributors

Margaret Alston, Professor and Head of the Department of Social Work; Director of the Gender, Leadership and Social Sustainability (GLASS) Research Unit, Monash University, Australia

Angie Carter, Teaching Fellow, Sociology, Augustana College, USA

Manase Kudzai Chiweshe, Centre for Development Studies, Chinhoyi University of Technology, Zimbabwe

Josephine Clarke, Postdoctoral Research Fellow, Gender, Leadership and Social Sustainability (GLASS) Research Unit, Department of Social Work, Monash University, Australia

Andrea M. Collins, Assistant Professor, Department of Environment and Resource Studies, University of Waterloo, Canada

June Corman, Professor, Department of Sociology, Brock University, Canada

Bryan Crawford-Garrett, Senior Consultant, Oxu Solutions, USA

Amber J. Fletcher, Assistant Professor, Department of Sociology and Social Studies, University of Regina, Canada

Venkatesan Gurumoorthy, Program Manager, Reliance Foundation, Sivagangai, India

Ashley Hand, Natural Resource Conservationist, Owensboro, Kentucky, United States

Carlyn James, McGill University, Canada

Jan Kainer, Associate Professor, School of Gender, Sexuality, and Women's Studies, York University, Canada

G. Kaleeswari, Nilakottai, Dindigul, India

E.D.I. Oliver King, Principal Scientist, M. S. Swaminathan Research Foundation, Chennai, India

Godbertha Kinyondo, Senior Lecturer in Economics, Mzumbe University, Dar es Salaam Business School, Tanzania

Wendee Kubik, Associate Professor, Centre for Women's and Gender Studies, Brock University, Canada

Clare Mbizule, Learning and Sharing Advisor, World Food Programme, Purchase for Progress

Andrea Moraes, Postdoctoral Researcher and Instructor, School of Nutrition, Ryerson University, Canada

Kudzai MacMillan Muzanago, Women's University in Africa, Zimbabwe

B. Raghini, Principal Scientist, M.S.Swaminathan Research Foundation, Chennai, India

Rengalakshmi Raj, Principal Coordinator, Gender and Grassroots Institutions, M.S.Swaminathan Research Foundation, Chennai, India

Cecilia Rocha, Associate Professor and Director, School of Nutrition, Ryerson University, Canada

Sabarmatee, Ph.D. Candidate, Wageningen University, Netherlands; Head, Sambhav (NGO), Odisha, India

Brian Sage, Principal, Oxu Solutions, USA

S. Abubaker Siddick, Hand in Hand, Chennai, India

Jessica Soulis, Sustainable Agriculture & Food Systems Consultant, Des Moines, Iowa, USA

Julie Théroux-Séguin, Gender, Advocacy and Communication Manager, Oxfam in Morocco

Norman Uphoff, Professor of Government and International Agriculture, and Senior Advisor, SRI International Network and Resources Center (SRI-Rice), Cornell University, NY, USA

Liette Vasseur, Professor, Department of Biological Sciences; Member, Department of Women's and Gender Studies; UNESCO Chair in Community Sustainability: From Local to Global – Brock University, Canada

Olivia Vent, SRI Liaison, Lotus Foods; former Director of Communications, Cornell International Institute for Food, Agriculture and Development (CIIFAD), Cornell University, USA

Maria-Stella Vettori, Professor, Graduate School of Business Leadership, University of South Africa, South Africa

Karin Wachter, Project Director, Institute on Domestic Violence & Sexual Assault, The University of Texas at Austin, USA

Betty Wells, Professor of Sociology and Sustainable Agriculture, Iowa State University, United States

Kerri Whittenbury, Senior Research Fellow, Gender, Leadership and Social Sustainability (GLASS) Research Unit, Monash University, Australia

Acknowledgments

The editors would like to thank Gower Publishing and Routledge for making this book possible. We are particularly grateful for the help of Kristina Abbotts, Sara Hutton, and copy editor Laura Macy. We are grateful for the support of Professor Kiymet Çaliyurt, series editor for the Women in Sustainable Business series, who invited us to produce this book for the series.

We would also like to thank Barbara James for helping us with the editing of the chapters. Her keen attention to detail and research skills enabled the book to be completed in a timely manner.

Introduction

Context and commonality

Women in agriculture worldwide

Amber J. Fletcher and Wendee Kubik

Around the world, women are important contributors to agriculture. Yet, at the same time, women are also the most marginalized farmers in the world. Their many contributions to food production are often invisible and unrecognized, despite the necessity, importance, and value of these contributions. The most recent *State of Food and Agriculture* report from the Food and Agriculture Organization of the United Nations (FAO) (2014) highlights ongoing challenges for women in agriculture, including lack of access to resources and infrastructure (resulting in lost productivity), lack of household decision-making power, and gender biases in policymaking and leadership. There is also a strong need for information about effective interventions to improve the situation for women in agriculture, including gender-based evaluations of particular policies and programs (World Bank, Food and Agriculture Organization, and International Fund for Agricultural Development 2008, 676).

This book is our contribution to a broader global effort to close the "knowledge gap" about gender in agriculture (Quisumbing et al. 2014, 5). Over the past two decades, existing anthologies related to gender in the agricultural sector have examined important topics, such as agricultural restructuring and land reform (Razavi 2002), international trade and the global food chain (Barndt 1999), land ownership and rural development in the global South (Sweetman 1999), and rural feminisms (Pini, Brandth, and Little 2014). Despite these important books (as well as a variety of scholarly articles) on women in agriculture, the rapid pace of change in this sector means that more knowledge is required. In their recent anthology, Quisumbing et al. (2014, 5) argued that, "by the end of the first decade of the twenty-first century, the evidence base on gender and agriculture remained woefully inadequate." Allen and Sachs (2007) also pointed out that, while there has been a significant amount of attention paid to the socio-cultural dimensions of gender and food (e.g., consumption and food preparation), far less attention has been paid to gender in the material aspects of food production, such as agriculture.

The importance of gender

As the title of this volume suggests, the following chapters provide gender analysis focused primarily on women in agriculture. This is not to suggest that gender is one-dimensional, nor is it meant to equate "gender" with "women." Rather, our focus on women is based on the recognition that women around the world continue to experience multiple structural inequalities in agriculture, and therefore a focus on practical strategies is needed to promote women's empowerment and equality in the sector. The authors in this collection share a commitment to recognizing and addressing ongoing gender inequalities in agriculture through their focus on women's diverse needs and responses.

Gender has been defined variously across the ontological spectrum. Definitions range from gender as the natural expression of biologically embedded differences based on physical sex (i.e., biological determinism), to a more sociological view of gender as a pattern of social relations and roles linked to reproductive bodies (e.g., Connell 2009), to a poststructuralist view of gender as a discursively constructed performance with no ontological basis in the "real" (e.g., Butler 1990). For the purpose of this book, we operate with an understanding of gender as a set of social relations and ideologies that have become embedded in – and have also come to shape – our social institutions, resource distribution systems, norms, and even individual identities and bodies. This definition recognizes both the material and ideological aspects of gender, which are interconnected and inseparable, as well as the ways gender shapes our societies at multiple levels, from the individual to the institutional. This definition also allows us to examine how gender affects agricultural women's lives at various levels, from the macro level of international or governmental policy (see for example the chapters by Collins; Moraes and Rocha, this volume) to community and household food production at the meso level (see for example the chapters by Chiweshe and Muzanago; Rengalakshmi et al.; Vasseur), and very micro-level issues like chronic pain caused by gendered farming practices (see the chapter by Vent et al.). The innovative theory of change presented by Crawford Garrett et al. offers a useful framework for this multi-level analysis.

Theorizing women's work in agriculture

This book presents practical strategies and solutions to address women's inequality in agriculture. Each chapter discusses an important intervention or makes concrete recommendations to challenge the ongoing invisibility and marginalization of women in this sector. Existing research has documented this invisibility in various contexts, and as these chapters show, it remains a persistent problem in many parts of the world. Dominant ideologies continue to naturalize agriculture as a masculine domain. In our own research, conducted in the highly industrialized agricultural context of rich countries, we have found that activities most recognized and valued as "farming" – tasks such as driving heavy equipment – are associated with men, while women's contributions to farms and farm households are more likely to be seen as peripheral, as "helping out" (Kubik 2004; Fletcher 2013). Although women in low-income countries often engage in fieldwork tasks, they are less likely than men to own, control, or hold rights to the land they farm (Lastarria-Cornhiel et al. 2014; Food and Agriculture Organization n.d.; Collins, this volume; Kinyondo, this volume). Studies have also shown gender inequality in access to labor-saving mechanized inputs. Women are more likely than men to use manual strategies, such as hand tools for harvesting and buckets for irrigation (World Bank, Food and Agriculture Organization, and International Fund for Agricultural Development 2008, 289; Van Koppen, Hope, and Colenbrander 2013).

Around the world, gendered divisions of labor also position women as responsible for other kinds of undervalued and invisible work: domestic work, caregiving work, and household food provision. For women in agriculture, these responsibilities exist in addition to farm work, and lines between home and farm are often blurred (Kubik 2004). Across the North and South, farm women's work defies categorization: consider the case of a Canadian prairie farm woman who drives 40 minutes each way, across the large expanse of an ever-growing and ever more industrialized family farm, to deliver meals to the field for farm workers (Fletcher 2013). Is this domestic work or farm work? In low-income countries, women often engage in household-based subsistence agriculture, such as the production of livestock and vegetables for home consumption, to support their families' nutritional needs. Such activities blur the lines between home and farm, illustrating the interconnection and inseparability of production and social reproduction.

The concept of social reproduction, drawn from feminist political economy, usefully illustrates the centrality of unwaged tasks – such as domestic food preparation and the raising of children, tasks which are most often done by women – to the ongoing reproduction of broader economic and social systems (Bezanson and Luxton 2006; Bakker 2007). While the activities encompassed by the concept of social reproduction are usually unwaged and seen as economically "unproductive," feminist theorizing has shown the true importance of these tasks to productive systems, thus challenging the binary division between production and reproduction. However, in agriculture the situation is more complex and less theoretically clear-cut. On family farms, there is often little separation between "waged" and "unwaged" labor, between "work" and "home." This situation complicates many of our existing feminist theories on work.

Nonetheless, the theoretical insights from feminist political economy shed light on a similar interdependence between production system and household system in agriculture. The chapters in this volume illustrate the important relationships between households and agricultural production. Agriculture is essential for the ongoing survival of rural and urban households, and around the world, agriculture remains a primarily household-based activity that is, in many ways, sustained by the farm family (Friedmann 1978). These interconnected and interdependent systems reflect the ongoing importance of both production and social reproduction. At the same time, as feminist theorists have shown, it is crucial to think beyond simply the household level. Gendered power relations exist within households and within agriculture. Many demographic and household surveys collect only household-level information, and the resulting lack of sex-disaggregated data has limited our knowledge base on gender and agriculture. It is crucial, then, to "lift the roof off the household": to view the gendered dimensions of power operating within agricultural households (Seager 2014, 275). The multiple levels and multiple contexts in which gender is part of agriculture become a key theme throughout this book.

Local contributions, global insights

This volume draws together authors from five continents. Their chapters discuss the situation for women in agriculture in 13 countries worldwide, with two chapters covering international contexts. Many of the existing books and reports about women and agriculture have focused on *either* high-income countries of the global North or low-income countries of the global South. Context is indeed important: extreme variation and diversity can be found in agricultural practices across different regions, countries, and even communities, and global economic inequality is an important determinant of agricultural producers' livelihoods and wellbeing around the world. Contextual considerations are important for understanding the best strategies and interventions for making change in a particular location. It is often useful, therefore, to view solutions in applied contexts or case studies. Accordingly, each chapter in this book examines a particular context, whether a specific country, region, or even a particular agricultural intervention or program. Many constitute the often-neglected evaluation phase of policies or programs, which can offer important insights and lessons. For this reason, we believe the book is unique and offers an important perspective.

Despite the importance of context, the North/South separation underpinning much of the literature often implicitly assumes that "developed" countries have little to learn from those in "developing" countries, or that there is little commonality across the global dividing line. This book is intentionally positioned at the intersection of context and commonality. We avoid a development discourse that promotes the highly industrialized agricultural paradigm currently dominant in many Northern countries as an ideal for all; in fact, several authors provide critical analysis of this paradigm (see the chapters by Clarke and Alston; Corman and Kubik). The authors in this text emphasize instead the contributions being made in a variety of countries. Although we identify ongoing gendered inequalities and problems, we emphasize effective strategies and innovations from around the world.

Diverse perspectives, concrete solutions

Although a significant amount of scholarly literature has identified key issues for women in the agriculture sector and has called for action and solutions, there is a tendency in such scholarly literature to sidestep a conversation about practical and concrete solutions to the problems. In contrast, practitioners and agricultural experts (including farm women around the world) have developed innovative solutions that may not reach the published literature. It is our contention that a focus on practical solutions can inform our theorizing about women in agriculture more broadly. Our goal is to present detailed contextual case studies with far-reaching implications: to address common problems through contextual insights. This conversation is most productive when it crosses organizational boundaries. Accordingly, contributors to this volume include university-based researchers, gender experts, agricultural consultants, and staff of agricultural research centers and international organizations (i.e., Oxfam, the United Nations World Food Programme). In fact, several chapters (see Carter et al.; Crawford-Garrett et al.; Vent, Sabarmatee, and Uphoff) represent collaborations between academic researchers and organizational experts working together on key problems. The common thread connecting these diverse authors is an emphasis on practical and concrete solutions.

Focusing on solutions means emphasizing agency and women's diverse knowledge. Women play a crucial role in agricultural innovation and new, beneficial practices. An emphasis on women's agency will re-frame the conversation about women in agriculture around the world. In this vein, many authors bring the voices of farm women directly to their chapters. The discussion contained in these pages is broadly framed by an emphasis on agency and the possibility of positive change.

Emphasizing sustainability

Sustainability is a pressing issue for the future of agriculture. Readers will notice another common thread running through this volume: sustainability in its three major forms – social, environmental, and economic. This book is part of a series with the theme "Women in Sustainable Business," edited by Professor Kiymet Çaliyurt. In keeping with this theme, each chapter in the book addresses an aspect of sustainability in agriculture, either explicitly or implicitly. Many of the chapters speak to social sustainability, a concept that (although variously defined) tends to promote principles like equity, democracy, strong social safety nets, and social interconnectedness as crucial for the long-term wellbeing of people and communities. Although social sustainability does not automatically translate into environmental sustainability (Fletcher 2016; Vallance, Perkins, and Dixon 2011), the two are often connected. All societies are ultimately dependent on the natural environment for their very existence; however, some writers have gone further to argue that "social sustainability is the only bedrock on which meaningful environmental sustainability can be grounded" (Dillard, Dujon, and King 2009, 1). Several of the authors in this collection (see for example Alston and Whittenbury; Clarke and Alston; Corman and Kubik) question the paradigm of industrialized agriculture so prevalent in the global North – a paradigm that privileges economic growth over other kinds of sustainability.

Alternative economic formations are possible, as authors like Carter et al. and Kainer (this volume) point out.

Our approach in this book suggests that we can create more sustainable agricultural societies and economies. We can create systems where all farmers have the resources to engage in environmentally sustainable practices that also sustain their families, communities, and livelihoods. A key step in this direction is to challenge global power relations that disadvantage farm families, while paying attention to the unequal power relations between men and women *within* those families. The chapters that follow speak volumes about the transformation of agriculture and the eventual elimination of gender inequality – one practical solution at a time.

The collection

Part I

Our book begins by discussing some ongoing equality issues that continue to affect women in agriculture. The chapters in this section go beyond simple issue identification, however; the authors highlight key strategies for addressing these inequality issues that have existed for far too long. In a chapter that sets the stage for the book's sustainability theme, Josephine Clarke and Margaret Alston discuss key challenges for social sustainability in Australian agriculture. Examining the gendered phenomenon of farm exits, the authors suggest that gender mainstreaming in agricultural policy can be an effective and transformative solution.

Also writing from the global North, June Corman and Wendee Kubik examine the changing nature of farm women's work in relation to the contemporary changes facing agricultural producers (i.e., industrial agricultural production, shifting farm ownership patterns, climate change, privatization of market relations, globalization, and the aging of the farm population). Corman and Kubik discuss how these changes may influence the future lives of farm women and their farms and the need for reliable indicators and knowledge regarding farm women's lives.

Maria-Stella Vettori's chapter reveals the ongoing legal and social discrimination against farm workers in South Africa, a phenomenon with important gendered dimensions. Vettori weaves together detailed legal analysis with revealing (and sometimes shocking) stories to shed light on important human rights issues for agricultural workers. Her discussion reveals the important intersections of gender, race, and class.

In their gender analysis of rice production methods, Olivia Vent, Sabarmatee, and Norman Uphoff illustrate how small-scale changes in production can have large-scale impacts on women's lives. After a revealing discussion about the sex-specific health impacts of conventional rice production, their chapter provides one of the first known gendered analyses of the System of Rice Intensification (SRI), a production method now being applied to a variety of crops around the world.

Part II

Section II is based on the recognition that agriculture is about more than productivity and profits. The chapters in this section highlight issues of sustainability and food security – issues often subsumed beneath the dominant contemporary discourses of industrialization and productivism as a way to "feed the world." The authors in this section challenge the dominant discourse, positing an alternative bottom line that emphasizes environmental responsibility, social sustainability, nutrition, and food security. In these chapters, we see the important contributions that can be made through localized and household efforts. Margaret Alston and Kerri Whittenbury examine how women's inequality undermines food security in Bangladesh and Lao PDR. The authors argue that macro-level trends such as outmigration and modernization have increased women's responsibility for agricultural production, but not necessarily their recognition as producers. Women's lack of access to agricultural resources thus serves to undermine food security in these contexts. Solutions to this challenge lie in gender mainstreaming and facilitating an enabling environment for women as food producers.

The focus on food security continues with a chapter by Manase Kudzai Chiweshe and Kudzai MacMillan Muzanago, who illustrate that agriculture is not always only rural: in Zimbabwe's urban spaces, women are sustaining their families and gaining financial independence by growing potatoes in sacks. Recognizing socio-economic class as an important intersection in the experience of urban potato farming, the authors point out the need for effective policy to ensure that even the poorest urban households have access to necessary inputs.

Taking us to Burkina Faso, Liette Vasseur illustrates how school gardens can strengthen both food security and social capital. The positive effects of the garden go far beyond nutrition, leading to improved educational outcomes for students and greater community cohesion. Vasseur's chapter speaks to the reclamation of valuable traditional practices that had been lost, submerged beneath an emphasis on agro-chemicals as the solution to production.

The chapter by Rengalakshmi Raj and colleagues similarly addresses the tension between traditional knowledge and modernist approaches. The authors discuss the negative health implications of market-oriented agriculture for the *Malyali* people in southern India. The authors describe a participatory garden initiative that successfully empowered women by reinvigorating their traditional knowledge and roles.

Part III

The third section of the book explores the potential and pitfalls of finance and policy for women's empowerment in agriculture. The section opens with a chapter by Andrea Collins, who examines two key tensions underlying gender-attentive international policy: formal versus substantive rights, and international policy versus customary practices. Analyzing the FAO's

Voluntary Guidelines on the Responsible Governance of Tenure of Land, Fisheries and Forests through a Tanzanian case study, Collins explores the tension between formal policy commitments to gender equality and the challenges of meaningful implementation.

Godbertha Kinyondo similarly highlights the difficulties associated with customary versus national laws regarding land rights in Tanzania. Through her economic analysis, Kinyondo effectively links women's access to land, credit, and other necessary inputs to much broader issues, including gender equality, food security, and economic development.

Taken together, the chapters by Kinyondo and Carlyn James highlight an important theme from eastern Africa: the important role of informal micro-finance for women in agriculture. Although significant attention has been paid to the positive and negative aspects of formal microcredit programs for women, less attention has been paid on the role of *informal* microcredit for women. James's chapter provides a rich, ethnographic study of such informal credit options in the Kenyan context. Her analysis reveals the important role of social capital in overcoming barriers caused by gender inequality and lack of formal infrastructure. It also reveals women's ongoing prioritization of, and responsibility for, social reproduction.

The chapter by Andrea Moraes and Cecilia Rocha takes us to South America, where targeted domestic food procurement policies have had positive outcomes for women in Brazil. Policies designed to economically value women's contributions to the Brazilian food system have strengthened women's position in agriculture while having other positive spin-offs throughout the country's social and economic fabric.

Continuing the discussion of food procurement policy, the chapter by Bryan Crawford-Garrett, Clare Mbizule, Karin Wachter, and Brian Sage further examines the potential for women's empowerment through carefully designed policy. Using a case study of the United Nations World Food Programme's Purchase for Progress (P4P) initiative, the authors examine both sides of the supply/demand relationship, discussing the importance of smallholder inclusion through supply-side supports. The authors' important Theory of Change provides an ideal bridge to the final section of our book, where we examine positive ways forward for women in agriculture.

Part IV

The final chapters in the book point us toward a more positive future. Julie Théroux-Séguin describes how female farm workers in Morocco are resisting the explicitly sexualized violence they experience at work in the strawberry fields. The chapter centers on women's voices in claiming their rights as workers and describes how local and international organizations are supporting the women's efforts. Examining tensions at the intersection of gender, religion, and culture, Théroux-Séguin's chapter introduces us to an intersectionality framework for understanding women's experiences in agriculture.

Writing from the American Midwest, Angie Carter, Betty Wells, Ashley Hand, and Jessica Soulis document the success of women's mentoring and information-sharing programs that are run through the non-profit Women, Food and Agriculture Network (WFAN). These programs are linked to a broader theoretical discussion that underpins the book as a whole: what is the relationship between context-specific interventions and broader structural change? Together, the chapters in this book help to address this pressing question and point to avenues for future change in agriculture.

Jan Kainer's chapter points to a desirable future for food systems. Kainer presents research conducted with farm women who offer youth internships on their operations in Ontario, Canada. The chapter highlights the importance of farm women's knowledge and expertise in training and supporting the next generation of farmers. Her analysis has implications for the sustainability of agricultural societies and points the way to a more socially, environmentally, and economically sustainable form of agriculture with women at the forefront.

The book concludes with Amber J. Fletcher's integrative discussion, which draws out common themes between these diverse chapters. The goal in this concluding chapter is to identify the relationship between concrete interventions and broader structural change. Drawing on the concepts of structure and agency, Fletcher identifies two interconnected themes emerging from this collection: the importance of everyday, situated actions and the potential of gradual transformation. The chapter summarizes the practical solutions presented in this book into four key themes: visibility and data; policy and gender mainstreaming; social capital and sustainability; and intersectionality. Each theme presents an important area for future focus in the field.

References

Allen, Patricia, and Carolyn Sachs. 2007. "Women and Food Chains: The Gendered Politics of Food." *International Journal of Sociology of Food and Agriculture* 15 (1): 1–23.

Bakker, Isabella. 2007. "Social Reproduction and the Constitution of a Gendered Political Economy." *New Political Economy* 12 (4): 541–56. doi:10.1080/13563460701661561.

Barndt, Deborah, ed. 1999. *Women Working The NAFTA Food Chain: Women, Food and Globalization*. Toronto: Sumach Press.

Bezanson, Kate, and Meg Luxton. 2006. *Social Reproduction: Feminist Political Economy Challenges Neo-Liberalism*. Montreal: McGill-Queen's University Press.

Butler, Judith. 1990. *Gender Trouble: Feminism and the Subversion of Identity*. New York: Routledge.

Connell, Raewyn. 2009. *Gender*. Cambridge: Polity Press.

Dillard, Jesse, Veronica Dujon, and Mary C. King. 2009. "Introduction." In *Understanding the Social Dimension of Sustainability*, edited by Jesse Dillard, Veronica Dujon, and Mary C. King, 1–12. New York, NY: Routledge.

Fletcher, Amber J. 2013. "The View From Here: Agricultural Policy, Climate Change, and the Future of Farm Women in Saskatchewan." Regina, SK: University of Regina.
———. 2016. "Women and Social Sustainability: The Case of Canadian Agriculture." In *Women in Sustainability in Business: A Global Perspective*, edited by Kiymet Çaliyurt. Farnham: Gower (Ashgate).
Food and Agriculture Organization of the United Nations. n.d. "Gender and Land Rights Database." www.fao.org/gender-landrights-database/data-map/statistics/en/.
Food and Agriculture Organization of the United Nations. 2014. *The State of Food and Agriculture 2014: Innovation in Family Farming*. Rome: Food and Agriculture Organization of the United Nations.
Friedmann, Harriet. 1978. "World Market, State, and Family Farm: Social Bases of Household Production in the Era of Wage Labor." *Comparative Studies in Society and History* 20 (4): 545–86.
Kubik, Wendee. 2004. "The Changing Roles of Farm Women and the Consequences for Their Health, Well Being, and Quality of Life." Regina, SK: University of Regina.
Lastarria-Cornhiel, Susana, Julia A. Behrman, Ruth Meinzen-Dick, and Agnes R. Quisumbing. 2014. "Gender Equity and Land: Toward Secure and Effective Access for Rural Women." In *Gender in Agriculture: Closing the Knowledge Gap*, edited by Agnes R. Quisumbing, Ruth Meinzen-Dick, Terri L. Raney, André Croppenstedt, Julia A. Behrman, and Amber Peterman, 117–44. Dordrecht: Food and Agriculture Organization; Springer Science & Business.
Pini, Barbara, Berit Brandth, and Jo Little. 2014. *Feminisms and Ruralities*. Lanham: Lexington Books.
Quisumbing, Agnes R., Ruth Meinzen-Dick, Terri L. Raney, André Croppenstedt, Julia A. Behrman, and Amber Peterman, eds. 2014. *Gender in Agriculture: Closing the Knowledge Gap*. Dordrecht: Food and Agriculture Organization; Springer Science & Business.
Razavi, Shara. 2002. *Shifting Burdens: Gender and Agrarian Change Under Neoliberalism*. West Hartford: Kumarian Press.
Seager, Joni. 2014. "Disasters Are Gendered: What's New?" In *Reducing Disaster: Early Warning Systems For Climate Change*, edited by Ashbindu Singh and Zinta Zommers, 265–81. Dordrecht: Springer.
Sweetman, Caroline. 1999. *Women, Land and Agriculture*. Oxford: Oxfam.
Vallance, Suzanne, Harvey C. Perkins, and Jennifer E. Dixon. 2011. "What Is Social Sustainability? A Clarification of Concepts." *Geoforum* 42 (3): 342–48. doi:10.1016/j.geoforum.2011.01.002.
Van Koppen, Barbara, Lesley Hope, and Willem Colenbrander. 2013. "Gender Aspects of Small-Scale Private Irrigation in Africa." Working Paper 153. Colombo, Sri Lanka: International Water Management Institute (IWMI). doi: 10.5337/2013.201.
World Bank, Food and Agriculture Organization, and International Fund for Agricultural Development. 2008. *Gender in Agriculture Sourcebook*. Washington, DC: The World Bank. http://elibrary.worldbank.org/doi/book/10.1596/978-0-8213-7587-7.

Part I

Women's agricultural work

Addressing inequality and invisibility

Australia

1 Understanding the "local" and "global"

Intersections engendering change for women in family farming in Australia

Josephine Clarke and Margaret Alston

Introduction

Agricultural restructuring in Australia continues as a result of multiple and intersecting challenges. These include declining terms of trade, globalization and its impacts on agricultural markets, ongoing structural adjustment pressures, changing technologies and reduced access to irrigation water, as well as ongoing drought and other weather events that suggest climate changes are escalating and permanent (Gray and Lawrence 2001; Alston and Whittenbury 2012; Smith and Pritchard 2014; Pritchard 2000). Yet, while family farming remains the dominant unit of production in Australian agriculture (Productivity Commission 2005; Commonwealth of Australia 2014), in recent decades structural adjustments have resulted in a reduction in the number of farmers in Australia: "Over the 30 years to 2011, the number of farmers declined by 106,200 (40%), equating to an average of 294 fewer farmers every month over that period" (Australian Bureau of Statistics 2012, 1). Nonetheless, family farming remains critical to the organization and embodiment of social and gendered roles and responsibilities that support commodity production in an evolving neoliberal economy.

Despite the falling numbers engaged in agriculture, this mode of production continues to ensure the persistence of agriculture as a male-dominated enterprise. For example, recent national statistics suggest that women comprised 28 percent of the farming workforce in 2011, representing a slight decline on 1981 statistics (30%). This is in stark contrast to women's increased participation in other workforce occupations (Australian Bureau of Statistics 2012) and suggests significant barriers have yet to be overcome. Regardless, the pressures of restructuring have significant consequences for women, particularly as many now work off-farm to facilitate the continuance of their family farm (Alston 2000). We argue that while women do participate in farming and the agricultural industry, there is increasing evidence that restructuring excludes women in new ways.

Recent social research has documented significant changes in agricultural industries and rural communities (Gray and Lawrence 2001; Cocklin and Dibden 2005). Australian rural communities reliant on agriculture are often described as sites where depopulation and farm restructuring are occurring, where farm exits are increasing, services and local businesses are withdrawing, and social relations within rural communities are evolving (Beer and Pritchard 2003; Pritchard and McManus 2000). Further, the impacts of ongoing restructuring include substantial wellbeing issues (Alston 2010; Alston 2012; Price 2010). Thus the interrelationship of agricultural and rural restructuring is an embodied social and gendered experience imbued with diverse responses to managing ongoing change.

Nonetheless, there are emerging efforts to innovate and inspire new relationships that support sustainable food production and new opportunities in rural localities. In this chapter we critique social relations, arguing that in their reshaping in a rapid period of change, these have become even more gendered, leading to an increasingly evident masculinization of Australian agriculture. As a result we argue there is an urgent need for gender mainstreaming in government and industry policies and practices.

Local and global components of agricultural restructuring

There is no doubt there are significant pressures on Australian agriculture – pressures that are not unique to our country, but that have shaped our industries in fundamental ways. While these are potentially economically advantageous for many, they continue to reduce the viability of a large proportion of family farms. Critical amongst these is globalization – the opening up of world markets to competition at the same time as local farmers become competitors in a highly volatile environment. The increasing marketization of agricultural produce keeps farmers on a treadmill of production, frequently involving increased use of chemicals and pesticides to sustain production levels. Price volatility is common and, while those farms that have expanded to be larger-than-family farms may be economically viable, many others are not. In Australia this has led to the need for alternative sources of income and a cost-price squeeze that places significant pressures on families. These pressures are exacerbated in an Australian context by a very evident increase in climate-related events including drought, widespread floods, cyclones, and bushfires. In this volatile environment, we have seen divisive debates over water usage, pitting irrigation farmers against environmentalists, and a questioning of the sustainability of agricultural practices (Alston et al., 2016). At the same time structural adjustments are reshaping communities that serve agricultural industries and family farms. Small communities across Australia have experienced declining populations, reduced services, low levels of transport and telecommunications access, and declining access to education and employment options. It is against this background that we examine the way Australian women engage in agriculture.

Women in Australian agriculture

Previous feminist social research has investigated the role of women in farming in Australia (Alston 1995; Alston 2000). This research has exposed women's on-farm roles and responsibilities and farming women's self-advocacy, and critiqued the power dynamics imbued in farm structure, family farming, rural social life, and more broadly in the agricultural industry (Pini 2004; Alston 2000; Alston 1998; Alston 2003; Liepins 1996). This research has investigated the extent to which women's work supports agricultural productivity and family-farm survival, and more recently has sought to understand how this operates in the context of experiences of managing drought and climate change (Alston and Whittenbury 2012; Alston 2006a; Alston 2006b). Women's work in farming is interpreted as involving both on-farm and off-farm work that supports family farming. This dichotomy of women's on- and off-farm work has also been interpreted as effectively a significant subsidy to food production (Kubik 2005).

Further, there is a gendered differential in the experience of agricultural and rural restructuring and climatic variations and this can involve substantial coping issues for women. For women involved in family farming – and this includes the many dimensions of their work to support the continuation of the family farm – managing the impacts of climate change and drought is a further component of industry and rural restructuring (Alston and Whittenbury 2012).

Concurrent with the research findings that document and value women's work on-farm, and promote opportunities for women in farming, there is emerging evidence that women have been leaving farming independently of their partners, either by physically moving away from the farm to work and/or disengaging from the enterprise (Clarke 2015). This turning away of women is further exacerbating the trend in Australia (and elsewhere) for agriculture to become increasingly masculinized (Alston and Whittenbury 2012; Clarke 2015; Brandth 2002). While the main feature of this "leaving" is women's participation in off-farm work as a farm survival strategy to address farm income shortfall, additional factors include new technologies that require less on-farm labor, objections to chemical use, and the patrilineal and patriarchal nature of farming practices more generally. Yet the farm/off-farm dichotomy is also challenged by changes in the social relations of agriculture such as the increasingly common practice of male farmers commuting to the farm, and women pursuing separate livelihood opportunities in rural communities (Clarke 2015). Thus the dominance of "the farm" is challenged not only in farm exit processes as a result of multiple restructuring pressures, but also as women increasingly do not participate in farming, or leave farming prior to their partner due to concerns for (and objections to) their view that the current social relations of farming are unsustainable. Many women perceive farming life as stressful, difficult, and lacking equitable opportunities, and hence view current arrangements as socially unsustainable (Alston and Whittenbury 2012; Clarke 2015).

To engender change for women in farming in Australia – and to promote equality of opportunity – the authors propose that the social sustainability of agricultural production urgently requires attention to gender-based inequalities within the industry and family farming to be addressed. On the one hand patrilineal inheritance practices and a male-dominated industry social norm significantly reduce women's access to farming as an occupation. On the other, in the face of multiple pressures and a nebulous recognition from industry and government of their efforts to support the agricultural industries, many women are losing their commitment to farming. Among a range of strategies, new opportunities for women to enter farming are required. Much research into the social impacts of restructuring focuses on mapping the detrimental aspects of globalization and neoliberalism, and the process of "leaving farming" is understood as a response to restructuring pressures. However, we extend our understanding of "leaving farming" to include acknowledging that women also leave farming often independently of their partner, due to objections to current practices in farming, and pressures associated with coping with, and managing, the impacts of drought and climate change, as well as their exclusion via inheritance practices.

This is an uncomfortable place in feminist rural social research: we wish not only to document gender inequality but also to advocate for new and equitable opportunities for women in farming, to improve the sustainability of farming in Australia. "Sustainability" is a varied discourse (see Black 2005) with multiple meanings contingent on the context whether it be industry, government policy in support of the agricultural industry, local community-based articulations of future scenarios, or individualized situated knowledge. Articulations of what is, is not, and can be sustainable, inform new opportunities in dynamic agricultural restructuring processes. Consequently, the authors note that working towards more socially sustainable farming practices requires attention to the processes that maintain gendered structures and practices in a time of significant agriculture and industry restructuring.

As Brandth (2002) notes, the discourse of the family farm has been a focus of much previous research seeking to understand gender relations in farming. This discourse and the hegemonic masculinity associated with it has, and continues to be, substantially critiqued by feminist social researchers (Alston 2000; Shortall 1999; Brandth 2002). The discourse of the family farm is by no means static: it reveals multiple gendered subject positions thereby suggesting change is possible, indeed necessary, to support gender equality in agriculture. In coming to terms with practical ways to address how family farming can be revised to support gender equality, we consider gender mainstreaming as a critical factor in building understanding, new knowledge, and new forms of social relations. We then examine recent government and industry documents that paradoxically reveal both the possibility of change and a lack of a gender mainstreaming framework that may make it this change unachievable.

Gender mainstreaming

Gender mainstreaming is a policy process adopted widely across the world as a result of the 1995 Beijing Women's conference. At this major global event, women from across the world expressed significant disquiet at the lack of action and progress around gender equality. As a consequence it was determined that signatories adopt gender mainstreaming to ensure that policies and the actions that flowed from them were assessed to determine that they did not adversely disadvantage women or men. The accepted definition of gender mainstreaming adopted across the world is that it is

> the process for assessing the implications for women and men of any planned action, including legislation, policies or programmes, in all areas and all levels. It is a strategy for making women's as well as men's concerns and experiences an integral dimension of the design, implementation, monitoring and evaluation of policies and programmes in all political, economic and societal spheres so that women and men benefit equally and inequality is not perpetuated. The ultimate goal is to achieve gender equality.
>
> (UN ECOSOC 1997)

Confusion exists about gender mainstreaming particularly in countries like Australia that have embraced the idea but not the intent of gender mainstreaming. Particularly in traditionally masculinized policy areas such as agriculture, there is a common view that acknowledging women by appointing a few women to boards addresses any obligations there might be to gender measures. Yet what is missing from this appraisal is that gender mainstreaming is much more than achieving greater representation for women and building their capacity. It is a far more complex process of attending to *all* issues that result in inequalities between men and women. In the case of agriculture in Australia, this should include an analysis of land ownership, of decision-making positions, and of the very nature of production systems that reduce sustainability and the capacity for farming units to be self-sustaining. When we examine government policy documents with gender mainstreaming in mind, we can see this process of gender blindness in action.

Representing agriculture – government and industry framing

First, in considering Australia's agricultural policy frameworks it is important to recognize structural change and adjustment priorities. "Structural adjustment" can be understood as an ongoing economic discourse informing industry reform policies and processes (see Productivity Commission 2001). In a recent Australian Government publication, *Australian Competitiveness Green Paper* (Commonwealth of Australia 2014: 101), success for the agricultural industry is expressed through evidence that Australian producers are some of the least protected in the world and that trade liberalization is an ongoing goal on a global scale that will benefit Australian producers. There is no mention of alternative income strategies that now must support agricultural production. Rather the role of government is articulated as supporting ongoing trade liberalization, including through the activity of free trade agreements, for example.

The recent *Australian Competitiveness Green Paper* is a good example of a document that lacks a gender mainstreaming framework. This paper overtly acknowledges the critical role farming families have in agricultural production, and advocates for support for the dominant mode of farming. Nonetheless this unit of production is undifferentiated and there is no gender analysis of economic contributions or ownership. Rather there is an implicit acceptance of patrilineal inheritance practices. For example:

> The question of the appropriate policy settings for a healthy agriculture sector extends beyond the economics of yields, productivity and prices; it also encompasses the issue of the ownership of the nation by the people in the most seminal and tangible form. Farming is a statement of who we are. Families on the farm are both the overwhelming driver of the economics of the farm as well as the owner of the asset. The concept of a family farm being small and inefficient is a misrepresentation of the reality that is today's business-oriented enterprises focused on market needs. Policy settings need to enable business success to be mindful of increasing returns to those who contribute most of the work and carry so much of the risk. Family farms are a cornerstone of Australian agriculture and rural communities and policy must reflect this fact, and the aspirations of those Australians who would seek to participate. Family farms are the best stewards of the land because they've been on it for generations and care about maintaining it for future generations.
>
> (Commonwealth of Australia 2014, x–xi)

This government policy document is part of a process currently working towards a final White Paper to define the role of the Australian government in the agricultural policy reform agenda. In many respects the articulation of the social significance of people and families as critical to agricultural production is timely, as awareness is increasing of the health and wellbeing issues in agriculturally dominated rural communities (and the Green Paper nominates supports for the latter). Moreover, this policy also acknowledges the social significance of the interface between production, family life, and attachment to, and care for, land that supports productivity. The above government policy statement is advocating for agricultural production reform that revives respect for an Australian agrarian and rural ideal – family farming – and also seeks to (re)value food production in Australia.

What is missing from this policy statement is a transparent appraisal of women's input, and of gender relations more generally. There is, for example, no discussion of ways inheritance and succession practices might be reformed to ensure gender equality. How are social and gender equity issues within family farming and agricultural production to be addressed to ensure reform and restructuring is imbued with a gender mainstreaming process? The paper reveals inherent biases in its lack of understanding of the social relations of agriculture.

A further document, *The Blueprint for Australian Agriculture 2013–2020* (National Farmers Federation and Sefton & Associates 2013) published by the dominant industry body, The National Farmers Federation, also outlines agricultural industry reform objectives. Similar to the Green Paper (above) this document is also the result of an extensive consultation process and, like the Green Paper, lacks gender analysis. *The Blueprint* suggests reform will involve farm consolidation that results in farm exits:

> New structures for owning and operating farms need to be encouraged to attract investment from domestic and foreign investors and capital markets. These structures might include rapidly evolving equity partnerships, modern variants of share farming and the use of off-take agreements like those used in the mining sector (Port Jackson Partners/ANZ, 2012). It is likely that because of the costs of remaining competitive, the trend towards smaller farm businesses consolidating will continue, and new farm ownership and operation structures, succession, and risk-sharing models will develop.
>
> (2013, 26)

Of note is that the *Blueprint* extensively discusses the theme of "People" and, albeit without a gendered analysis, describes the challenges of ageing farmers, labor shortages, farm exits, and succession challenges. The report also acknowledges estimations of women's contribution to real farm income, and discusses the significance of having rural women in leadership positions (National Farmers Federation and Sefton & Associates 2013, 45, 49). Following this discussion, the "People Theme" articulates strategies specifically targeted at providing more opportunities for women: first, to "Expand the numbers of women in leadership positions in agriculture" and second, to "Encourage the participation of women in rural skills training" (National Farmers Federation and Sefton & Associates 2013, 47).

The *Blueprint* recognizes women's role in supporting agricultural production and articulates strategies that promote opportunities for women in agriculture. However, despite these broad sentiments, industry-based articulations of future scenarios for sustainable agriculture do not incorporate gender mainstreaming processes to achieve these admirable goals. They remain platitudes that pass over the challenges and shift the blame for their absence to women. Moving beyond these motherhood statements requires agricultural policymakers not only to recognize women's vital contribution to supporting agricultural production but also to move beyond strategies associated with farm business restructuring and economic rationalism. What is omitted in this industry and government policy narrative is an examination of ways to improve women's lives as well as their opportunities to engage in agriculture. There is no discussion of flexible off-farm work practices, child care, and transport infrastructure in any discussion of the economic viability of family farming thus rendering invisible, and difficult, the significant economic contribution women make through their off-farm income. There are no examples of strategies to break down patriarchal structures and processes. There is no discussion of land ownership or sustainable agriculture. These are significant opportunities missed.

We would argue that policies must move beyond economic parameters to embrace sustainable agricultural practices, new forms of social relations, and an awareness of gender barriers. This would allow new opportunities for women and men and provide the opportunity for alternative social relationships. There are inherent dangers in a business-as-usual approach. In fact, this is touched on in the Green Paper where reference is made to the need to support industry change by including the provision of mental health services. This is an important acknowledgment of the coping and wellbeing issues embedded in current agricultural practices. Certainly adequate social supports are required to assist people to manage the challenges of agricultural restructuring. There is cause for concern when a major policy document acknowledges the need for social supports consequent on current practices without unpacking the relationship between these practices and social and health impacts.

We would argue that current production practices are socially unsustainable. However we wish to move beyond a crises-response narrative (Lockie 2000) and argue for industry policy and ambition to consider social alternatives that promote gender and social equity, which in turn will support wellbeing and enhance agricultural production.

What is required is a critical and transparent assessment of agricultural production and embedded social relations. Drawing on the ECOSOC (1997) definition of gender mainstreaming, this requires an assessment of the implications of current practices for women and men in order to make women's and men's concerns and expectations an integral dimension of the design, implementation, monitoring and evaluation of policies and programs in all political, economic and societal spheres so that women and men benefit equally and inequality is not perpetuated.

To enhance sustainable agriculture and the social relations that make it possible, no issue should be off the agenda – access to arable land, succession, inheritance, intra-family relationships, health and wellbeing, flexible work arrangements, service infrastructure, local employment etc. Such an appraisal will not only provide a platform for more sustainable agriculture, it will support social relations and community revitalisation.

Conclusion

This chapter has considered how social and gender relations in agriculture in Australia are adapting to intersecting challenges to agricultural production.

Further, the authors discussed the opportunities for women to further contribute to agricultural industry restructuring at this critical time. This chapter considers these issues with respect to women's advocacy for sustainability in farming and food production. We argue there is a critical need for gender mainstreaming across all facets of agricultural production and the policies that shape industry development, in order to achieve a more economically, environmentally and socially sustainable agriculture. We have illustrated this need through a consideration of industry-based policies in order to demonstrate the inherent gender blindness in current frameworks and to promote gender equality and further opportunities for women in the agricultural industry. There is also an international dimension to our argument – much research in the global North illustrates gender inequities in agricultural production. While we acknowledge the diversity of social experiences and gender relations in farming, we argue gender mainstreaming is a strategy that can support the agricultural industry in multiple localities. Further, it is timely to consider equitable opportunities and gender equality in agricultural restructuring as social and gender relations are globalized given restructured food systems.

References

Alston, M. 1995. *Women on The Land: The Hidden Heart of Rural Australia*. Kensington: UNSW Press.

———. 1998. "Farm Women and Their Work: Why Is It Not Recognised?" *Journal of Sociology* 34: 23–34.

———. 2000. *Breaking Through The Grass Ceiling*. Amsterdam: Harwood Academic Publishers.

———. 2003. "Women in Agriculture: The 'New Entrepreneurs'." *Australian Feminist Studies* 18: 163–71.

———. 2006a. "The Gendered Impact of Drought." In *Rural Gender Relations: Issues and Case Studies*, edited by B. B. Bock and S. Shortall, 165–180. Wallingford: CABI Publishing.

———. 2006b. "'I'd Like to Just Walk Out of Here': Australian Women's Experience of Drought." *Sociologia Ruralis* 45: 154–70.

———. 2010. "Gender and Climate Change in Australia." *Journal of Sociology* 47 (1): 1–18. doi: 10.1177/1440783310376848.

———. 2012. "Rural Male Suicide in Australia." *Social Science & Medicine* 74 (4): 515–22.

Alston, M. and K. Whittenbury. 2012. "Does Climatic Crisis in Australia's Food Bowl Create a Basis for Change in Agricultural Gender Relations?" *Agriculture and Human Values* 30: 115–28.

Alston, M., K. Whittenbury, D. Western, and A. Gosling. 2016. "Water Policy, Trust and Governance in The Murray-Darling Basin." *Australian Geographer* 47 (1): 49–64.

Australian Bureau of Statistics. 2012. *Australian Social Trends*, Cat. no. 4102.0. www.abs.gov.au/AUSSTATS/abs@.nsf/Lookup/4102.0Main+Features1Dec%20 2012?OpenDocument.

Beer, A., A. Maude, and B. Pritchard. 2003. *Developing Australia's Regions: Theory and Practice*. Sydney: UNSW Press.

Black, A. 2005. "Rural Communities and Sustainability." In *Sustainability and Change in Rural Australia*, edited by C. Cocklin, and J. Dibden, 20–37. Sydney: University of New South Wales Press.

Brandth, B. 2002. "Gender Identity in European Family Farming: A Literature Review." *Sociologia Ruralis* 42:181–200.

Clarke, J. 2015. "A Gender Analysis of Agricultural and Rural Restructuring in The Mallee Region." PhD diss., Monash University.

Cocklin, C., and J. Dibden, eds. 2005. *Sustainability and Change in Rural Australia*. Sydney: UNW Press.

Commonwealth of Australia. 2014. *Australian Competitiveness Green Paper*. Canberra: Commonwealth of Australia.

Gray, I., and G. Lawrence. 2001. *A Future for Regional Australia: Escaping Global Misfortune*. Cambridge: Cambridge University Press.

Kubik, W. 2005. "Farm Women: The Hidden Subsidy in Our Food." *Canadian Woman Studies/ Les Cahiers De La Femme* 24: 85–90.

Liepins, R. 1996. "'Women in Agriculture:' A Geography of Australian Agricultural Activism." PhD diss., University of Melbourne.

Lockie, S. 2000. "Crisis and Conflict: Shifting Discourses of Rural and Regional Australia." In *Land of Discontent: The Dynamics of Change in Rural and Regional Australia*, edited by B. Pritchard and P. McManus, 14–32. Sydney: UNSW Press.

National Farmers Federation and Sefton & Associates. 2013. *The Blueprint for Australian Agriculture 2013–2020*. www.nff.org.au/blueprint.html.

Pini, B. 2004. "Farm Women and Off-farm Work: A Study of the Queensland Sugar Industry." *Labour and Industry* 15: 53–64.

Price, L. 2010. "The Damaging Impacts of Patriarchy on UK Male Family Farmers." In *Geographical Perspectives on Sustainable Rural Change*, edited by D. G. Winchell, D. Ramsey, R. Koster and G. M. Robinson, 61–77. Manitoba: Brandon University (Rural Development Institute).

Pritchard, B. 2000. "Negotiating The Two-Edged Sword of Agricultural Trade Liberalization: Trade Policy and Its Protectionist Discontents." In *Land of Discontent: The Dynamics of Change in Rural and Regional Australia*, edited by B. Pritchard and P. McManus, 90–104. Sydney: UNSW Press.

Pritchard, B., and P. McManus, eds. 2000. *Land of Discontent: The Dynamics of Change in Rural and Regional Australia*. Sydney: UNSW Press.

Productivity Commission. 2001. *Structural Adjustment – Key Policy Issues*. Commission Research Paper. AusInfo: Canberra.

———. 2005. *Trends in Australian Agriculture*. Commission Research Paper. Commonwealth of Australia: Canberra.

Shortall, S. 1999. *Women and Farming: and Property Power*. Houndmills, Basingstroke: Palgrave.

Smith, E. F., and B. Pritchard. 2014. "Water Reform in The 21st Century: The Changed Status of Australian Agriculture." In *Rural Change in Australia: Population, Economy, Environment*, edited by R. Dufty-Jones and J. Connell, 169–86. Farnham: Ashgate Publishing Ltd.

UN Economic and Social Council (ECOSOC). 1997. September 18. *Gender Mainstreaming Extract from Report of The Economic and Social Council for1997* (A/52/3, 18). www.un.org/womenwatch/daw/csw/GMS.PDF.

Canada

2 Who's counting … on the farm?

June Corman and Wendee Kubik

Introduction

The food sovereignty movement uses strident language and questions to force our attention on food. Who has access to and control over agricultural land and hence food production? How will changing forms of land ownership affect food production? What effect will climate change have on food production? Looking at agriculture from a gendered perspective, we ask: how has women's work in food production and in supporting the family farm changed in these contexts and what does it mean for the future of farming?

The Canadian prairies are a useful case for examining these questions. In the late 1800s and early 1900s the Canadian national government deliberately settled the prairies in family units, to grow food to export to consumers. Measuring the success of this experiment depends on vantage point. If success is measured in food produced, the policy was successful. In the 1900s, the abundance of wheat grown on the prairies bestowed it the name "Bread Basket of the World." Today, in addition to grains, the prairies export oil crops such as canola and pulse crops such as lentils and chickpeas. Other measures of success are not positive. First Nations peoples were forcibly pushed aside: moved off their land without involving them in developing a viable alternative way of life.[1] Most of the descendants of homestead families were not successful in reproducing the family on the farm as the economics of agriculture could not sustain all these families.

Examining the contributions of women to the family farm has always been complicated by the intertwining of women's household labor, off-farm labor, and agricultural work on farm (Ghorayshi 1989; Sachs 1996; Alston 1998; Kelly and Shortall 2002; Kubik 2004; Luxton and Corman 2011; Fletcher 2013). Patriarchal relations on the farm and in farm communities add further complications (Shortall 1999; Corman 2005; Alston 2006). Some progress was made in tracking aspects of household labor in the 2001 and 2006 Canadian census, but by 2011, with the demise of the long-form census, this information is not available. In the twenty-first century farm women's contributions became even more conceptually muddied by the changing nature of land ownership. From the uniformity of homesteaders owning and living on quarter sections with rights to an additional 120 acres, ownership arrangements today include but are not confined to families farming their land, farmer owned corporations (utilizing their own and paid labor), First Nation partnerships with corporate capital (employing wage labor),[2] as well as corporations and the Canadian Pension Plan owning land and leasing back to local farmers (Atkins 2013; Desmarais et al., 2015).

This chapter is broadly concerned with assessing the important contributions that women make to the twenty-first century version of family farms and, more specifically, women who report as farm operators on the agricultural census.[3] Many family farms would not exist or be viable without the contributions of farm women (Storey 2002; Martz and Brueckner 2003; Kubik 2004). These contributions can be, as previous research has argued, direct labor-producing agricultural commodities, household labor reproducing the labor power of the family from day to day and generation to generation, self-employment, and more commonly, off-farm waged or salaried jobs. We argue that women's contributions, even those of women farm operators, continue to remain "invisible" for many reasons and cannot be determined given the format of the federal census. We examine how women's relationship to prairie agriculture is tied directly to the initial settlement practices and to the on-going changes in the forms of land ownership and production practices. Women's labor is placed in the context of gendered patterns of control of farm land, the gendered division of agricultural labor, and gendered patterns of household labor. We speculate that diversity in forms of land ownership and production practices has now created greater diversity amongst the contributions of women to farm households. We conclude with an analysis of what might be the future effects of industrial agricultural production, shifting ownership patterns, globalization and privatization of market relations on the contributions of farm women.

From homesteads to differentiated farm types

During the late 1800s, the Canadian national government recruited people of European descent to settle the prairies, with the goal of producing grains to export and of establishing a market for manufactured goods produced in eastern Canada (Fowke 1957). These policies ensured that homesteaders did not become subsistence producers but were integrated into the money economy: selling agricultural commodities to buy inputs. The initial land grant, given to male homesteaders only, was not sufficient to make a living. Done deliberately, this federal policy motivated homestead families to clear land, produce commodities for sale, and invest the money to buy more land and machinery.

From the homestead period to the present, farmers have faced a cost/price squeeze, with input costs often higher than receipts. Given that large multinationals provide the inputs, farmers have never had latitude to bargain input costs down. Although farmers determine how much land to crop each year, they cannot control how much they will produce, due to pests, disease, frost, hail, wind, floods, or drought.

Farm families developed differentiated responses to decades of uncertain returns, increasing inputs and surviving on low net incomes. These strategies have had consequences for the type of work done by women and men to contribute to the livelihood of the family. Some families have responded to the cost/price squeeze by acquiring more land to produce greater yields, by diversifying into oil seeds and pulses, applications of fertilizer, herbicides, pesticides, and fungicides, and by investing in large-scale equipment. The proportion of land owned by large-scale farmers is constantly increasing.

Other families operate on a smaller scale, producing specialty items such as organic produce, or continuing to grow wheat in a holding pattern until ill health or death. Organic field crop operations are not commonplace (according to Statistics Canada's Report on Agriculture, only 1.8 percent of farms in Canada were organic in 2012). The transition to organic often comes with the cost of low yields at low non-organic prices during the four-year transition period. The differential response of farm families to market uncertainty has increasingly contributed to differentiation in the size of farms and farm management practices.

Every year fewer farm families reproduce themselves on the farm; some have had no children, others had children without an interest or incentive to farm, and others could not assist their children to farm. Some were forced to leave when the farm became non-financially viable. In many cases in the twentieth century, a neighboring farmer would buy the land in hopes of achieving economies of scale or to assist their child (almost always a son) to farm.[4] Increasingly, local farmers compete with large farming consortiums, out-of-province investors and the Canada Pension Plan for access to this land (Magnan 2011; Atkins, 2013).

Concentration of ownership resulted in fewer farms, with some farms increasing in size and others remaining small (see Figure 2.1). The number of farms increased from the homestead period to a high of 142,391 in 1936, dropped to 44,329 in 2006 and further declined to 36,952 in 2011 (Statistics Canada 2011). Unless agricultural policies change, this trend will continue. The decline in the number of farms combined with the increase in size of farms is tied to significant differences among farms in the value of commodities produced for sale as measured by gross farm receipts. In 2006, 12 percent of farms sold less than $10,000 while 15 percent sold over $250,000; by 2011 the gap had increased, with 10 percent of farms selling less than $10,000 and 27 percent of farms selling over $250,000.[5]

Although most farms are still family operations in which the farm operator owns, manages, and works on the farm, divergent operating arrangements are becoming increasingly common. Among farm operators, only 62 percent remain as sole proprietorships, while 19 percent are partnerships and 17 percent are family corporations. In 2011, 2.1 percent of farms were non-family corporations or were owned by another type of non-farm family arrangement (see Table 2.1). Hiding behind the figures on farm types is lack of published information on the proportion of land held by each ownership

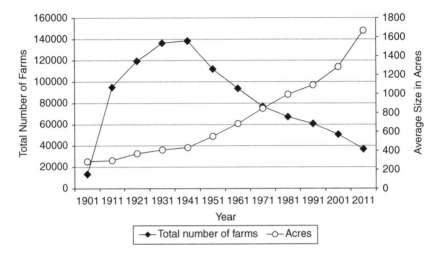

Figure 2.1 Number of farms and average farm area (Saskatchewan 1901–2011).
Source: Compiled by authors from Census of Agriculture data, Statistics Canada.

Table 2.1 Operating arrangements, Saskatchewan farms for 2006 and 2011

	2006		2011	
	#	%	#	%
Individual or family farm	28,860	65	22,756	62
Partnership, no written agreement	8,401	19	6,044	16
Partnership, written agreement	980	2	1,068	3
Family corporation	5,380	12	6,304	17
Non-family corporation	525	1	542	1.5
Other	183	0.4	238	0.6
Total number of farms	44,329		36,952	

Source: CANSIM 004-0007 for both years.

arrangement and in particular the prevalence of off-farm investors. As forms of ownership become more diverse, the position of women in relationship to the land and their contributions to the agricultural operation becomes increasing difficult to determine.

In summary, Saskatchewan farms are increasingly differentiated by ownership arrangements, size, capital value, gross sales, commodities produced, and production practices. These changes have ushered in considerable variation in the contributions farm women make to the household regarding operating the farm, producing commodities, self-provisioning, and off-farm work.

Women at work on the farm

In contrast to today, for the first half of the twentieth century, all agricultural land was farmed by family households and these families lived on the farms. The vast majority of farm women worked only on the farm, and contributed by provisioning for the family, household labor, and assisting with production of commodities for sale. Women followed the same pattern in their daily lives, dictated by the weather and seasons, doing more or less of the same kind of work depending on the prosperity of the farm. The more food that could be sourced on the farm, the less money was needed to be spent at the grocery store and this saving could be directed toward farm inputs.

June Corman recalls growing up on her parents' farm in Saskatchewan in the 1960s:

> We sprouted potatoes all winter to ensure they stayed firm, we churned milk into butter and baked our own bread: from farm to table through my mother's labor. A typical evening meal consisted of roast chicken (raised from a new born chick, butchered, cleaned, and frozen), mashed potatoes (grown in the garden), peas (frozen from the garden) or beans (canned from the garden), bread (baked by my mother), milk (from our cow), butter (churned by my mother), dill pickles (made by my mother from cucumbers grown by my mother) and a cake (baked by my mother). I should note that my sister and I helped my mother while my brothers were outside helping my father. Almost everything we ate embodied my mother's labor. We ate none of the grain, largely wheat, produced for sale while our beef and pork were sourced from our farm livestock produced for an income.

Uniformly throughout the prairies, until farms had access to electricity in the 1940s and 1950s, food production was very labor intensive: pumping water, lighting wood/coal stoves, hauling wood, hand churning butter, and ice block food storage. Access to electricity introduced the immediate heat of electric stoves, year round refrigeration, vacuum cleaners, and electric mixers. Women could grow enough vegetables to feed the family throughout the year by canning on the electric range, keeping other vegetables in the freezer and storing root vegetables – potatoes, carrots, onions, beets – in the cold room. Hens could lay eggs almost year round, while older hens were canned for sandwich meat and younger roosters were frozen for roasts throughout the winter.

On the farms, families needed money to invest in agricultural production: buying land and equipment. Women spent their working day looking after animals and helping where needed to ensure the financial viability of the farm. This was invisible work that was expected of farm women; they were not seen as farmers or as contributing to the farm (Reimer 1986; Sachs 1987, Smith 1992; Kinnear 1998; Kubik 2005; Roppel, Desmarais, and Martz 2006;

Fletcher 2013). Their husbands labored to produce commodities such as grain and livestock for sale, through agribusiness companies, to national and international consumers. Both forms of food production – commodities for sale and food for the family – during the homestead period and even up to the 1940s was what is known today as organic. The invention of pesticides, herbicides, fungicides, and chemical fertilizers were a thing of the future. Every year farmers lost crops to grasshoppers, cutworms, and other insects as well as to diseases and molds. Manure was the only source of fertilizer and there was never enough to cover all the land. The amount of moisture was a critical determinant of crop yields. Livestock lived or died without the intervention of inoculations and medicines. The Corman farm in the 1960s was not unique. Other studies of prairie farm households during the 1960s found a rigorous gendered division of labor and patterns of deferred consumption (Kohl 1983; Wiebe 1987). Almost all land in Saskatchewan was owned and farmed by families who lived on their land. The domestic activities of women were intimately connected to the economic production processes of the enterprise although this was a "taken for granted" and not factored into the economic accounting of farm production.

By the turn of the twenty-first century, economic, demographic, and social conditions combined to provide a different set of financial inducements for prairie farm women. The amount of money that could be saved by self-provisioning fell in relationship to the capital costs of running the farm. While at the same time, taking employment in a local urban center provided a paycheck larger than needed to replace self-provisioned goods. Women's labor was more efficiently used bringing home a paycheck than canning beans and freezing peas. Better roads and cars made the trip to town convenient even on snowy winter mornings. Women also gained financial independence and more autonomy by taking jobs and working in urban centers. Employment for married women was commonplace and childcare was available (even though more difficult to find in a rural area) and socially acceptable.

By 2011, more differentiation was evident among farm women. A large number of farm women were employed for at least some of their married life, and with less time available, they had cut back on self-provisioning labor. There was also less incentive to provide their own food because the number of people to feed per farm unit had declined. The number of people living in each farm household had diminished by half from 4.7 in the baby boom period of 1951 to 2.4 in 2001 (Statistics Canada 2001). Many farm homes had no children living with them. The adult population on Saskatchewan farms was aging, rising from a median age of 39 in 1921 to 54.2 years in 2011. With usually only two adults at the table, there were diminishing returns to keeping a milk cow and chickens. Less food was consumed and as farm women aged, purchasing rather than gardening and storing became an option.

The transition from self-provisioning gardener to consumer removes women from a direct connection to the land. While many farm women worked off the farm, the labor involved in producing, packaging, and storing food transferred to unknown people in far-off places: tomatoes from Mexico, potatoes from Atlantic Canada, pork from feedlots, and chickens from cells in large metal buildings.

In contrast to the homestead period, by the twenty-first century farm women were no longer a homogeneous group providing similar types of contributions to the farm operation. Some women who are married to farm operators have no interaction with their husband's work, similar to a wife of a dentist. In this case, the family may live in town and the husband drives to the farm or they may live on the farm but the woman may not engage in operating the farm. At the other end of the continuum are women who own, manage, and operate their own farm, some as sole operators (in Saskatchewan in 2011, 3.9 percent of all farms were run solely by women). Many women fall in between these two extremes, doing more or less of all labor types: self-provisioning of food, paid employment, engaging in commodity production, and doing the marketing and book keeping. As Kubik and Moore (2003) observed, these "farm families are both an economic and kinship unit who live and work together in order that their means of subsistence – the farm – remains viable in a context of rapidly changing market conditions" (26).

The contemporary arrangement of the Corman farm represents one form of the diversity in the twenty-first century. Three brothers and one son farm collaboratively with various forms of labor and financial relations. Two Corman sisters live in cities and are not involved in the farm. Some of the land and crop sales are managed through a brother-owned corporation. Other land is owned individually or where present, with their wives. Neither wife, apart from providing household labor, is involved in any direct agricultural work or management-related decisions. One brother and his wife live on a farm and the wife drives to the nearby town to work five days a week. A brother and his wife live in town where she recently retired from owning, managing, and working in her restaurant. One brother lives alone on his farm. None of the brothers' daughters (one lived on a farm and the other two lived in town) participated in any agricultural work. The son of one of the brothers lives on a nearby farm and, although he labors collaboratively alongside his father and uncles, he owns his land outside the brother-owned corporation due to financial complexities. All crop-related equipment is jointly owned and the crop-related labor is done on a shared basis, with each of the four men developing their own specialties. Two brothers and one of their sons own, care for, and incur the expenses and revenue for the beef cattle, while the third brother assists with cutting hay for these cattle.

The family farm of the 1960s, each family with their own farm, has a new form in direct response to the necessity to grow big or to sell out. In this case, both the wives and their daughters are employed independently of the farm and contribute to the livelihoods of their households much as any urban woman does. Standard production of food for the household from the farm is limited to consumption of their own beef, which is provided by the men. None of the families raise chickens, provision vegetables, or milk a cow.

This example shares typical and atypical features with other family farm arrangements. In the vicinity of this farm, 29 families lived on farms in the 1960s; each farm was constituted by a man, woman, and their children. All labor, with rare exceptions, was done by family members and only one woman of the 29 had an off-farm job. In cases where children were not available, women assisted in agricultural production. Thirty children rode the bus to school in the nearby town. Today, 13 families work this land either through ownership or rental arrangements. Three of these families live off the farm. One child under 18 lives in the neighborhood. Only two men are under 50. Only one woman is under 50 and only one of the seven women who live on the farm has never had off-farm employment. Three of these women, ages 51, 68 and 75, still operate equipment in the field during periods of peak demand for labor. None of those living on farms keep a milk cow or chickens for family use. From 29 traditional family farms in the 1960s, only four in 2014 could be loosely considered family farms and in these cases, the children are all now non-resident adults.

Determining the contribution of women and men to operating the farms in Saskatchewan is difficult due to the varied nature of their contributions, the difficulty of measuring various types of "invisible" contributions and the lack of available statistics and information.[6] The types of contributions also vary across the life cycle according to the age of adults and the age and presence of children.

Farm women recognized as farm operators[7]

In keeping with the patriarchal structures in place in the British world in 1900, homesteads were granted to men and the descent line on the farm for the next hundred years was largely to sons. Generally, women moved to farms only as wives of male farmers. Some farm women participated in farm management decisions and also assisted in producing agricultural products for sale. However, it was not until 1991 that farm women could identify themselves as a farm operator in the Canadian Census and at the same time, up to three operators could be associated with one farm.

According to the Census of Agriculture, in 2011 Saskatchewan had 49,475 farm operators on 36,952 farms, 16.4 percent fewer than in 2006 and down from 78,025 in 1991. In 2011, women formed 22.9 percent of Saskatchewan farm operators, while nationally this percentage was 27.4 percent (see Figure 2.2) (Statistics Canada 2011). Many of these women were operating farms alongside their husband or son; only 5.2 percent operated farms independently of men (1,385 operators/36,952 farms). Although both the number of male and female operators has fallen significantly from 1991 to 2011, the number of female operators has not fallen as sharply, a drop of 30.3 percent as compared to male operators at a drop of 38.3 percent. This lower trend may be reflected in the larger proportion of remaining farm women claiming the status of farm operator. Sole women farm operators declined the least in this period, down to 28.9 percent.

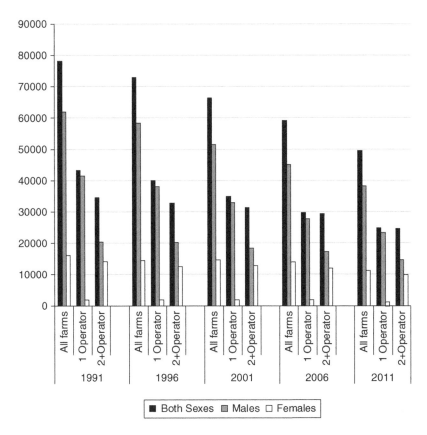

Figure 2.2 Number of Saskatchewan female and male farm operators 1991–2011.

Source: Compiled by authors from Census of Agriculture data, Statistics Canada.

The average age of female and male farm operators in Canada is increasing. By 2011, the average age for women was 53.4 years, while for men it was 54.4 (Statistics Canada, 2011). A greater proportion of women farm operators were under 35 years, at 21.6 percent, compared to only 9.0 percent of men operators under 35 years. Fifty percent of male operators were over 55 years in comparison to 46.6 percent of women operators (Table 2.1) (Statistics Canada 2011).

According to the Census of Agriculture, in 2011 44.2 percent of all Saskatchewan male farm operators had an off-farm job or business compared to 52.5 percent of women. Men were more likely to work longer hours on the farm, with 52.6 percent working over 40 hours a week on the farm compared to 26.3 percent of women. Data are no longer available on caring work and domestic labor because the long-form census was abandoned in 2011, but past data suggest women did more of this kind of work (Statistics Canada 2011).

Table 2.2 Selected farm operator variables classified by sex of farm operators, Saskatchewan, 2011

Operator variables	All operators	Male operators	Female operators
Total number of farm operators	49,475	38,150	11,320
Under 35 years	4,375	3,445	930
35 to 54 years	20,705	15,585	5,125
55 years and over	24,395	19,130	5,270
Average age of farm operators	54.2	54.4	53.4
Farm work in 2010:			
More than 40 hours per week	23,055	20,065	2,985
30 to 40 hours per week per week	7,270	5,685	1,590
20 to 29 hours per week	6,830	4,830	2,000
Less than 20 hours	12,325	7,570	4,750
Paid non-farm work in 2010			
0 hours per week	26,650	21,275	5,375
More than 40 hours per week	8,710	7,350	1,355
30 to 40 hours per week	6,570	4,520	2,055
20 to 29 hours per week	3,150	2,035	1,115
Less than 20 hours	4,395	2,970	1,425

Source: 2011, Census of Agriculture, Statistics Canada.

There are striking differences in the size of farms managed by sole women operators compared to joint women-men operators and male-only operations. Sole women operators are more likely to manage smaller farms, with 66 percent of them managing farms under 560 acres. Men are less likely to manage smaller farms, only 36 percent of joint women-men operations and 35 percent of sole men operators are of this size (Statistics Canada 2011).

Given that women are more represented on smaller farms, there are also striking differences in the types of farms on which women self-report as operators.[8] In Saskatchewan, the following farms are more likely to have male-only operators: oil seed and grain at 74 percent, beef at 66 percent, miscellaneous at 66 percent, and vegetable/melon at 61 percent. Sole women operators have their largest share in green houses, at 24.8 percent. Sole women operators manage less than 10 percent of all other farm types. Joint women and men operators manage 51 percent of sheep/goat farms, 48 percent of dairy farms, 45 percent of green houses, and 42 percent of poultry/egg farms. The financial status of farms managed solely by women is considerably different from those farms managed solely by men or in a joint female-male arrangement. The average total gross farm receipts for sole female operators is $86,081 as compared with $222,062 for sole male-managed farms and $259,379 for joint operations. Similarly the operating income (gross farm receipts subtract operating expenses) for sole female operators is $19,200 as compared with $62,600 for sole male managed farms and $62,700 for joint operations (Statistics Canada 2011).

External forces

The marketing and distribution of food to consumers around the world by multinational conglomerates, whose primarily motivation is maximizing profits, has established a series of economic and political pressures on farm operators, be they female or male, to adopt industrial agricultural practices. Thousands of these individual farmers, confronting the same set of marketing relations, have moved to increase production by buying more land, investing in big machines and heavy chemical inputs, and by diversifying their crops.

Buying inputs and selling their commodities to multinationals leaves individual farmers with little flexibility. Equality of opportunity for women to operate the farm is not enough. Marketing possibilities tie farm families to production practices. Saskatchewan farmers will remain compelled to embrace industrial agricultural practices as long as their livelihoods depend on multinationals to purchase their products. Among the inevitable structural outcomes of a capitalist marketplace and the dynamics of market-based production are the concentration and centralization of capital. In the farming sector this is apparent by the growth in the size of farms, the decline in the number of family farms, and the challenge to retain youth in farming.

The period from World War II into the early 1970s encompasses what some scholars (Lawrence, Knuttila and Gray 2001; Qualman 2007; Winson 2013 call the Second International Food Regime, marked by efforts to facilitate international trade through trade agreements, the growing importance of large multinational capital in virtually every aspect of food production, and increased processing and increasing productivity in many parts of the world that generated a new problem – commodity surpluses (McMichael 2009). By the 1970s, Western nations including Canada entered an era of deregulation, market supremacy, denigration of the public sphere, and cuts to public expenditures except those directly beneficial to capital or backed by powerful political forces. In Canada, post 1970s when the Federal Task Force on Agriculture suggested elimination of excess producers, neo-liberalism meant abandonment of transportation systems and support, abrogation of support such as the elimination of the Crow's Nest Pass Agreement (a transport support program for farmers), dilution and elimination of the Canadian Wheat Board's single-desk sales capacity, cuts to many support programs, and so on (Conway 2006). The general move to allow the market to do what the market will do – concentrate and centralize production in fewer but larger producers – meant many farm families gave up and left the land while others attempted to survive. Survival strategies were varied and involved different members of the family in different ways. Women contributed by directly working on the farm, taking off-farm work to subsidize the farm and feed the children, running the household (nearly single-handedly), volunteering in the community, and emotionally supporting the family as it experienced the vagaries of farming.

In this context, women's work on the farm and their interactions with the land have changed. From solely working on the farm to combining work that supports the farm with paid off-farm work, many farm women with off-farm jobs orient their lives toward urban centers with the consequence that they do not have the time or energy for food production either for the farm or the market. As their own food consumption is increasingly tied to the grocery store rather than the farm yard, the tie between women and nature is not cultivated and without direct involvement in food production, women's material and emotional connection to the land is increasingly weakened.

The future?

What are future options? If we continue on this course, the dramatic changes in ownership relations and production practices call into question both the sustainability of farm land and also the quality of food produced in Saskatchewan. Given that the average age of farm operators in Canada is increasing each year, there is a realistic concern that young people are not available or not able to take over the farm. Unless policies change, large corporate interests and pension plan concerns will likely continue to amass Saskatchewan farm land. Given that, as DiPerna and Norsigian argue, "the expanding global food system is characterized by environmental problems resulting from large-scale, chemical-intensive agriculture" (quoted in Sachs 2003, 372), what are the consequences of soil erosion, pesticide use, and contaminated water for the composition of our food? Will the high cost of fuel and chemical inputs, with the resultant financial implications for farm input costs, generate a different set of financial inducements for farm families? Will this different set of financial inducements favor management practices without a reliance on chemical inputs? Is the energy crisis the motivational factor that will assist the sustainable agricultural movement, and, as Sachs (2003, 372) has hoped, generate a production and marketing system "that protects the environment, is economically profitable for farmers and is socially just"? Or will the higher price of agricultural commodities lead to non-family corporate ownership of farm land, a disembodied ownership that leads to short-term profitable land use strategies that are detrimental to long-term land fertility?

The necessity of food for human life is a given, and humans continue to be more numerous. The United Nations (2013) predicts that the population of the world will reach 9.6 billion by 2050. The long-term feasibility of producing enough healthy food is at a crossroads. Fortunate people demand and can afford organic food while many around the world are still malnourished. Even within Canada a two-tiered food system is emerging where the poor buy one type of food while the wealthy can afford a healthy alternative. Traditional producers, such as Saskatchewan farmers and their families, are increasingly losing control over their operations because of land speculation, high input costs, and inability to control market forces. If these trends continue large corporations and wealthy investors will control an ever-increasing portion of our food production. Many of these companies are now horizontally and vertically integrated multinational corporations whose main concern is with their bottom line. Our control of our food security and sustainability, food systems, and environment are increasingly at risk.

Farm women and family farms are key to sustainable and secure food in Saskatchewan. Family farms are much more invested in producing healthy sustainable high-quality food in the long term, but for them to do so these families must be supported by the public and governments. Research has consistently illustrated that women do more work on farms than agricultural statistics indicate (Reimer 1986; Machum 2006). We need much more reliable census data regarding women's contribution to farm households, to on-farm labor, off-farm income, and to their communities. These data should be sensitive to life-cycle changes and to whether women indicate themselves as farm operators. Currently, no research exists to indicate the circumstances under which women embrace this affiliation.

We need farm policies that support the farm family with long-term sustainable and secure food practices. Corporations and external investors, focused as they are only on short-term gain (or else they leave), are not the best way to produce secure, healthy, and sustainable food for Canadians. Farmland ownership legislation needs to deter ownership by the Canada Pension Plan, non-farm consortiums, and certainly out of country investors if we want to ensure food sustainability and security. We need to support farm families and particularly the work of farm women. As land degradation and climate change rapidly transform the prairies and as food demands increase, the urgency required for progressive farm policies (from ownership statuses, income supports, to reliable census data, and support/recognition for farm women) are drastically and immediately needed.

Notes

1 The Federal Government instituted policies that restricted farming for status Indians and contributed to the failure of agricultural production and marketing on reserves (see Indian Policy and the Early Reserve Period in Nestor 2006).

2 Toronto-based Sprott Resources terminated its leasing agreement with Saskatchewan reserves and no longer participates in farming 200,000 acres of First Nations-owned farm land. Instead they are focusing on cattle ranching (Cross 2014).

3 Beyond the scope of this chapter is women's ownership, management and laboring roles on Hutterite colonies and in First Nations/corporate co-ventures, and other forms of corporate owned farm and ranch land.

4 The vast majority of grain farms and ranches in Saskatchewan are owned and operated by people born into farm families or those who marry farmers. By 2001, 97.6 percent of farm operators were Canadian born to families of European descent that had lived in Saskatchewan for two or more generations (Statistics Canada 2001).

5 Gross farm receipts include sales of agricultural products, program payments and custom work. Data for 2006 were sourced from Census of Agriculture, 2006. Data for 2011 are sourced from a private run provided by Statistics Canada. Table Name: Gross farm receipts, operating expenses and operating income classified by farm type.

6 According to Reimer (1986, 153), "focus on productive labor caused women's indirect contribution to the production of goods to be overlooked." This finding is supported in a variety of contexts, see: Kinnear 1998; Rosenfield 1985; Sachs 1987;
Shortall 1993; Smith 1988, 1992; Whatmore 1991; Wiebe 1995.

7 All data for this section were commissioned from a custom run on the 2011
Agricultural Census and were provided by Statistics Canada in 2014.

8 Data on women farm operators are from a custom run on the 2011 Agricultural
Census and were provided by Statistics Canada in 2014.

References

Alston, Margaret. 1998. "Farm Women and Their Work: Why Is It Not Recognized?"
Journal of Sociology 34 (1): 23–34.

———. 2006. "The Gendered Impact of Drought." In *Rural Gender Relations: Issues and
Case Studies*, edited by Bettina Barbara Bock and Sally Shortall, 165–80. London:
CAB International.

Atkins, Eric. 2013. "CPPIB buys Saskatchewan farms in $128 million deal." *The Globe
and Mail*, December 12.

Conway, John. 2006. *The West: The History of a Region in Confederation*. Toronto:
Lorimer Books.

Corman, June. 2005. "The 'Good Wife' and Her Farm Husband: Changing Household
Practices in Rural Saskatchewan." *Canadian Woman Studies* 24 (4) (Summer): 69–74.

Cross, Brian. 2014. "One Earth Farms Restructures." *Western Producer*. Posted May 15.
www.producer.com/2014/05/one-earth-farms-restructures.

Desmarais, Annette; Darren Qualman, Andre Magnan, and Nettie Wiebe (2015)
"Land Grabbing and Land Concentration: Mapping Changing Patterns of
Farmland in Three Rural Municipalities in Saskatchewan, Canada." *Canadian Food
Studies/ La Revue canadienne des études sur l'alimentation [Online]* 2 (1): 16–47.

Fletcher, Amber. 2013. "The View from Here: Agricultural Policy, Climate Change,
and the Future of Farm Women in Saskatchewan." PhD diss., University of Regina.

Fowke, Vernon. 1957. *The National Policy and the Wheat Economy*. Toronto: University
of Toronto Press.

Ghorayshi, Parvin. 1989. "The Indispensable Nature of Wives' Work for the Farm
Family Enterprise." *The Canadian Review of Sociology* 26 (4): 571–95.

Kelly, Roisin, and Sally Shortall. 2002. "'Farmers' Wives': Women Who are Off-farm
Breadwinners and the Implications for On-farm Gender Relations." *Journal Of
Sociology* 38 (4): 327–43.

Kinnear Mary. 1998. *A Female Economy: Women's Work in a Prairie Province,
1870–1970*. Montreal and Kingston: McGill-Queens University Press.

Knuttila, Murray, and Bob Stirling. 2007. *The Prairie Agrarian Movement Revisited*.
Regina: Canadian Plains Research Center.

Kohl, Seena. 1983. "Working Together: Husbands and Wives in the Small Scale
Family Agriculture Enterprise." In *The Canadian Family*, edited by K. Ishwaran,
234–43. Toronto: Gage Publishing Limited.

Kubik, Wendee. 2004. "The Changing Roles of Farm Women and the Consequences
for Their Health, Well Being, and Quality of Life." PhD diss., University of Regina.

———. 2005. "Farm women: The Hidden Subsidy in our Food." *Canadian Woman
Studies* 24 (4) (Summer): 85–90.

Kubik, Wendee, and Robert Moore. 2003. "Farming in Saskatchewan in the 1990s: Stress and Coping." In *Farm Communities at the Crossroads: Challenge and Resistance*, edited by Harry P. Diaz, JoAnn Jaffe, and Robert Stirling, 137–48. Regina, SK: Canadian Plains Research Center.

Lawrence, Geoffrey, Murray Knuttila, and Ian Gray. 2001. "Globalization, Neo-liberalism, and Rural Decline Australia and Canada." *In Writing Off the Rural West, Globalization, Governments, and the Transformation of Rural Communities*, edited by Roger Epp and Dave Whitson, 89–105. Edmonton, AB: University of Alberta Press.

Luxton, Meg, and June Corman. 2011. "Families at Work: Individual versus Collective Strategies for Making a Living." In *Canadian Families: In the 21st Century*, edited by Ann Duffy and Nancy Mandell, 211–42. Toronto: Nelson.

Machum, Susan. 2006. "Commodity Production and Farm Women's Work." In *Rural Gender Relations: Issues and Case Studies*, edited by Bettina Bock and Sally Shortall, 47–63. London: CAB International.

Magnan, Andre. 2011. "New Avenues of Farm Corporatization in the Prairie Grains Sector: Farm Family Entrepreneurs and the Case of One Earth Farms." *Agriculture and Human Values* 29 (2): 161–75.

Martz, Diane, and Ingrid Brueckner. 2003. *The Canadian Family at Work: Exploring Gender and Generation*. Muenster, SK: Centre for Rural Studies and Enrichment, St. Peter's College. www.nfu.ca/sites/www.nfu.ca/files/The_Canadian_Farm_Family_at_Work.pdf.

McMichael, Phillip. 2009. "A Food Regime Genealogy." *Journal of Peasant Studies* 36 (1): 139–69.

Nestor, Rob. 2005. "Indian Policy and the Early Reserve Period." In *Encyclopedia of Saskatchewan*, 480–81. Regina: University of Regina.

Qualman, Darrin. 2007. "Farmers and Farm Organizations: The Effects of Trade Agreements and Globalization" In *The Prairie Agrarian Movement Revisited*, edited by Murray Knuttila and Bob Stirling, 251–62. Regina: Canadian Plains Research Center.

Reimer, Bill. 1986. "Women as Farm Labour." *Rural Sociology* 51 (2): 143–55.

Roppel, Carla, Annette Aurelie Desmarais, and Diane Martz. 2006. *Farm Women and Canadian Agricultural Policy*. Ottawa: Status of Women Canada. www.aic.ca/gender/pdf/Farm_Women.pdf.

Rosenfield, Rachel. 1985. *Farm Women: Work, Farm, and Family in the United States*. Chapel Hill: The University of North Carolina Press.

Sachs Carolyn. 1987. "American Farm Women." In *Women and Work: An Annual Review*, edited by Ann Stromberg, L. Laurwood and B.A. Gutak, 2:233–48. Newbury Park, California: Sage Press.

———. 1996. *Gendered Fields: Rural Women, Agriculture, and Environment*. Boulder: Westview Press.

———. 2003. "Rural Women: Sustaining Farms, Feeding People." In *Sisterhood Is Forever: The Women's Anthology for a New Millennium*, edited by Robin Morgan 368–77. New York: Washington Square Press.

Shortall, Sally. 1993. "Canadian and Irish Farm Women: Some Similarities, Differences and Comments." *The Canadian Review of Sociology and Anthropology* 30 (2): 172–90.

———. 1999. *Women and Farming Property and Power*. Basingstoke: Macmillan Press.

Smith, Pamela. 1988. "Murdoch's, Becker's and Sorochan's Challenge: Thinking again about the Roles of Women in Primary Agriculture." In *The Political Economy of Agriculture in Western Canada*, edited by Gurcharn Basran and David Hays, 157–74. Toronto: Garamond Press.

———. 1992. "Beyond 'Add Women and Stir' in Canadian Rural Society." In *Rural Sociology in Canada*, edited by David A. Hay and Gurcharn S. Basran, 155–70. Don Mills, ON: Oxford University Press.

Statistics Canada. 2001. *Census of Agriculture*. Ottawa, ON. Government of Canada.

———. 2006. Table 004-0007. *2006 Census of Agriculture farms classified by operating arrangements, Canada and provinces*. CANSIM (database). Last modified December 10, 2012. www5.statcan.gc.ca/cansim/a26?lang=eng&id=40007.

———. 2011. *Census of Agriculture*. Ottawa, ON. Government of Canada.

Storey, Shannon. 2002. "Neoliberal Trade Policies in Agriculture and the Destruction of Global Food Security: Who can feed the world?" *Canadian Woman Studies* 21 (3) (Spring): 190–95.

United Nations, Department of Economic and Social Affairs, Population Division. 2013. *World Population Prospects: The 2012 Revision*, www.un.org/en/development/desa/news/population/un-report-world-population-projected-to-reach-9-6-billion-by-2015.html.

Whatmore, Sarah. 1991. *Farming Women: Gender, Work, and Family Enterprise*. Basingstoke: Macmillan.

Wiebe, Nettie. 1987. *Weaving New Ways: Farm Women Organizing*. Saskatoon: National Farmer's Union.

———. 1995. "Farm Women: Cultivating Hope and Sowing Change." In *Changing Methods, Feminists transforming Practice*, edited by Sandra Burt and Lorraine Code, 137–162, Peterborough, ON: Broadview Press.

Winson, Anthony. 2013. *The Industrial Diet, the Degradation of Food and the Struggle for Healthy Eating*. New York: New York University Press.

South Africa

3 The plight of female farm workers on South African farms

Maria-Stella Vettori

Introduction

Women represent almost two thirds of those engaged in some form of agriculture in South Africa (Hart and Aliber 2012). Many women do this as a main source or as an extra source of household food. The women who are involved in agriculture as a main source of food exceed men by 37 percent, while those women who are engaged in agriculture as a means of acquiring an extra source of household food exceed the men by 65 percent (Hart and Aliber 2012). According to this research, female and male agricultural roles and responsibilities are different because women are generally responsible for the supply of food. Given the large proportion of women involved in agriculture in South Africa, and given the fact that their roles in agriculture differ from their male counterparts, it is important that policies and legislation created to reduce inequalities in the agricultural sector take these differences into account. Legislation and policies should be designed to address the differences between men and women farm workers as well as the unique needs of women involved in agriculture.

The first democratically elected government of South Africa has made concerted efforts to develop South Africa's agricultural sector. The post-1994 policies and programs of the government also sought to diminish both racial and gender inequality in the agricultural sector. Many of these policies and programs, including the *1995 White Paper on Agriculture*, the *1998 Agricultural Policy in South Africa* discussion document, the *2001 Strategic Plan for South African Agriculture*, and the 2004 *Comprehensive Agricultural Support Programme*, "have exemplified the criticism that there is an evident shift away from supporting the poor and more vulnerable farmers, especially female farmers, towards an overwhelming focus on the better resourced and more commercially orientated black farmers" (Hart and Aliber 2012, 1). The post-1994 government has also attempted to reduce gender and racial discrimination in the agricultural sector through the introduction of legislation, specifically through land tenure legislation and labor legislation.

The purpose of this chapter is to set out the extent of poverty, abuse, discrimination, and utter desperation that fills the lives of women in the agricultural sector in South Africa, to examine the land tenure and labor legislation put in place to redress these social problems, and to ascertain whether the legislation has been successful in improving the lives and status of these women.

South Africa's history of slavery and colonialism

Farm workers are amongst the poorest people in South Africa. They rank as the poorest people in South Africa in terms of education levels, cash income, and nutritional status (Hall, Kleinbooi, and Mvambu 2001). This results in a cycle of poverty, the consequences of which include lack of access to justice, lack of access to farms, and the social and economic effects of alcohol abuse. The poverty of farm workers is rooted in South Africa's history of slavery and colonialism. Many farm workers can trace their ancestry to the slaves of the seventeenth and eighteenth centuries in slave plantations in the Cape of Good Hope. In 1652 the Dutch East India Company set up at the station in Table Bay (Cape Town) in order to provide necessary provisions for passing ships. Beginning in 1657, the European settlers were allotted farms by the colonial authorities in the arable regions around Cape Town. In response to the European settlers' need for labor, the Dutch East India company imported slaves from East Africa, Madagascar and the East Indies. By the mid-1700s there were more slaves in Cape Town than European colonists (South African History Online, 2015).

After the abolition of slavery in 1834, farm workers became subject to legally enforced racial segregation and exploitation culminating in the formalization of racial segregation and oppression in terms of apartheid legislation. The Acts that made up the apartheid legislation were passed between 1856 and 1904. Amongst other things it was a criminal offence to breach a contract of employment and to partake in a strike. Insolence, drunkenness, desertion, and negligence at work all constituted criminal offences. Although in theory these laws applied to all races, in practice the court held that the laws were applicable only to unskilled work, which was performed mostly by black people (Dugard 1978). The notorious Natives Land Act of 1913 outlawed the ownership of land by blacks in areas designated for white ownership. In essence, this legislation ensured that the distribution of land that emerged from the era of colonial wars against indigenous tribes remained intact. The outcome was that 80 percent of land became white owned whilst blacks were relegated to the remaining 13 percent. The remaining seven percent of the land was owned by the State. This state of affairs remained in place until 1994 when the first democratic government of South Africa was elected.

Historically, farm workers' families have worked for the same farm owner family for many generations. From generation to generation, farm workers' children step into their parents' shoes, stuck in the same cycle of poverty and dependence. By the same token the children of the farm owners also step into their parents' shoes. In this way the mindset of both farm owner and worker is passed on from generation to generation. The problem is that the human psyche perceives this way of doing things as normal, in a sense of being morally correct, and acceptable simply because that is what they know in their own experience. People simply accept things and circumstances without question because that is the way things have been done for centuries.

> The fact that many farm worker families have lived on the same farm for generations has undoubtedly resulted in a unique bond between employers and workers on commercial farms, but this relationship is inherently unequal – it derives originally from slavery, and allows farmers to continue to treat 'their' workers paternalistically at best, and as legal minors at worst. Within this paternalistic system, farmers are invariably male, and farmworkers' families are seen (often inaccurately) as headed by men who are primarily income earners. This patriarchy and paternalism have interacted to marginalise farm women.
>
> (Devereux and Solomon 2011, 10)

The harsh reality of farm workers' socio-economic circumstances serves to exacerbate the situation so that they are, in effect, powerless to change the circumstances even when they do realize that the manner in which they are treated and exploited is morally reprehensible and illegal. Even if farm owners do see the moral malaise of their ways, some simply continue doing what they do because it renders their life easier and because their obligations are not properly enforced allowing them to act illegally and immorally regarding their tenancy and labor law obligations. In a most pervasive manner, the fact that many farm workers' families have lived on the same farm for generations has created a bond between employers and workers on commercial farms (Devereux and Solomon 2011, 10). Naturally this relationship is a paternalistic one where farm workers are entirely dependent on their employers rendering the relationship inherently unequal. In short, the historical background to the deplorable conditions endured by farm workers in South Africa lies in South Africa's history of colonial conquest and disposition of the land occupied by indigenous people.

A woman's place

The poverty of women is exacerbated by social customs, illiteracy, inequality, isolation and low mobility levels, ignorance, and lack of access to justice and other resources. Women are subordinate and subservient not only to the farm owner family but also to their husbands or partners. Women in rural areas are bound by cultural, paternalistic traditions that are prevalent both in the culture of the traditionally white farm owner, and also in the culture of black and colored farm workers. (In South Africa "colored" refers to an ethnic group that is essentially of mixed origins who possess ancestry from Europe, Asia, and various indigenous ethnic groups of Southern Africa.) The traditions regarding tenancy and women's work on farms have emanated from this sexist and paternalistic culture. A woman's access to housing is dependent on her husband's contract of employment. Since housing is provided as a benefit in a contract of employment, termination of the contract of employment means the end of access to housing and the eviction of an entire family (Dladla 2000). Therefore a woman occupier is in a dependent position vis-à-vis her spouse or partner regarding access to houses and tenancy. The male laborer as occupier determines who will live with him on the farm.

> In South Africa, the history of colonialism and apartheid rule has resulted in a significant overlap of race and poverty. Because poverty and inequality are so strongly gendered, the most disadvantaged and marginalized in our society are black women. A substantial number of black women are further disadvantaged by their exposure to cultural and religious regimes that make the struggle for gender equality even more complex. Specifically, African customary law – which is essentially patriarchal in both character and form and has been interpreted in a way that allocates crucial benefits according to male primogeniture has had a particularly detrimental effect on the social economic power and well-being of rural women.
>
> (Mokgoro 2003, 565–66)

Wages

Women farm workers are generally paid less than men, not only because of the patriarchal customs and practices, but because women typically do casual work and because female labor is viewed as less skilled. Female workers also do not get as much payment in kind as their male counterparts. On average women farm workers earn 25 percent to 50 percent less than their male counterparts (Husy and Samson 2001). The trend towards increased casualization continues (Brown-Luthango 2006). All seasonal workers, usually women, who were interviewed in the research of Brown-Luthago and who had been working on the same farm for more than five years, and even as long as 13 years, had not been appointed on a permanent basis.

Furthermore, Brown-Luthago's research discovered an increase in the number of labor brokers in the agricultural industry in the Western Cape. Seasonal workers are either employed directly by the farm or recruited through labor brokers or temporary employment services (TES). Those recruited by TES were found to be even worse off than those who were employed directly by the farm. The research conducted also highlighted and commented on the insecurity and vulnerability of farm workers in general and seasonal women workers in particular. The researchers identified the harsh reality of the daily lives of female seasonal workers. The circumstances of one seasonal worker is described in the research as follows:

> A seasonal worker in the Grabouw area's husband died towards the end of 2005. She was left behind with two small children to support. The farmer informed her that since she did not have a husband anymore, she

could no longer live on the farm. She had no choice, but to evacuate the home and move in with her father on a neighboring farm. This meant that she had no transport from her new place of residence to her place of work and she could no longer take her youngest child to the crèche on the farm where she used to live. In addition to losing her home, she was now forced to give up her job as she did not have the means to get to work and had no one to look after the baby.

(Brown-Luthango 2006, 4–5)

Tenure

Labor tenants in South Africa depend on farm owners for access to land, housing, and income. Many families have lived on farms for generations (Bosch 1994), and most permanently employed farm workers live on the farm (Kritzinger and Vorster 1997). According to research by Human Rights Watch (2011), which involved more than 260 interviews with farm workers, farm owners, civil society members, industry representatives, government officials, lawyers, union officials, and academic experts, housing for farm workers is often so deplorable that it is unfit for living, with lack of access to toilets or drinking water. One farm worker showed Human Rights Watch the former pig stall, which lacked electricity, water, or protection from the elements, where he had lived with his wife and children for ten years. The report also describes insecure tenure rights and threats of eviction for long-time residence on farms.

The 2003 South African Human Rights Commission (SAHRC) report, which was the result of a comprehensive national enquiry into human rights violations in farming communities, found that an estimated 1.4 million people were evicted from farms in South Africa between 1950 and 1980. The SAHRC's (2008) report referred to the Nkuzi Development Association/ Social Surveys study (Wegerif, Russell, and Grunding 2005), which is the only large-scale national survey that assessed evictions since 1994 when the first democratic elections in South Africa were held. The survey found that more evictions have occurred since 1994 than before 1994. It found that there was a steady increase in evictions up until 2004. According to the survey, close to one million farm workers were evicted in the ten years immediately after the 1994 elections and approximately three quarters of evictees were women. Human Rights Watch found that according to civil society estimates, more than 930,000 people were evicted from South African farms between 1994 and 2004 (Human Rights Watch 2011). Evicted workers who spoke with Human Rights Watch had not been given suitable alternative housing or adequate compensation to find new accommodation. According to the Human Rights Watch report, farm owners sometimes still resort to illegal tactics to get farm dwellers to leave including cutting off electricity or water. Security guards are paid to harass families in the middle of the night with dogs (Human Rights Watch 2011).

Violence

The history of colonialism, slavery, and apartheid legislation has ensured that farm workers are dependent on farm owners, not only for employment, but also for accommodation, land, housing, education, basic necessities, food, and social services including health and electricity. This allows farm owners extensive power over farm workers and their families. This dependence results in a significant imbalance of power between farm owner and farm worker. Violence against farm workers has been a fact of life since colonial times in South Africa. Numerous cases of violence, including rape of farm workers, have been reported. In July 2002, the Centre for Rural Legal Studies in Cape Town conducted a survey and found that farm owners regarded it as their right to "discipline workers." This included severe beatings, and some farm workers regarded it as normal to receive a beating (Dladla 2000). This is accompanied by a very low rate of conviction as many assaults go unreported as a result of lack of transport and communications systems as well as a lack of faith in the police (SAHRC 2003).

The abuse and violence perpetrated against farm workers of both sexes spills into the dwellings of the farm workers. Women become victims of violence not only from the farm owners but also from their husbands or partners who are farm workers. The violence against women is intensified as a result of alcohol abuse. This was confirmed by the SAHRC report of June 2003. In this report, the SAHRC found further that alcoholism is rife amongst farm workers and locks them into cycles of poverty and abuse. Alcohol abuse diverts money from being spent on food and thus plunges the family even deeper into a cycle of debt, poverty, and violence. This research was followed by the SAHRC report in 2008 in order to assess progress with respect to tenure security, safety, and labor in the agricultural sector in South Africa. Regarding violence in the agricultural community, the SAHRC report found that "there continues to be unacceptably high levels of violent crime which persist in farming areas" (2008, 35). A report by Human Rights Watch (2011, 15) states that "farm workers and other rural dwellers are more vulnerable to violence, including from their white employers and are the least likely to get help from the police and courts."

Legislation

Security of tenure

The Land Reform (Labour Tenants Act) was passed in 1996 in order to give effect to the Constitution and secure tenure or comparable redress for those who had insecure land tenure as a result of discriminatory laws. This legislation made provision for labor tenants to apply to own the land they lived on and used. The cut-off date to make such application was March 31, 2001. By that date about 19,000 applicants had made application to the Department of

Rural Development and Land Reform. To date these applications have yet to be processed (Hornby 2015).

The Extension of Security of Land Tenure Act (ESTA) was enacted in order to prevent arbitrary evictions; to ensure that people who live on land belonging to other people are guaranteed basic human rights; to promote long-term security either on the land where people are living or on other land and; to recognize and protect the existing rights of ownership (Department of Land Affairs 1997). Unfortunately the legislation had some unintended adverse effects, as many farm owners evicted farm workers and were discouraged from keeping labor tenants and taking on new families, especially extended families of workers (Murray 2000). Farm owners perceived ESTA as a disincentive to invest in decent housing standards as the law stipulates that alternative housing of the same standards has to be accessible if the residence is terminated (Hall, Kleinbooi, and Mvambu 2001).

Furthermore, the paternalistic and sexist attitude has unfortunately been reinforced by the courts in the interpretation given to the provisions in ESTA, which were intended to protect farm workers from evictions. For example, in the case of *Landbounavorsingsraad v Klaasen* 2001 ((NPO) unreported case number ZALCC 83R/01 of October 29), Gildenhuys AJ held that the female spouse of a farm worker occupies under or through the head of a household and that therefore she does not qualify as an "occupier" as intended by ESTA, unless the land owner explicitly consented to her staying on the farm. In short the court made it clear that a wife or partner cannot derive occupier status on grounds of her family ties with the head of the household. The judgement reinforced the existent patriarchal system. Secondly, if a male occupier is dismissed or falls ill and can no longer work or dies, his spouse or partner automatically also loses her tenancy rights since these rights are inextricably linked to her spouse's or her partner's employment by the land owner. This interpretation of the legislation is a violation of human rights. As stated by Hattingh: "To uproot women who are working on farms with their children without even considering all the relevant factors, is a violation of their constitutional rights. Even more so because farm evictions take place in the context of increasing poverty and illness" (2008, 526).

This interpretation of ESTA also blatantly attributes to a neutral concept such as "occupier" contained in ESTA, a sexist meaning that infringes the right to equality contained in section nine of the Constitution (South Africa, 1996). This type of decision also has no regard to the purpose and intent of the legislation given the socio-economic reality the legislation was intended to address and remedy. In short, the reality is that access to housing for a woman is determined by her relationship with a male farm worker despite legislation put in place to protect the vulnerable, especially women.

Although it is against the law for landowners to evict occupiers from land without following the required procedures, the authorities rarely initiate criminal proceedings. In 2001 Hall, Kleinbooi, and Mvambu observed that evictions were still taking place with little fear of consequences since there is no supervision or implementation of the law. This does not seem to have changed and according to the Human Rights Watch (2011) report, evictions continue without procedures being followed. Even when the farm owners follow legal procedures evicted farm dwellers often have no place to go. This is because municipal governments are generally unprepared to assist them. It is clear that tenure security legislation has not improved the lot of farm workers, especially women. In fact it may have made matters worse.

Labor legislation

Post-apartheid labor laws are progressive by global standards. However, the law is premised on a corporatist model of labor where big business and big unions negotiate conditions of employment for standard employees. In other words, atypical employees who do not have permanent secure employment are often excluded to a large extent. "Atypical," "non-standard," or even "marginal" are terms used to describe "those engaged, for instance, in part-time work, contract work, self-employment, temporary, fixed term, seasonal, casual, piece rate work, or to employees supplied by employment agencies, home workers and those employed in the informal economy" (Fourie 2008, 111).

The primary and inherent imbalance of power between employer and employee in the employment relationship is addressed by the legislative provisions that provide employees with rights and by the exercise of collective power of unions in the setting of terms and conditions for the employees they represent. The legal framework comprises four sources of law, namely, the Constitution, legislation, common law, and customary law. The Constitution contains a Bill of Rights which entrenches a range of labor rights for workers and employees; for example, section 23(1) of the Constitution (1996) provides that "everyone has the right to fair labor practices." The other provisions in the Constitution provide for collective labor rights including the right to join and form trade unions and the right to strike. The Bill of Rights binds the state as well as employers. Section 8 of the Constitution permits courts to develop the common law rules and remedies to give effect to the rights contained in the Bill of Rights to the extent that there is no legislation giving effect to the right.

The common law is important because it is the contract of employment that creates the basis or foundation for the edifice of the employment relationship. Without a contract of employment there is no employment relationship.

The centerpiece of South African legislation concerning labor relations is the Labour Relations Act (1995) (LRA). This Act encourages collective bargaining inter alia by creating fora for collective bargaining, by creating means of achieving organizational rights, and providing for the right to strike. It also protects employees against unfair labor practices and unfair dismissal. Other significant labor legislation includes the following:

1. The Basic Conditions of Employment Act (1997) (BCEA), which provides for minimum standards such as hours of work and leave. The BCEA sets out minimum standards for most employers, excluding minimum wage requirements. The BCEA also provides for state-legislated Sectoral Determinations which regulate wages, hours, and basic conditions for vulnerable or special sectors. Under this Act the ANC government, in some cases for the first time, has set minimum standards, including minimum wages and benefits for vulnerable workers including farm workers;
2. The Employment Equity Act (1998) (EEA), which prohibits discrimination in the workplace and places an obligation on employers who employ more than 50 employees to implement affirmative action measures in order to redress the inequities of the past and achieve equity in the workplace;
3. The Skills Development Act (1998), which seeks to improve the skills of South African workers by imposing a training levy on employers;
4. The Occupational Health and Safety Act (1993), which sets minimum health and safety standards in most workplaces;
5. The Compensation for Occupational Injuries and Diseases Act (1993), which establishes a compensation fund to which all employers are obliged to contribute and from which loss of wages and medical expenses of employees injured at work, or who were suffering from an occupational disease, are paid out; and
6. The Unemployment Insurance Fund Act (2001), which establishes an unemployment insurance fund to which both employers and employees contribute for the purpose of providing benefits to the unemployed who contributed for a limited period.

In order to benefit from the rights contained in the above pieces of legislation a worker has to qualify as an employee. Only employees can become union members. Therefore it is not only the individual rights granted in the legislation that are limited to employees but also the mechanisms put in place to enable employees acting jointly to bargain collectively with the employer to better their working terms and conditions. According to a Human Rights Watch (2011) report, farm workers in South Africa remain the most poorly organized sector in the country with a mere three percent of workers in the Western Cape being represented by unions compared to 30 percent of those with formal employment in South Africa as a whole. Given the isolation of farm workers from cities and central places where gatherings can take place combined with the proportionately high number of informal and atypical employees, the unionization of farm workers is even more daunting. Given the corporatist nature of the underlying legislation and the importance of union power in the determination of wage and other employment conditions, the low percentage of union members in the agricultural sector makes it very difficult for unions to negotiate a better deal for workers in the agricultural sector, especially for atypical employees such as seasonal workers.

Widespread strikes occurred in the agricultural sector in South Africa in 2013. Strikers demanded increased wages to R150.00 per day, which resulted in a 52 percent increase in minimum wages for farm workers. This brought the paltry R69.00 per day minimum wage up to R105.00 per day. However, this amount is still paltry, rendering it impossible to make ends meet even if one lives a frugal and simple life. The increase in minimum wage brought about by the strikes was a hollow victory for farm workers. As a result of this increase in the wage bill, farmer employers made unilateral changes to workers' conditions of employment. These changes included increases in working hours, meal breaks reduced and deducted from the workers' hours of work, farm workers charged rent or increased rental fees for their accommodation on the farm, electricity and transport costs increased, and workers who in the past did not pay doctors' and medical services were made to pay them. Farmer employers are also now charging farm workers who reside on the farm for the maintenance of the accommodation. Furthermore, full-time workers' weekly rates have been unilaterally changed to piece labor rates (Kleinbooi 2013). In addition to this, farm owners have applied for an exemption to pay the new minimum wage. There is no certainty as to whether employers have been granted exemption by the Department of Labor or not as the Department of Labor does not share this information with employees. The Department of Labor also does not monitor the exemption or implementation of minimum wages and there is a lack of transparency regarding the periods for which exemption has been granted. Furthermore, the increase in wages is being used as a justification for changing the conditions of employment for women workers by withholding benefits and threatening tenuous security. After the promulgation of the new minimum wage many farm workers reported that farm owners forced them to sign blank papers in support of the owners' application for exemption (Kleinbooi 2013). It is clear that all this has further eroded the rights of vulnerable workers, especially women who are now in a worse position than before.

While receiving little protection from trade unions, atypical employees including seasonal workers are also generally not well protected by the legislation. Even though certain categories of atypical employees may qualify as employees – for example, part-time employees, fixed-term employees, and those employed by temporary employment services (TES) – they nonetheless are often treated less favorably than their "typical" counterparts.

The use of atypical employees or workers who do not qualify as employees in terms of the legislation is very prominent in the agricultural sector, especially amongst women farm workers. As explained by Devereux and Solomon:

> One way that employers have cut costs is by 'feminization' of the workforce – replacing permanent male workers with temporary female workers. … Women are preferred for 'nimble fingered' tasks, such as picking and sorting fruit, while men are allocated heavy manual tasks such as fencing and operating machinery – and partly because there remains a gendered wage hierarchy (in defiance of equity legislation) with women

earning less than men for performing the same tasks. But seasonal or casual employment, being temporary, is lower paid and less secure than permanent employment.

(2011, 6)

The use of atypical forms of employment including the use of TES is common throughout the South African economy and specifically so in the agricultural sector. In order to cast the net of protection provided for in terms of the centerpiece of labor legislation, the LRA, the legislature saw fit to introduce amendments which came into force on January 1, 2015.

LRA amendments 2015

The latest amendments to the LRA seek to protect three categories of non-permanent employees, namely employees employed by TES, employees on fixed-term contracts, and part-time employees.

Regarding employees of TES, the new section 198(A) of the LRA provides that employees who earn below a certain threshold who work for more than three months for the client are considered to be employees of the client, unless the employee works as a substitute for somebody who is temporarily absent. Furthermore, the section provides that termination of the employee's services by the TES, whether at the insistence of TES or the clients in order to avoid "deemed employment," is considered to be a form of unfair dismissal. The section also provides that "deemed employees" must on the whole be treated not less favorably than comparable employees unless justifiable reasons exist for differentiation in treatment. In terms of section 198(D)(2) justifiable reasons include seniority, experience, length of service, merit, quality or quantity of work and any other similar criteria. The provision specifically provides that affordability on the part of the employer is not a justifiable reason.

Section 198(B) provides protection for employees on fixed-term contracts. In terms of the section an employee may only be employed on a fixed-term contract for more than three months in circumstances where the nature of the work is of a limited or definite duration or there is a justifiable reason for fixing the term. Justifiable reasons include replacing an employee who is temporarily absent; where there is a temporary increase in work that is longer than 12 months; so that a student can gain experience; where a person is engaged for a specific and limited duration project; work for a non-citizen with a work permit; seasonal work; a public works scheme; where there is external funding; or the person has reached retirement age. An employee who is on a fixed-term contract the duration of which is longer than three months may on the whole not be treated less favorably than permanent employees performing the same or similar work, unless there are justifiable reasons. Justifiable reasons are the same as those mentioned above. Employees on fixed-term contracts must be provided with equal access to opportunities for vacancies from the first day of their employment with the employer. Employees on fixed-term contracts the duration of which is longer than 24 months are entitled to severance pay unless alternative employment on similar terms and conditions is provided or offered prior to the expiry of the fixed-term contract. These protective provisions are not applicable to employees who earn above the threshold, or where there is a collective agreement, statute, or sectoral determination which allows for a fixed period. These provisions are also not applicable for employers who employ fewer than ten employees or for employers employing fewer than 50 employees whose business has been in operation for less than two years.

In terms of section198(C), a "part-time employee" is defined as an employee who works shorter hours than a comparable full-time employee and is paid according to the time worked. A "comparable full-time employee" is an employee who is paid for a full day and is identifiable as a full-time employee in terms of custom and practice. This section is not applicable during the first three months of employment. It is also not applicable if the employee earns more than the threshold, or works less than 24 hours per month, if the employer employs fewer than ten employees or if the employer employs fewer than 50 employees and the business has been in operation for less than two years.

Part-time employees may not be treated less favorably than equivalent full-time employees unless it is justified. The justifiable reasons are the same as those mentioned above. After three months, part-time employees must be provided with the same access to opportunities for vacancies as well as access to training and skills development.

As progressive as this legislation might be, it is no guarantee that the vulnerable seasonal employees will be protected. It has been documented that implementation of the LRA, especially on remote farms, has been problematic (Devereux and Solomon 2011). Research conducted by Human Rights Watch (2011) found that in the Western Cape, 107 labor inspectors are responsible for inspecting over 6,000 farms and all other workplaces in the province. The research also found that an agreement between the Department of Labour, Agri South Africa (an association that represents farmers), and other parties requires labor inspectors to give farm owners notice of inspections. Clearly this undermines inspectors' capacity to identify violations.

Furthermore, even if these legislative protections are implemented, seasonal workers will often be excluded from such protection because the protection only comes into force when an employment contract lasts for longer than three months. The duration of seasonal workers' contracts is often less than three months thus excluding seasonal workers from the protection provided in terms of the amendments to the LRA.

Amendments to the Employment Equity Act

Section 6 (1) of the Employment Equity Act (1998) (EEA) prohibits direct and indirect unfair discrimination on grounds of gender, sex, pregnancy, marital status, and family responsibility in both access (recruitment) and treatment (job classification, remuneration, employment benefits, employment terms and conditions, promotion, and dismissal). Where discrimination is alleged on one of the listed grounds, the employer bears the burden of proving that the discrimination is fair or justified. Discrimination can be justified or fair if it is necessary as an inherent requirement of the job or the reason for the discrimination is affirmative action.

The 2014 amendments to the EEA added the words in section 6(1) "or on any other arbitrary ground" after the list of prohibited grounds for discrimination. This addition leaves no doubt that claims for equal pay based on discrimination can now be brought in terms of section 6(1) of the EEA. The following sections have also been added to section 6 of the EEA:

> (4) A difference in terms and conditions of employment between employees of the same employer performing the same or substantially the same work or work of equal value that is directly or indirectly based on any one or more of the grounds listed in subsection (1) is unfair discrimination.

Unfortunately this addition seems to address only one aspect of gender pay discrimination, namely the situation in which women and men do the same or similar work, or work of similar value. Therefore the law does not address the concentration of women in sex-typed jobs, which are concentrated in lower paying occupations such as farm workers or the disproportionate share of low-ranking positions held by women and the lower earnings relative to those of men with similar training and experience.

Since the 2014 amendments to the EEA, section 10(6) of the EEA provides that if an employee earns less than the threshold determined by the Minister in terms of section 6(3) of the Basic Conditions of Employment Act, that employee may refer a dispute about discrimination, which includes sexual harassment, to the Commission for Conciliation Mediation and Arbitration (CCMA). This provision renders access to justice accessible to the poorer members of community since access to the procedures provided by the CCMA free of charge. This is very significant given the SAHRC findings in their enquiry that, "workplace sexual harassment remains under reported and poorly prioritised by many employers, law enforcement and government agencies" (2008, 56).

Conclusion

Despite progressive post-apartheid laws and policies designed to provide protection for the most vulnerable in society, the relationship between farm workers and farm owners has remained largely unchanged. The following have constituted some of the obstacles facing farm workers, especially women in enforcing their rights:

1. Lack of knowledge of the labor rights and entitlements, largely as a result of the paternalistic relationship with the farmer employer, low union activity, physical isolation, low literacy and education levels, fear

of retribution and violence by the farmer employer, and fear of loss of their jobs. According to the SAHRC (2008, 69) report: "On the whole the majority of agricultural workers remained uninformed about fundamental rights in relation to labor legislation.";

2. Lack of economic resources needed to enforce their rights;
3. Weak government monitoring and enforcement of the legislation;
4. Non-compliance by farmer employers who have devised ingenious ways to circumvent the labor law obligations; and
5. The might of the unwritten laws of slavery based on centuries of oppression that undermines the ability of modern labor legislation to protect employees especially the more subservient and oppressed ones.

The reforms implemented by the post-apartheid ANC government have not been properly implemented. What is clear is that the promulgation of legislation alone is insufficient to ensure the basic human rights of those in precarious work relationships who have limited access to socio-economic resources and who have been historically disadvantaged. Only when these vulnerable people are empowered on multiple fronts so as to fundamentally alter the skewed balance of power that allows paternalistic relationships to flourish, will it be possible to protect the farm workers by means of progressive labor and tenure security legislation. To this end the following are necessary:

1. Access to socio-economic resources that are essential for a dignified life;
2. Proper monitoring and enforcement of legislation, in particular labor legislation;
3. Proper implementation of the criminal law system to protect farm workers against violence; and
4. Comprehensive union mobilization and representation of all farm workers including casual seasonal employees.

References

Bosch, D. 1994. "Another Change to Agricultural Labour Law: Addressing the Concerns of Farmers and Farm Workers." Briefing Paper No. 2, Stellenbosch, South Africa: Centre for Legal Studies.

Brown-Luthango, M. 2006. "Rotten Fruits 2: South African Farm Workers Pay a High Price for Profits." Women on Farms Project (WFP) and ActionAid. www.wfp.org.za/publications/research-publications.html.

Department of Land Affairs. 1997. "White Paper on South African Land Policy." Pretoria: Department of Land Affairs.

Devereux, S., and C. Solomon. 2011. "Can Social Protection Deliver Social Justice for Farmwomen in South Africa?" Paper presented at the Social Protection for Social Justice Conference, Institute of Development Studies, UK, April 13–15.

Dladla, S. 2000. "Trapped in Feudal Times." *Land and Rural Digest* 13: 31–32.

Dugard, J. 1978. *Human Rights and the South African Legal Order*. Princeton: Princeton University Press.

Fourie, E. 2008. "Non Standard Workers in the South African Context, International Law and Regulation by the European Union." *Potchefstroom Electronic Law Journal* 11 (4): 110–52. www.nwu.ac.za/sites/www.nwu.ac.za/files/images/2008x4x_Fourie_art.pdf.

Hall, R., K. Kleinbooi, and N. Mvambo. 2001. "What Land Reform has Meant and Could Mean to Farm Workers in South Africa." Paper presented at the Land Reform and Poverty Alleviation in Southern Africa, Human Sciences Research Council (HSRC) Conference, 2001 Pretoria, South Africa, June 4–5.

Hart, T., and M. Aliber. 2012. "Inequalities in Agricultural Support for Women in South Africa." Policy Brief. Cape Town, South Africa: Human Sciences Research Council. www.hsrc.ac.za/uploads/pageContent/3025/InequalitiesLR.pdf.

Hattingh, S. 2008. "African Agriculture Uprooted by Economic Policies." *Inter Press Service*, June 18. www.ipsnews.net/2008/06/development-african-agriculture-uprooted-by-economic-policies/.

Hornby, D. 2015. "Government Cocks a Snook at the Courts over Labour Tenants." *Tshintsha Amakhaya*. https://sites.google.com/site/tshintshaintranet/key-issues/Farm-Dwellers/labour-tenants.

Human Rights Watch. 2011. "South Africa: Farmworkers' Dismal, Dangerous Lives: Workers Protected by Law but not in the Field." Human Rights Watch. www.hrw.org/news/2011/08/23/south-africa-farmworkers-dismal-dangerous-lives.

Husy, D., and C. Samson. 2001. "Promoting Development and Land Reform on South African Farms." Paper presented at the South African Regional Poverty Network (SARPN) Conference on Land Reform and Poverty Alleviation in Southern Africa, Pretoria, June 4–5.

Kleinbooi, K. 2013. "Farm Workers' Living and Working Conditions." Workshop Report. Bellville, South Africa: Institute for Poverty, Land and Agrarian Studies (PLAAS). www.plaas.org.za/sites/default/files/publications-pdf/farmworkers%20living%20working%20conditions.pdf.

Kritzinger, A., and J. Vorster. 1997. "The Conceptualistion of Farm Family Business: Deciduous Fruit Farming in South Africa." *Socilogica Ruralis* 37 (1): 114–33.

Mokgoro, Y. 2003. "Constitutional Claims for Gender Equality in South Africa: A Judicial Response." *Albany Law Review* 67 (2): 565–73.

Murray, C. 2000. "Changing Livelihoods, The Free State, 1990s." *African Studies* 59 (1): 115–43. doi.10.1080/713650975.

Pienaar, J., N. Olivier, and W. Du Plessis. 2011. "Land Matters and Rural Development." *Southern African Public Law* 26 (2): 523–65. http://hdl.handle.net/10520/EJC153192.

South Africa. 1993a. Compensation for Occupational Injuries and Diseases Act, No. 130 of 1993. Gazette No. 337(15271). October 6. Pretoria: Government Printer.

———. 1993b. Occupational Health and Safety Act, No. 85 of 1993. Government Gazette No. 337(14918). Pretoria: Government Printer. July 2.

———. 1995. Labour Relations Act, No. 33 of 1995. Government Gazette No. 366(16851). Pretoria: Government Printer. December 13.

———. 1996. Constitution of the Republic of South Africa as adopted by the Constitutional Assembly May 8 and as amended October 11. Government Gazette No. 17678. Pretoria: Government Printer.

———. 1997a. Basic Conditions of Employment Act, No. 75 of 1997. Government Gazette No. 390(18491). Pretoria: Government Printer. December 5.

————. 1997b. Extension of Security of Land Act of 199, No. 62 of 1997. Government Gazette No. 389(18476). Pretoria: Government Printer. November 28.

————. 1998a. Employment Equity Act, No. 55 of 1998. Government Gazette No. 400(19370). October 19. Pretoria: Government Printer. October 19.

————. 1998b. Skills Development Act, No. 97 of 1998. Government Gazette No. 401(19420). Pretoria: Government Printer. October 20.

————. 2001. Unemployment Insurance Fund Act, No. 63 of 2001. Government Gazette No. 439(23064). Pretoria: Government Printer. January 28.

South Africa Human Rights Commission (SAHRC). 2003. "Final Report on the Inquiry into Human Rights Violations In Farming Communities." SAHRC. www.gov.za/sites/www.gov.za/files/farming_complete_0.pdf.

————. 2008. "Progress Made in Terms of Land Tenure Security, Safety, and Labour Relations in Farming Communities Since 2003." SAHRC. www.sahrc.org.za/home/21/files/Reports/Farming%20Inquiry%20Report_2008.pdf.

South African History Online. 2015. "History of Slavery and Early Colonisation in South Africa," accessed July 6, 2015, www.sahistory.org.za/south-africa-1652–1806/history-slavery-and-early-colonisation-sa.

Wegerif, M., B. Russell, and I. Grundling. 2005. *Still Searching for Security: The Reality of Farm Dweller Evictions in South Africa*. Polokwane, South Africa: Nkuzi Development Association; Johannesburg: Social Surveys. PDF e-book.

4 The System of Rice Intensification and its impacts on women

Reducing pain, discomfort, and labor in rice farming while enhancing households' food security

Olivia Vent, Sabarmatee and Norman Uphoff

Introduction

> We know that we have to work. It is our way of life. We not only work in our fields, also in our homes. In rice season, the workload is so much that we don't have time to think about it. Since we are farming women, hardly anyone cares about it.
>
> Mami, an Indian woman rice farmer in Odisha state

Rice is the world's most important food commodity, feeding half of its population. Most rice is produced on some 250 million small family farms, providing income and employment for an estimated 1 billion people (Bouman et al. 2007). Given that women provide 27–84 percent of the labor and predominate in transplanting and weeding (Romero-Paris 2010), women who are engaged in rice production may be the largest single livelihood group in the world.

These days women are taking on ever more responsibility in managing rice production, as more men seek work off-farm to generate needed household income, a process characterized as the "feminization of agriculture" (De Schutter 2013). Women are thus central not just to sustaining global food security and nutrition, but also for the environmental management of a large portion of the world's cultivable land.

Rice is mostly grown under flooded conditions and mainly in the wet or summer season, requiring women to work long hours under hot sun or in rain, in standing water, under unhygienic conditions, and exposed to numerous chemicals, parasites, and various disease vectors. These conditions almost guarantee chronic illness and pain. These women must also tend other crops, care for livestock, sometimes do wage labor or market small products, collect wood and water, process food, bear and rear children, and care for family members.

Current strategies that seek higher yield and productivity through using new seeds and agrochemicals are premised on the continued availability and utilization of cheap women's labor. Such strategies also often result in the dislocation of women and smallholders through consolidation of farms and expanded commercialization and mechanization.

Women engaged in rice production are often overlooked by policymakers, researchers, and extension personnel, and they are accordingly underrepresented in their access to land, credit, training, and setting development priorities (FAO 2004). A recent index published on women's empowerment in agriculture for assessing the impact on women of agricultural innovations and policies considered resource allocation, income, leadership, and time (USAID, IFPRI, and OPHI 2014). However, no attention was given to the impacts that such policies and practices have on women's health and bodies.

Women's bodies ultimately are the human capital required to produce most of the rice eaten in the world. Development strategies that do not consider their impact on women and women's bodies will suffer from losses in productivity that derive from women's diminished health due to such working conditions. Assessing such impacts will give more accurate accounting of the actual consequences, net costs, and net benefits of technological alternatives.

This chapter addresses these issues in the context of an agroecological methodology for rice production known as the System of Rice Intensification (SRI), which is improving the lives of women involved in rice growing in over 50 countries. SRI does this through multiple entry points: increased yields and incomes; reduced workloads, pain, and exposure to occupational hazards; nutritional benefits; and enhanced personal status. In particular, we consider the implications of SRI for women's physical well-being, drawing on Sabarmatee's detailed investigations in three villages in Odisha state of India during 2011–2012. Using both quantitative and qualitative methods, she assessed the impact of SRI on the physical well-being of over 200 men and women rice field workers.

Women's risks and exposures in standard rice production

Is there a way of producing rice without experiencing pain in the body?

Mami

For centuries, the nature of women's labor in rice farming has remained essentially unaltered and unquestioned. Rice-growing requires physically demanding work by both men and women throughout the cropping season. Labor allocations by sex vary in different rice-growing ecosystems depending on whether it is rice-livestock, rice-fish, rice-vegetable, rice-wheat or some other rice-based system, and whether women are cultivating their own land or are hired laborers (FAO 2004). Traditionally, in Africa and Asia men do plowing, make bunds (embankments around rice paddies to contain water), prepare seedbeds, and apply synthetic fertilizers and pesticides. Women generally select the seeds, sow and manage nurseries, remove seedlings and transport them to the field, transplant them, weed, harvest, thresh, winnow, clean, sort and bag the grain, process it, and save seeds for the next crop. They work in a wet environment performing repetitive motions in painful postures for long hours, with rudimentary tools such as hand hoes, sickles, and hatchets. When carried out by women laborers, such tasks are considered unskilled, and they command only the lowest wages. Hardly any changes have occurred in women's work in rice farming since Mencher and Saradamoni observed in 1982:

> If one stops to think of it, one might even argue that higher wages should be paid for work which requires bending over most of the time while standing knee-deep in water, having one's legs attacked by leeches, and often not being allowed to straighten out one's back even for a few minutes by an over-zealous supervisor.
>
> Transplanting is both a hazardous and skilled job. It is hazardous because of the illness to which it exposes the women, which include a variety of intestinal and parasitic troubles, infections, splitting heels (from standing in muddy water for hours on end), severe pain from leech bites, and ultimately the possibility of crippling ailments like rheumatic joints, arthritis. It is not rare to find old women who have spent more than 40 or 50 years of their life transplanting paddy, permanently bent over and unable to stand up straight at all.
>
> (A-153)

A study of women rice field workers in West Bengal, India, found that musculoskeletal disorders were widespread among women (Kar et al. 2012). Almost 100 percent presented shoulder and lower back problems, followed by 90 percent presenting thigh and neck disorders due to the long hours performing repetitive operations such as uprooting and transplanting seedlings and weeding (Kar et al. 2012).

Flooded rice fields and irrigation canals are a favorable environment for the growth of bacteria, viruses, fungi, and different parasites which in developing countries cause malaria, tetanus, hookworm, dermatitis, conjunctivitis, and various other diseases (IRRI 1988; Hassan, Scholes, and Ash 2005). They are major habitats of the freshwater snail that carries the schistosomiasis parasite, which causes painful and debilitating conditions affecting the bladder, liver, intestines, and reproductive organs (Boelee and Madsen 2006). In Africa, women growing rice are especially vulnerable to female genital schistosomiasis, a widespread cause of gynecological disorders that can also increase women's risk of acquiring HIV/AIDS (Nour 2010; Yirenya-Tawiah et al. 2011; Hotez 2013). Kar et al. (2012) found that 56 percent of Indian women who worked in flooded rice fields reported having menstrual problems. Based on her research in Odisha state, Sabarmatee estimates that, each season, women spend about 400–500 hours per acre in bent or sitting positions in flooded fields on uprooting, transporting seedlings, transplanting, and weeding.

As women take over more of men's agricultural tasks, this will increase their exposure to various pesticides, insecticides, and herbicides. The links between acute and chronic ailments, associated health costs and the extent of farmers' and laborers' exposure to agrochemicals are well-documented (Rola and Pingali 1993; Huang et al. 2001; Joshi 2002). Women are already exposed by washing pesticide-soaked clothes, cleaning containers, buying and mixing chemicals, and pesticide drift (Tanzo 2005). Adding the spraying of rice crops to their tasks has serious health implications.

Women are more vulnerable to the ill effects of these chemicals than are men because most of these toxins are stored in fat, and women often have a higher percentage of body fat. Chemical pollutants can be stored in the body for many years after exposure, causing harm distant in time and space. Also, children can suffer the impact of "hand-me-down" toxins during fetal development and later through breast milk (Lu 2011).

By the time a season's weeding operations are finished, Sabarmatee noted that women laborers reported being exhausted and fatigued. Besides musculoskeletal pain throughout their bodies, they suffered from fungal and other skin infections like candidiasis and tinea (ringworm) due to prolonged exposure to muddy water. Such infections were worse if agrochemicals like urea or chlorofluorocarbons were applied, intensifying the pain.

Sabarmatee found malnourishment to be highest among women during the rice-growing season, combined with greater incidence of diseases and excessive domestic and farm workloads. Despite being ill, many women laborers postpone buying medicine due to the urgent need for cash for other things. This can exacerbate problems and they have to spend more on treatment later on.

Malnutrition, undernourishment, and diseases undermine long-term agricultural productivity not just from women's illness or weakened ability to tend their crops, but also from loss of wages. To cope with health crises, households often have to withdraw savings, sell or mortgage important assets (such as jewelry, livestock, farm equipment, and land), withdraw children from school, and/or reduce the nutritional value of their food. All these responses have adverse effects both on the well-being of household members and on agricultural output locally and nationally.

Alternative rice cultivation methods: the System of Rice Intensification

> SRI shows the path of enhanced income and healthy life to small and marginal farmers.
>
> Odisha women farmers, quoted in Panigrahi (2010)

The System of Rice Intensification (SRI) is a set of agroecological practices developed some 30 years ago in Madagascar as an alternative to prevailing practices for irrigated rice production by small-scale farmers (Box 4.1). Key changes include transplanting individual young seedlings at wider spacing rather than crowding many older seedlings together in clumps, and keeping soils mostly aerobic rather than continuously flooded. Organic matter replaces or reduces the use of inorganic fertilizers. The improved growing environment – especially healthier aerobic soils – promotes larger, more effective root systems. These support more and stronger grain-bearing tillers and leaves that are capable of more photosynthesis, which consequently produces more and often heavier grains (Thakur, Uphoff and Antony 2010).

Box 4.1 SRI practices

SRI practices include:

1. **Transplanting young seedlings 8–15 days old**, instead of 21–45 days, thereby minimizing transplant shock and conserving inherent growth potential
2. **Transplanting one seedling per hill**, instead of multiple seedlings in a clump, reducing competition among plants for light, water, and nutrients
3. **Transplanting seedlings** carefully into moist but not flooded soil, not pressing them in deeply, which delays their resumption of growth
4. **Planting with wider spacing** and in a square pattern, not at random, giving both roots and canopy more room to grow and facilitating mechanical weeding between rows
5. **Maintaining unflooded, aerobic soil conditions** so as not to suffocate the plants' roots and beneficial aerobic soil organisms
6. **Weeding several times with a weeder** instead of using herbicides or hand weeding; the weeder buries the weeds as it churns and aerates the soil's surface
7. **Enhancing soil structure and fertility with organic matter**, in preference to synthetic fertilizers
8. **Using integrated pest management methods** when needed, instead of chemical insecticides and pesticides

---

There is strong and growing scientific evidence for the effectiveness of SRI (e.g., Mishra and Salokhe 2008; Lin et al. 2009; Zhao et al. 2009; Thakur, Uphoff, and Antony 2010; Ndiiri et al. 2013; Thakur, Rath, and Mandal 2013). These sources have shown that SRI methods increase yield, irrespective of variety, by at least 20–50 percent, and sometimes by 100 percent or even more, with greatly reduced requirements for seed (70–90% less), with 20–50 percent less irrigation water, and usually (or eventually) less labor.

Growing more robust plants minimizes the need for using chemicals for crop protection, and plants are generally better able to resist climatic stresses such as drought, extremes of temperature, flooding, and storm damage (Uphoff 2011). SRI concepts and practices are also being adapted for rainfed cropping, with yields often doubled (Kabir and Uphoff 2007; RRA 2015).

Socio-economic impacts of SRI are well documented. For example, since 2008 the government of Bihar, one of India's poorest and most populous states, has been promoting SRI and SCI (SRI principles applied to other crops like wheat, millet, mustard, etc.) under a World Bank-supported program. An evaluation in 2012, when over one hundred thousand households were using SRI and related methods, reported an average yield increase of 86 percent for rice, with profitability of rice cultivation increased by 250 percent (Behera et al. 2013).[1]

Published literature on SRI and gender, however, is scarce, and there is even less literature connecting SRI, gender, and health. This is, in part, because SRI has been largely extended through civil society organizations with tight budgets focused on adoption and enhancement of yield, not generating and publishing data on the issue. Nonetheless, there is some information in technical reports, project evaluations, videos, media articles, blogs, and our own research to draw on. The following two sections draw on Sabarmatee's research in Odisha, India, to illustrate how SRI can change both the amount and kind of work required, in particular for those tasks normally done by women, and how this influences the pain and drudgery experienced by women in rice production.

Changes in work patterns with SRI and their implications for women

> We now have more time to look after our children, sew and clean more. We now only spend 1–2 hours in the field. ... We can work during the hours when sunlight is not too strong, unlike in conventional farming, when we have to spend all morning and most of the afternoon in the field.
>
> Cambodian woman farmer, quoted in Resurreccion,
> Sajor, and Sophea (2008)

Debates on labor issues mostly focus on whether SRI requires more labor and the role of labor requirements in adoption of SRI (e.g., Moser and Barrett 2003; Barrett et al. 2004; Resurreccion, Sajor, and Sophea 2008; Rao 2011; Dill, Deichert, and Le 2013; Berkhout, Glover, and Kuyvenhoven 2014). Usually labor is discussed as a homogeneous entity without paying much attention to the gendered nature of labor and to the gender implications of changed practices. While Schipper et al. (2014) and Resurreccion, Sajor, and Sophea (2008) found that SRI leads to lighter workloads for women, the important aspect missing in these discussions is implications of SRI on women's physical well-being.[2] An analysis of the following parameters can shed some light on how different methods have different effects, particularly for women:

1. Work environment, and time spent in that environment;
2. Posture, and time spent in that posture;
3. Volume of materials handled;
4. Area of work (size of nursery);
5. Distance that laborers walk;
6. Gendered work participation.

Changes in rice management practices that improve women's health and ease their physical discomfort will have broad implications whether women are working on their own paddy lands or on others' fields as wage laborers.

Transplanting practices: making the work easier and lighter

Typically, rice seeds are sown in a nursery to grow for a period before being transplanted into the main fields. Under SRI, planting only one or two younger seedlings per hill and at wider spacing means that less seed and land are required for the nursery. Only 3–5 kg of seeds (instead of 30–40 kg) are sown in a nursery of 0.01 acre (instead of 0.10 acre). Seedlings are removed 8–15 days after sowing instead of 30 days or more; hence much less time is needed to manage the nursery.

Traditionally women pull up seedlings in bending (70°–80° angle) postures, or sitting in the flooded nurseries, cleaning the soil from the roots, and then bundling the seedlings. Much larger numbers of older, heavier seedlings require a lot more energy and time to pull up. Then the bundles are transported to main fields, often at some distance, on people's heads, shoulders, slings or bicycles, and spread over the fields to be transplanted. Men and women transport on average 400 to 1,200 kg of seedlings per acre. At one time men carry bundles weighing between 8–100 kg, while women carry 7–30 kg bundles depending on the transport method.

Under SRI, younger seedlings are removed carefully with soil kept intact around the roots and then carried directly to the field for immediate transplanting, eliminating the task of spreading. Farmers generally raise their SRI nurseries inside or near the main field, so they make fewer trips and walk less distance. Containers of SRI seedlings weigh around 5–6 kg, or at most 13–15 kg if older. The total weight transported is between 80–145 kg per acre, and up to 200–250 kg if the seedlings are somewhat older due to various reasons.

With SRI, women spend much less time in stressful postures carrying out repetitive movements. It takes only 7–25 hours for uprooting and transporting seedlings (instead of 80–150 hours normally) and 70–90 hours per acre for transplanting in SRI (instead of 120–150 hours in the prevailing conventional method). Sabarmatee observed wide variation in work hours with conventional and SRI methods depending on work group size, age and gender of the laborers, soil-water consistency, and so on. Further, with SRI, the seedlings women hold in their hand for transplanting weigh 150–300 grams instead of 1–1.5 kg. They insert the young seedlings into the mud at wide spacing at an average rate of 6–10 times/minute, rather than plunging their hands and wrists deep into the mud 40–50 times/minute as when they plant more and older seedlings at closer spacing.

Weeding practices: from bending to standing

Under aerobic soil conditions, weeds can be more prolific than in conventionally flooded rice paddies. Thus, it is strongly recommended with

SRI to use a simple mechanical weeder to control weed growth. The weeder not only buries the weeds, which turn into green manure, but also aerates the soil. Despite the flooding for weed control in conventional fields, Sabarmatee observed that farmers do manual weeding after the weeds become big enough to hold in their fists. It takes women around 130–160 hours to weed an acre, moving at an average speed of 1 square meter per minute. Weeding with a mechanical weeder takes 16–25 hours/acre. Farmers normally do weeding 2–3 times. A one-time supplementary manual weeding can take another 5–9 hours.

An evaluation done by researchers in Andhra Pradesh in India found that women need 76 percent less time for mechanical weeding with SRI. Moreover, it "optimized the human effort through improved postures and reduced the muscular fatigue as compared with the hand weeding process" (Mrunalini and Ganesh 2008, 58). Sabarmatee measured 15 women's physiological responses during both mechanical and manual weeding. Although their heartbeat rate per minute increased with mechanical weeding, the overall burden on their bodies was reduced because of adjustments to work–rest rhythms, reduced work hours, changing from bending to erect posture, and the increased participation of men in mechanical weeding.

Introduction of the weeder can alter the gender division of labor depending on the context (Hansda 2014; Sabarmatee 2014). In some cultures, men are expected to do any agricultural operations involving mechanical/motorized implements. This is the case in Timbuktu, Mali, where men took over mechanical weeding almost entirely. This freed women to tend vegetable gardens, which did not reduce their total labor time but enhanced family nutrition (Hauser 2010).

An evaluation in Tamil Nadu, India, with 100 farmers found that SRI increased men's labor inputs into rice cultivation by 60 percent per hectare, while women's days of labor in rice production were reduced by 25 percent as men took over mechanical weeding (Thiyagarajan 2004). This was a positive change for women engaged in their own household rice production; however, it represented a loss of wage labor opportunities for women of the lowest castes or *dalit* group. This illustrates that, as with many matters of evaluation, attention must be given also to class or social affiliations and not just gender (Hansda 2014).

Not all weeder designs are gender-neutral or woman-friendly, and not all perform equally well in all kinds of soils. Women's participation in the design and evaluation of weeders is critical because implements that are too large or too heavy, or are not appropriate for the particular soils, can cause various kinds of stresses and injuries.

Water management practices: potential benefits of not flooding rice fields

With SRI, rice fields are no longer kept constantly flooded, reducing or eliminating women's prolonged exposure to water-borne disease vectors (e.g., mosquitoes, snails, and leeches [see Figure 4.1]). According to a Philippine NGO introducing SRI among rural women in Isabela province, the high

Figure 4.1 Women in Timbuktu, Mali, often sit for days in flooded fields pulling up
rice seedlings for transplanting, which can lead to multiple maladies.

Source: Erika Styger.

water level maintained in fields with conventional rice cultivation contributes
to vaginal and urinary tract infections, whereas women reported that with
SRI methods their incidence of such infections diminished (Uphoff 2003).
There is very little discussion and literature on this particular aspect of rice
production, and further research is needed.

In the Philippines, intermittent irrigation has been used as a strategy for
reducing snail populations, with the number of snails reduced from 200 to less
than one per square meter (IRRI 1988). This would suggest that practices such
as SRI's could be effective in controlling schistosomiasis. Intermittent irrigation of rice fields has already been identified as an effective strategy for reducing the incidence and impact of malaria (Keiser, Utzinger, and Singer 2002;
Cameron and Lorenz 2013). A study of SRI water management in the Mwea
Irrigation Scheme in Kenya showed all mosquito larvae introduced in the SRI
plots died within two days after draining the water, while 98 percent of the
larvae introduced in the flooded plots survived to adulthood (Omwenga 2014).

A male Malian farmer, and also president of the Federation of the Union
of Cooperatives of Goundam District, summarized the impact of water management practice under SRI on women this way:

> Before, in the flooded fields, women sat in the water for days, transplant-
> ing and weeding. They would get fever or diarrhea from sitting in the

water. Now, because the fields do not need to be flooded, the men do most of the weeding with a weeder, and the women only do some by hand.

(Hauser 2010, n.p.)

Soil and crop health management: reducing health hazards of agrochemical exposure

As women take over more of men's agricultural tasks, their contact with agrochemicals increases. Exposure to these chemicals is especially high among rice farmers in Asia (Huang et al. 2001; Chiong-Javier 2009; Phung et al. 2012). Concern about the negative impacts of chemical inputs on people's health and the environment has been a major impetus for introducing SRI in both Cambodia (Environmental Justice Foundation 2002) and Vietnam (Dill, Deichert, and Le 2013). In Vietnam, the government agency that took the lead in promoting SRI was the integrated pest management (IPM) program in the Ministry of Agriculture and Rural Development. With SRI, farmers significantly reduce or eliminate their exposure to inorganic fertilizers and pesticides (Tech 2006).

Rapid comparative pain assessment by rice field workers

While interacting with villagers as a facilitator and practitioner of SRI, and also during fieldwork for her PhD, Sabarmatee repeatedly heard women reporting positive health impacts with SRI and men complaining of greater workload, at least in the initial stages. Table 4.1 summarizes the experiences reported to her by women.

To better comprehend and compare actual differences in drudgery and pain (D&P) experienced by women, men, and children when working in rice fields under SRI and/or conventional rice management, Sabarmatee devised and used a participatory visual diagnostic tool she called Rapid Comparative Pain Assessment (RaCoPA). This methodology seeks agreement among participants about the impacts on physical well-being of different rice-growing practices.

RaCoPA exercises were carried out in three villages of Odisha state in 2011–2012 with around two hundred participants who worked in rice fields. During focus group discussions, a body map was drawn enabling participants to point to locations on the body where pain is experienced and reenact positions and activities to make comparative assessments of D&P. An example of such a map is shown in Figure 4.2.

Although D&P is considered to be a personal experience, Sabarmatee found that a group of people doing similar work in a similar work environment are likely to experience and report similar kinds of D&P in their bodies, which can be identified and compared with some objectivity. Information collected from the map is later converted into tables that summarize information for different sex and age groups across villages. Focus-group data were

Table 4.1 Health-related impacts of SRI reported by women in Odisha state

Direct effects of SRI methodology		Indirect effects of SRI methodology	
Reported	*Reasons given*	*Reported*	*Reasons given*
Reduction in infections on hands and legs (if chemical fertilizers and pesticides are not applied in SRI fields)	Laborers do not have to put their hands and legs in muddy water for long periods	Get more time to cook and eat comfortably	Changes in the nature of the rice cultivation work
Reductions in muscle, bone, and other pains	Reduced work hours	Get more time to rest at home and hence to feel better	Changes in working hours More participation of men in rice cultivation, which relieves women of some of their workload
SRI is less strenuous overall	Men share women's work due to introduction of mechanical weeders Changes in posture Changes in type of work		

Source: Group discussions during 2011–2012 in Odisha, India, recorded by Sabarmatee.

supplemented with story-telling and visual documentation such as photographs and videos. The RaCoPA exercises helped inform the quantitative data collected, as described in the previous section.

The RaCoPA data-gathering made clear that SRI results in a significant reduction in women's workload and in the D&P associated with rice production if its recommendations are followed. While testing the RaCoPA tool in 2013 in villages of Uttarakhand in India, each having different agroecological and social features, Debashish Sen from People's Science Institute in Dehradun found that farmers reported the same assessments (personal communication).

Both women and men reported that SRI methods contributed to their overall well-being. Women reported more time to eat their meals and more time to rest, and fewer stomach ailments. They felt strongly that practicing SRI with organic methods led to a reduction in health problems, as they no longer stayed for long periods in fields sprayed with chemical pesticides, which caused skin ailments, headaches, and dizziness. This is similar to the findings of Panigrahi (2010).

However, these experiences varied by gender, age, variation in practices, and types of tools. Most elderly women continued to do manual weeding

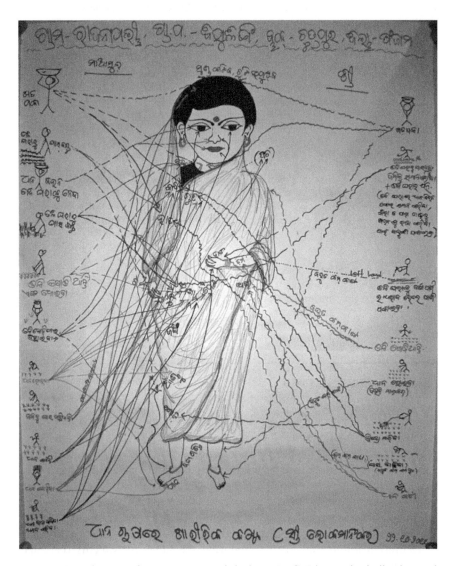

Figure 4.2 Body map of woman prepared during a RaCoPA exercise indicating and assessing D&P associated with different rice-cultivating activities that affect specific body parts.

Source: Sabarmatee (2011).

instead of using weeders, so they experienced no pain reduction in weeding. They did, however, report less pain with removing and transporting fewer and lighter SRI seedlings from the nursery. Men reported more D&P associated with mechanical weeding as they had not done this task previously and also while land leveling and making drainage channels. And, while women and men were generally happier about SRI methods producing more rice, those who worked as laborers reported that the harvested bundles of SRI rice were heavier to handle. Further investigation by epidemiologists, ergonomists, economists, gender scholars, and extension educationists will help to assess and understand such experiences more thoroughly.

Other benefits for women

Although documentation of SRI's socio-economic impacts is increasing, gender is rarely disaggregated in the data. Although not precisely measured with regard to women's health and well-being, the findings have important implications for women's health and deserve consideration by governments, researchers, and decision-makers.

Increased food security and income

Access to enough food is critical for women to have the energy to perform the physically demanding tasks of growing rice along with all of their other responsibilities. Consuming not just more calories but essential nutrients is especially vital for women who are pregnant and nursing. Just the 70–90 percent reduction in seed required with SRI frees up considerable rice for household food needs, and it can release some of the family's budget spent on food to meet other household and farm needs, including more protein- and vitamin-rich foods that they cannot grow for themselves.

When evaluating its introduction of SRI among small and marginal farmers in the state of Jharkhand, the National Bank for Agriculture and Rural Development in India found that use of the new methods, compared with traditional cultivation practices, greatly reduced the number of days of family food insecurity, calculated for typical households having five members (NABARD 2012). Ultra-poor households with less than 0.4 hectares of land were able to grow enough rice with SRI for 294 days a year instead of just 176 days; farmers with somewhat more land produced enough surplus to meet the annual rice needs of additional households. Similar findings have been reported in many other countries.

Diversification of farming systems contributing to better nutrition and health

With higher yields per unit of land with SRI methods, many farmers can convert part of their land to growing more nutritious and more profitable crops such as fruits, vegetables, legumes, and small livestock. With reductions in chemical use, irrigation canals become habitable again for fish and ducks. Substantial gains in diversity, productivity, and quality of food production have been reported from Cambodia (Lim 2007) and Ethiopia (Araya et al. 2013) as well as India.

Micronutrient deficiency is a worldwide problem, with women affected particularly by dietary deficiencies of iron (causing anemia) and zinc. Recent research in India has indicated that use of SRI methods can enhance rice plants' uptake of important nutrients (iron, zinc, copper, and manganese) from the soil and can increase the concentration of these nutrients in rice grains, especially in conjunction with the enhancement of soil microorganisms (Adak et al. 2016).

SRI production methods are found to increase significantly the yields of traditional, so-called "unimproved" varieties, many of which have much higher levels of iron and protein than do "modern" varieties (Frei and Becker 2005).[3] Research shows that red and black pigmented rices, for example, have more antioxidant capacity than almost any other grain (Dykes and Rooney 2007). They have potential for reducing the risk of diseases such as cardiovascular disease and cancer (Deng et al. 2013). Of particular interest, the β-carotene content of some unmilled black rice varieties is similar to that of transgenic Golden Rice, and they supply the lipids necessary to transform β-carotene into vitamin A (Frei and Becker 2005).

As many households, especially poor ones, prefer traditional rices due to taste and other qualities, promoting such locally available rices could be a more efficient strategy to boost the nutrition of marginalized rural households than current investments for breeding and delivering new biofortified varieties. Most of the current knowledge about such varieties resides with village women.

In some countries, concentration of arsenic in rice grains is a serious health concern. It is well documented that growing rice with alternate wetting and drying of fields, rather than continuous flooding, reduces the uptake of arsenic (As) from soils and water (Roberts et al. 2011; Senanayake and Mukherji 2014; Shah et al. 2014). SRI practices should thus mitigate the uptake of arsenic in rice through its water management practices.

Enhancement of women's status and security

Due to the many ways that introduction of SRI can improve women's lives, it is often integrated into civil society projects that seek to improve the incomes, status, and security of marginalized rural women. These projects create and/ or support village self-help groups, with training programs tailored to women. When trained as farmer-leaders, women gain confidence and enhanced status in the family and community (Panigrahi 2010; Behera et al. 2013). Much of the grassroots leadership for the dissemination of SRI has come from women, who actively promote SRI village-to-village (Castillo, Minh, and Pfeifer 2012).[4] In India, women have begun receiving national recognition for their achievements for high productivity.[5]

As a consequence, women are starting to exert their influence in political arenas for policies that support sustainable farming (Menon 2014). One woman SRI farmer/trainer/activist in Bihar state of India, coming from one of the lowest and poorest social groups in her society, was elected to that state's Legislative Assembly (Kumar 2010). In Madhya Pradesh, India, in 2012, 5,600 women organized a march to demand access to more resources for improving their farming operations, including training on SRI (Philipose 2012).

Outlook for the future

Women bear an unequal burden for producing the world's food supply, with major consequences for their health and bodies. Enhancing women's health as well as labor productivity is thus a crucial production issue. Agriculture and health policies and strategies need to acknowledge this and be revised accordingly. Assessments of current and future agriculture development programs should factor in their impact on acute and chronic ailments, injury, health costs, and days lost to illness that undermine women's productivity and income potential. Any modifications in rice cultivation that reduce women's workload and exposure to parasitic infestation and musculoskeletal disorders deserve systematic investigation, especially if the methods also offer other benefits such as resistance to adverse climate stresses (see Figure 4.3).

SRI simultaneously fulfills several important development priorities, namely food security, women's empowerment and well-being, and sustainability of both livelihoods and the environment. However, to date, few international agencies have prioritized SRI as a development strategy, perhaps due to an emphasis on varietal development (e.g. Thompson et al. 2007). Moreover, public–private partnerships in which large seed, fertilizer, and agrochemical corporations leverage public funds earmarked for development to expand the use of their products or to gain or enlarge market presence can overwhelm community-led initiatives that promote local innovations and agroecological solutions.

Extension of SRI is not only very affordable as a development strategy but can enhance households' food security and income within one to two cropping seasons. The Bihar state government has estimated that an investment of US$4.50 per household resulted in US$34 additional household income (Behera et al. 2013: table 7). This calculation did not include the value of the additional rice produced for family consumption. Most obstacles to rapid and widespread adoption of SRI crop management methods can be overcome by quality training and follow-up, especially for women, by increasing the availability of organic fertilizers, and by developing and manufacturing affordable mechanical and motorized tools that are ergonomically appropriate for women as well as men.

Public policies need to recognize the central role of women in participating in and promoting beneficial innovations such as SRI, and should leverage investments to develop gender-need-responsive tools, improve their access to

Figure 4.3 Vietnamese farmer in Dông Trù village north of Hanoi showing typical SRI rice plant on left and the same variety conventionally-grown on right in front of their respective fields after a tropical storm. Due to stronger and larger roots, the SRI plants were not devastated by the heavy winds and rain.

Source: Elske van de Fliert, at the time with FAO/IPM program in Vietnam.

these tools, assist them to enhance their skills, and create livelihood opportunities for women. In this way, the ill-being of millions of women working in rice production can be turned into well-being.

Acknowledgments

Sabarmatee expresses thanks to NWO-WOTRO, Netherlands, for its financial support for the study reported here that was undertaken under the auspices of Wageningen University.

Notes

1 Behera et al. (2013) report that the use of SRI concepts and methods is contributing to large increases in yield of other crops: oilseed crops (50%), legumes (56%), and vegetables (20%), in addition to the 86 percent average increases in yield of SRI rice and 72 percent increase in yield of SWI wheat.

2 Resurreccion, Sajor, and Sophea (2008) found that as a result of lighter workloads, women have more time to do other things, such as backyard livestock-raising, fish-farming, and vegetable-growing, which also enhance their status as income earners. Lightening workloads made it possible for other family members to seek non-farm employment, contributing to household income and more diverse livelihood options.

3 Sambhav, a NGO in Odisha state evaluating over 400 traditional varieties under SRI management, has found that most of them yield five tons per hectare or more. In fact, some exceed the yields of "improved" high-yielding varieties grown with conventional methods.

4 The leadership of women in SRI in Madagascar, Rwanda, and Burundi is made visible and accessible by videos produced with support of the International Fund for Agricultural Development (IFAD): www.youtube.com/watch?v=J3N4 qrhADQo.

5 In 2013 a woman farmer from Tamil Nadu received a prestigious national award with cash prize of 100,000 rupees from the President of India for her harvest of 18,143 kg/ha of rice using SRI practices (*The Hindu* 2013).

References

Adak, A., R. Prasanna, W. Bidyarani, S. Verma, M. Pal, Y. S. Shivay, and L. Nain. 2016. "Micronutrient Enrichment by Plant-Microbe Interactions and Rice Cultivation Practices." *Journal of Plant Nutrition*. doi: 10.1080/01904167.2016.1148723.

Anthofer, J. 2004. "Potentials of the System of Rice Intensification (SRI) in Cambodia." Food Security and Nutrition Policy Support Project. Phnom Penh: GTZ. www.foodsecurity.gov.kh/sri/documents/Potential-SRI Cambodia-ENG.pdf.

Araya, H., S. Edwards, A. Asmelash, H. Legasse, G. H. Zibelo, E. Mohammed, and S. Misgina. 2013. "SCI: Planting with Space." *Farming Matters* 29: 35–37.

Barrett, C. B., C. Moser, J. Barison, and O. McHugh. 2004. "Better Technology, Better Plots, or Better Farmers? Identifying Changes in Productivity and Risks among Malagasy Rice Farmers." *American Journal of Agricultural Economics* 86: 869–88.

Behera, D., A. K. Chaudhury, V. K. Vutukuru, A. Gupta, S. Machiraju, and P. Shah. 2013. "Enhancing Agricultural Livelihoods through Community Institutions in Bihar, India." South Asia Livelihoods Learning Series. Joint publication of the World Bank and JEEViKA. www-wds.worldbank.org/external/default/WDSContentServer/WDSP/IB/2013/04/02/000333037_20130402105225/Rendered/PDF/763380NWP0P09 00030Note10Box0374379B.pdf.

Berkhout, E., D. Glover, and A. Kuyvenhoven. 2014. "On-Farm Impact of the System of Rice Intensification (SRI): Evidence and Knowledge Gaps." *Agricultural Systems* 132: 157–66.

Boelee, C., and H. Madsen. 2006. "Irrigation and Schistosomiasis in Africa: Ecological Aspect." Research Report 99. Colombo, Sri Lanka: International Water Management Institute.

Bouman, B., R. Barker, E. Humphries, and T. P. Tuong. 2007. "Rice: Feeding the Billions." In *Water for Food, Water for Life: A Comprehensive Assessment of Water Management in Agriculture*, edited by D. Molden, 515–49. London: Earthscan; and Colombo: International Water Management Institute.

Cameron, M., and L. Lorenz, eds. 2013. *Biological and Environmental Control of Disease Vectors*. London: CABI International.

Castillo, G.E., Minh N. L., and K. Pfeifer. 2012. "Oxfam America: Learning from the System of Rice Intensification in Northern Vietnam." In *Scaling Up in Agriculture, Rural Development, and Nutrition* series, Policy Brief No. 19. Washington, DC: International Food Policy Research Institute.

Chiong-Javier, M. E. 2009. "Health Consequences of Rural Women's Productive Role in Agriculture in the Philippines and Other Developing Countries." *Journal of International Women's Studies* 10: 95–110.

Deng, G. D., X. R. Xu, Y. Zhang, D. Li, R. Y. Gan, and H. B. Li. 2013. "Phenolic Compounds and Bioactivities of Pigmented Rice." *Critical Review in Food Science and Nutrition* 53: 296–306.

De Schutter, O. 2013. "The Agrarian Transition and the 'Feminization' of Agriculture." Conference Paper 37. Center for Agrarian Studies, Yale University, New Haven, CT.

Dill, J., G. Deichert, and T. N. T. Le, eds. 2013. *Promoting the System of Rice Intensification: Lessons Learned from Trà Vinh Province, Viet Nam.* Joint publication of the German Organization for International Cooperation (GIZ) and International Fund for Agricultural Development (IFAD): Hanoi. http://infoagro.net/archivos_ Infoagro/Regatta/biblioteca/VN-GIZreportonLesson.pdf.

Dykes, L., and L. W. Rooney. 2007. "Phenolic Compounds in Cereal Grains and Their Health Benefits." *Cereal Foods World* 52: 105–11.

EJF. 2002. *Death in Small Doses: Cambodia's Pesticides Problems and Solution.* London: Environmental Justice Foundation. http://ejfoundation.org/sites/default/ files/public/death_in_small_doses.pdf.

FAO. 2004 "Report of the Regional Consultation on Gender Dimensions in Asian Rice Livelihood Systems in the Changing Milieu of Technologies and Economy." Bangkok, Thailand: UN Food and Agriculture Organization.

Frei, M., and K. Becker. 2005. "On Rice, Biodiversity and Nutrients." Institute of Animal Production in the Tropics and Subtropics. Stuttgart: University of Hohenheim. www.greenpeace.org/international/en/publications/rep.

Hansda, R. 2014. "Sustainable Agriculture for All? The Complex Cases of the System of Rice Intensification (SRI) and Conservation Agriculture (CA)." In *In Our Common Dream: A Secure Food Future for All*, edited by A. Radl, and J. Rycroft, 18–21. Cambridge, UK: Cambridge University Press.

Hassan, R., R. Scholes, and N. Ash eds. 2005. *Ecosystems and Human Well-being: Current State and Trends.* Findings of the Condition and Trends Working Group of the Millennium Ecosystem Assessment. Washington, DC: Island Press.

Hauser, K. 2010. "Interview: Malian Rice Farmer Uses SRI to Get More from Less." *One* (blog). www.one.org/us/2010/10/22/interview-malian-rice-farmer-uses-sri-to-get-more-from-less/.

Hotez, P. 2013. "Female Genital Schistosomiasis (FGS): Sub-Saharan Africa's Secret Scourge of Girls and Women." *PLOS* (blog), May 6. http://blogs.plos. org/speakingofmedicine/2013/05/06/female-genital-schistosomiasis-fgs-sub-sah aran-africas-secret-scourge-of-girls-and-women/.

Huang, J., F. B. Qiao, L. X. Zhang, and S. Rozelle. 2001. "Farm Pesticide, Rice Production and Human Health." Research Report. Penang, Malaysia: Joint publication of the Economy and Environment Program for Southeast Asia (EEPSEA) and World Fish Center.

IRRI. 1988. Vector-Borne Disease Control in Humans through Rice Agroecosystem Management: Proceedings of the Workshop on Integrated Vector-Borne Disease Control in Riceland Agroecosystems of Developing Countries. Los Baños, Philippines: International Rice Research Institute.

Jagannath, P., H. Pullabhotla, and N. Uphoff. 2013. "Meta-analysis Evaluating Water Use, Water Saving, and Water Productivity in Irrigated Production of Rice with SRI vs. Standard Management Methods." *Taiwan Water Conservancy* 61: 14–49.

Joshi, S. K. 2002. "Rice Field Work and the Occupational Hazards." *Journal of Kathmandu Medical College* 4: 111–14.

Kabir, H., and N. Uphoff. 2007. "Results of Disseminating the System of Rice Intensification with Farmer Field School Methods in Northern Myanmar." *Experimental Agriculture* 43:.463–76.

Kar, S. K., S. Ghosh, R. Paul, S. De, and P. C. Dhara. 2012. "Ergonomical Evaluation of Occupational Problems of Women Workers in Agricultural Tasks." *International Journal of Basic and Applied Physiology* 1: 103–08.

Keiser, J., J. Utzinger, and B. H. Singer. 2002. "The Potential of Intermittent Irrigation for Increasing Rice Yields, Lowering Water Consumption, Reducing Methane Emissions, and Controlling Malaria in African Rice Fields." *Journal of the American Mosquito Control Association* 18: 329–40.

Kumar, N. 2010. "Beyond the Rat Race." *The Times of India*, December 29. http:// timesofindia.indiatimes.com/city/patna/Beyond-the-rat-race/articleshow/7182371. cms.

Lim, S. 2007. "Experiences in Multi-Purpose Farm Development: Raising Household Incomes by Utilizing Productivity Gains from the System of Rice Intensification." Phnom Penh: Center for Study and Development of Cambodian Agriculture (CEDAC). http://sri.ciifad.cornell.edu/countries/cambodia/cambSidMPREng.pdf.

Lin, X. Q., D. F. Zhu, H. Z. Chen, S. H. Cheng, and N. Uphoff. 2009. "Effect of Plant Density and Nitrogen Fertilizer Rates on Grain Yield and Nitrogen Uptake of Hybrid Rice (Oryza sativa L.)." *Journal of Agricultural Biotechnology and Sustainable Development* 1: 44–53.

Lu, J. L. 2011. "Relations of Feminization of Agriculture and Women's Occupational Health: The Case of Women Farmers in the Philippines." *Journal of International Women's Studies* 12 (4): 108–18.

Mencher, J., and K. Saradamoni. 1982. "Muddy Feet, Dirty Hands: Rice Production and Female Agricultural Labour." *Economic and Political Weekly* 17 (52) (December 25): A149–A167.

Menon, A. 2014. "In Bengal, Women Agriculturalists Take Charge." *Women's Feature Service*, July 14. www.readperiodicals.com/201407/3384660481.html#ixzz3QYxv p5Kf.

Mishra, A., and V. M. Salokhe. 2008. "Seedling Characteristics and the Early Growth of Transplanted Rice under Different Water Regimes." *Experimental Agriculture* 44 (3): 365–83.

Moser, C., and C. B. Barrett. 2003. "The Disappointing Adoption Dynamics of a Yield-Increasing, Low External-input Technology: The Case of SRI in Madagascar." *Agricultural Systems* 76: 1085–1100.

Mrunalini, A., and M. Ganesh 2008. "Workload on Women Using Cono Weeder in SRI Method of Paddy Cultivation." *Oryza* 45: 58–61.

NABARD (National Bank for Agriculture and Rural Development). 2012. "SRI in Jharkhand 2012: A Pilot Project in Jharkhand." Ranchi, India: National Bank for Agriculture and Rural Development. www.indiawaterportal.org/articles/nabard s-report-system-rice-intensification-sri-2011-2012-jharkhand.

Ndiiri, J., B. Mati, P. Home, B. Odongo, and N. Uphoff. 2013. "Adoption, Constraints and Economic Returns of Paddy Rice under the System of Rice Intensification in Mwea, Kenya." *Agricultural Water Management* 129: 44–55.

Nour, N. M. 2010. "Schistosomiasis: Health Effects on Women." *Reviews in Obstetrics and Gynecology* 3 (1): 28–32.

Omwenga, K. G. 2014. "Assessment of the Impact of the System of Rice Intensification (SRI) on Mosquito Survival at Mwea Rice Irrigation Scheme, Kenya." Master's thesis, Jomo Kenyatta University of Agriculture and Technology, Nairobi.

Panigrahi, K. 2010. "Creating Space for Women Farmers' Voices: Institutional and Capacity Building Interventions." Paper for 3rd International Rice Congress, Hanoi, November 8–12.

Philipose, P. 2012. "Rural Champions of Change." *The Hindu*, February 28. www.thehindu.com/news/national/other-states/rural-champions-of-change/article2941702.ece?css=print.

Phung, D. T., D. Connell, G. Miller, M. Hodge, R. Patel, R. Cheng, M. Abeywardene, and C. Chu. 2012. "Biological Monitoring of Chlorpyrifos Exposure to Rice Farmers in Vietnam." *Chemosphere* 87 (4): 294–300.

Rao, I. V. Y. Rama. 2011. "Estimation of Efficiency, Sustainability and Constraints in SRI (System of Rice Intensification) *vis-à-vis* Traditional Methods of Paddy Cultivation in North Coastal Zone of Andhra Pradesh." *Agricultural Economics Research Review* 24 (2): 325–31.

Resurreccion, B. P., E. E. Sajor, and H. Sophea. 2008. *Gender Dimensions of the Adoption of the System of Rice Intensification (SRI) in Cambodia.* Phnom Penh: Oxfam America.

Roberts, L. C., S. J. Hug, A. Voegelin, et al. 2011. "Arsenic dynamics in porewater of an intermittently irrigated paddy field in Bangladesh." *Environment, Science and Technology* 245: 971–76.

Rola, A. C., and P. L. Pingali. 1993. *Pesticides, Rice Productivity and Farmers' Health: An Economic Assessment.* Washington, DC: Joint publication of the World Resources Institute and the International Rice Research Institute.

Romero-Paris, T. 2010. "Women's Roles and Needs in Changing Rural Asia with Emphasis on Rice-based Agriculture." Food and Fertilizer Technology Center. www.agnet.org/htmlarea_file/library/20110725165454/eb593.pdf.

RRA (Revitalizing Rainfed Agriculture). 2015. "System of Rice Intensification (SRI) with Rainfed Tribal Farmers in Malkangiri." Secundarabad, India: Revitalizing Rainfed Agriculture Network. www.wassan.org/sri/documents/SRI_Malkangiri_RRAN.pdf.

Sabarmatee. 2014. "Understanding Dynamics of Labour in System of Rice Intensification (SRI): Insights from Grassroots Experiences in Odisha, India." Presented at International SRI Research Seminar, New Delhi, India, June 19–21. National Consortium on SRI (NCS) and Wageningen University. www.sri-india.net/event2014/presentations.htm.

Schipper, R., A. Ravindra, Sabarmatee, D. Sen, and E. Berkhout. 2014. "The System of Rice Intensification in India: Results of Rapid Rural Appraisals in 62 Villages in Telangana, Odisha and Uttarakhand." Presented at International SRI Research Seminar, New Delhi, India, June 19–21. National Consortium on SRI (NCS) and Wageningen University.

Senanayake, N., and A. Mukherji. 2014. "Irrigating with Arsenic-Contaminated Groundwater in West Bengal and Bangladesh: A Review of Interventions for Mitigating Adverse Health and Crop Outcomes." *Agricultural Water Management* 135: 90–99.

Shah, A. L., U. A. Naher, Z. Hasan, Q. A. Panhwar, and O. Radziah, 2014. "Influence of Arsenic on Rice Growth and its Mitigation with Different Water Management

Techniques." *Asian Journal of Crop Science* 6: 373–82. http://scialert.net/abstract/? doi=ajcs.2014.373.382.

Tanzo, I. R. 2005. "Women and Pesticide Management in the Philippines: An Assessment of Roles and Knowledge." PhD diss., Pennsylvania State University.

Tech, C. 2006. *Ecological System of Rice Intensification (SRI) Impact Assessment in 2001–2005*. Phnom Penh: Center for Study and Development of Cambodian Agriculture (CEDAC).

Thakur, A. K., N. Uphoff, and E. Antony. 2010. "An Assessment of Physiological Effects of System of Rice Intensification (SRI) Practices Compared with Recommended Rice Cultivation Practices in India." *Experimental Agriculture* 46 (1): 77–98.

Thakur, A. K., S. Rath, and K. G. Mandal. 2013. "Differential Responses of System of Rice Intensification (SRI) and Conventional Flooded Rice Management Methods to Applications of Nitrogen Fertilizer." *Plant and Soil* 370 (1–2): 59–71.

The Hindu. 2013. "Woman Farmer Honoured for Record Rice Yield." *The Hindu*, January, 22. www.thehindu.com/todays-paper/tp-national/tp-tamilnadu/woman-farmer-honoured-for-record-rice-yield/article4331136.ece.

Thiyagarajan, T. M. (2004). "On-farm Evaluation of SRI in Tamiraparani Command Area, Tamil Nadu, India." Presentation at World Rice Research Congress, Tsukuba, Japan, November. http://ciifad.cornell.edu/sri/wrrc/wrrcppts/wrintnseveraju.ppt.

Thompson, J., E. Millstone, I. Scoones, A. Ely, F. Marshall, E. Shah, and S. Stagl. 2007. "Agri-food System Dynamics: Pathways to Sustainability in an Era of Uncertainty." STEPS Working Paper 4. Brighton: STEPS Centre. www.ids.ac.uk/files/agriculture.pdf.

Uphoff, N. 2003. "Trip Report from SRI Visit to the Philippines, March 12–19." Ithaca, NY: Cornell International Institute for Food and Development (CIIFAD). http://sri.ciifad.cornell.edu/countries/philippines/philstrep03.pdf.

———. 2011. "Agroecological Approaches to 'Climate-Proofing' Agriculture While Raising Productivity in the 21st Century." In *Sustaining Soil Productivity in Response to Global Climate Change*, edited by T. Sauer, J. Norman, and M. Sivakumar, 87–102. Hoboken, NJ: Wiley-Blackwell.

USAID, IFPRI, and OPHI. 2014. "Women's Empowerment in Agriculture Index." Washington, DC: Joint publication of the US Agency for International Development, International Food Policy Research Institute, and Oxford Poverty and Health Development Initiative. http://feedthefuture.gov/sites/default/files/resource/files/weai_brochure_2012.pdf.

van de Hoek, W., R. Sakthivadivel, M. Renshaw, J. B. Silver, M. H. Birley, and F. Konradsen. 2001. "Alternate Wet/Dry Irrigation in Rice Cultivation: A Practical Way to Save Water and Control Malaria and Japanese Encephalitis?" Research Report No. 47. Colombo: International Water Management Institute.

Yirenya-Tawiah, D., C. Amoah, K. A. Apea-Kubi, M. Dade, M. Ackumey, T. Annang, D. Y. Mensah, and K. M. Bosompem. 2011. "A Survey of Female Genital Schistosomiasis of the Lower Reproductive Tract in the Volta Basin of Ghana." *Ghana Medical Journal* 45: 16–21.

Zhao, L. M., L. H. Wu, Y. S. Li, X. H. Lu, D. F. Zhu, and N. Uphoff. 2009. "Influence of the System of Rice Intensification on Rice Yield and Nitrogen and Water Use Efficiency with Different Application Rates." *Experimental Agriculture* 45 (3): 275–86.

Part II

Gendering sustainability and food security

Bangladesh and Laos

5 Women and food security in South Asia

Margaret Alston and Kerri Whittenbury

Introduction

Food security is one of the global community's most challenging concerns, and one that critically implicates agricultural production across the world. According to the United Nations High Level Panel on Global Security (2012, 13), an increasing population (expected to reach 9 billion by 2040) will necessitate an increase in food production of 50 percent by 2030. If this is to be achieved significant attention to strategies and actions designed to improve food production will be required. Yet while this remains a critical global challenge, the number of under-nourished people is growing, and food insecurity is unevenly distributed. The most critically affected are those areas where poverty levels are high and those most disproportionately affected are women and children in rural areas (De Schutter 2011). Particularly vulnerable are countries across South Asia where food insecurity is exacerbated by a number of additional factors including climate changes, processes of modernization, globalization, rising levels of fundamentalism, high levels of poverty, and ongoing rural area restructuring (Alston 2015).

In this chapter we focus on the gendered aspects of food security and production in South Asia by drawing on research conducted with local researchers in two countries, Lao PDR and Bangladesh (Alston 2015; Alston et al. 2014; Alston and Whittenbury 2015). The Bangladesh research was conducted from 2011 to 2014, in three diverse areas of the country. Interviews and focus groups were conducted in the three regions (nine villages) during 2012, and a quantitative survey of 617 respondents was conducted in 2013. The Lao study was a smaller scoping study and took place in 2014; it included key informant interviews in Vientiane and two site visits to rural villages.

While we note the significant vulnerability of women in South Asia, we focus beyond this on policies, practices, and strategies to build the capacity of women to be key players in food production into the future. In developing this chapter we note the FAO's (2013) bold prediction that if women had equal access to resources, technology transfer, credit, and extension advice, global food production would be boosted by 2.5–4.0 percent in the developing world, reducing the number of undernourished people in the world by 100–150 million, or 12–17 percent.

Food security

In defining food security, the FAO (1996) argues it exists "when all people, at all times, have physical and economic access to sufficient, safe and nutritious food that meets their dietary needs and food preferences for an active and healthy life." However as Oxfam (2014) notes, this definition fails to nuance *food justice* and unequal access between and within countries. De Schutter (2011) argues that food insecurity is differentially experienced, linked with poverty, over-represented in rural areas, and more likely to affect women and children. De Schutter (2013, 1) has developed a more nuanced definition of food security that argues for the inclusion of the right to food.

Many people across the world do not have adequate access to food; the vast majority of the world's hungry are from developing countries (FAO, IFAD and WFP 2014), and one in eight people in these countries are chronically undernourished (FAO et al 2014). Particularly vulnerable are populations in the Asian region, where approximately 60 percent of the world's hungry and malnourished live in extreme poverty (ADB 2013), and where women and girls face even greater challenges (De Schutter 2011). Critical to the future are processes and practices that address food production in these vulnerable areas.[1] In this context, the empowerment of women to more fully engage in food production is a crucial element of global food security.

Factors shaping food security in South Asia

A number of processes are underway across South Asia that in combination are revolutionizing food production and indirectly affecting food security in the region. These include processes of modernization, climatic changes affecting both the location and the methods of food production, globalization, rising religious fundamentalism, high levels of poverty, agricultural restructuring, a growing trend to outmigration from rural areas, greater reliance on remittance income, the resultant impacts on the agricultural workforce, a growth in urban slums on the fringes of major cities, a breakdown in the traditional social relations of agriculture, a growth in the numbers of female-headed households (FHH), and a rise in the feminization of agriculture (Alston 2015). Together these processes are having a critical impact on agricultural production, food security, nutrition, and health (UN 2010).

The two countries in which we have conducted our research, Lao PDR and Bangladesh, are classified as Least Developed Countries (LDC) and both rely heavily on agriculture as a major industry base. In Lao PDR 80 percent of the population is dependent on agriculture, while in Bangladesh it is nearly 50 percent (DFAT 2015). Food security is recognized as a national priority goal (see for example FAO and MAF 2010) in both countries, particularly in rural areas where poverty levels are high and where malnutrition affects 26 percent of Bangladeshis (Sudo et al. 2004) and approximately 14 percent in Lao PDR (FAO 2011).

Modernization

Both Lao PDR and Bangladesh are members of the World Trade Organization – Bangladesh since 1975 and Lao PDR since 2013 – and this has had an impact on the marketing of agricultural products and the move from subsistence agriculture to a market based system affecting small-scale producers. This move to the production of commercial crops and products has changed the methods of production at the same time as it has added to the complexity of livelihoods. For example, in many areas of Bangladesh, small producers have become dependent on loans to access inputs required to grow crops (Alston 2015).

The trend to market-based agriculture is more evident in Bangladesh where there is greater access to markets and where modernization appears to be further advanced. In Lao PDR the process of marketing agricultural products is made more difficult by the geographic variation of the country – the mountainous terrain and inaccessible areas, lack of water for irrigation, restricted access to markets and lack of road infrastructure in many parts of the country (FAO and MAF 2010). In some more isolated areas the only market for agricultural produce is accessed on foot and limited to what one can carry. Nonetheless there are significant infrastructure issues in both countries affecting levels of isolation and access to markets. Roads, transport, and telecommunications issues make access to many areas difficult or, at times, impossible.

Globalization is evident in the extensive spread of telecommunications, including mobile phone access across large areas of both countries. However the integration into international markets has been slow to develop. This is gradually changing particularly with the growing demand for products that are high-value, fair trade, socially responsible, organic, ethical, and environmentally-friendly (FAO and MAF 2010; see also Leung, Sethboonsarng, and Stefan 2008).

Climate changes

Across the South Asian region climate-induced challenges are having major impacts on food production, the types of food grown, how often crops are grown, soil salinity levels, erosion, and the amount of food produced (Alston 2015). Major climatic events vary across the region but include storm surges, erratic rainfall, major cyclonic and flood events, river erosion, droughts, and sea level and air temperature rises (Gass, Hove and Parry 2011; Khatun and Islam 2010). In Lao PDR these pressures are compounded by deforestation and the development of large hydropower plants.

Climate predictions for the South Asia region include temperature rises, increased vulnerability to flooding and sea level rises, more monsoon activity, shorter rainy season, and increased droughts (IPCC 2007; IPCC 2013; Khatun and Islam 2010). These changes will have a significant impact on the capacity of small-scale producers to produce food for their families and/ or the market. At the same time, the increasing value of labor is changing the way that families use their labor capacity. This has led to a growing trend towards outmigration to earn alternative income for the family.

Outmigration

There are a number of push and pull factors that shape outmigration from rural areas to the cities within country or internationally. The pull factors include the increasing numbers of jobs available in the Asian cities that are experiencing rapid modernization. As a result men are more likely to find work on large construction sites while women labor either in the burgeoning garment industry in the many factories dotted across Asia or as domestic workers in their own countries or abroad. The growing numbers of people moving from villages to cities provides an additional chain migration effect that attracts others and builds familiarity in the often-temporary communities on the edges of the cities.

The push factors relate to the need for families to source alternative income. Family members move away temporarily, seasonally, or permanently for work and remit income back to the family in the village. In Lao PDR and Bangladesh the initial dominance of outmigration processes by men (FAO and MAF 2010) is matched by a growing trend for young women to move away – a "feminisation of rural-urban migration" (Phouxay and Tollefsen 2011, 421) evident in both countries (Ahmed 2004).

This significant growth in workforce mobilization has a number of impacts on both the family left behind and the person migrating. Those who migrate have significant obligations to their family and, because much of their income is remitted, are often forced to live in poverty in the alien environment of the cities. The growth of urban slums on the edges of cities, where sanitation and safe water are lacking, can have deleterious effects on health. There is also evidence that living and working conditions may compromise health and welfare and of a constant threat that rogue employment agents may traffic young women into sexual slavery (Alston 2015). An emerging development amongst migrating men is the increase in polygamous relationships entered into in the city, a practice that over time leads to less income being remitted back to the village (Alston 2015). There are also rising levels of HIV/AIDS as a result of the movement of people from rural areas to the cities and back again.

The impacts on the family left behind are also extensive. One particular consequence of migration trends across South Asia is the rise in the number of FHH particularly in rural areas (NIPORT et al 2009) and the extreme poverty levels of this group (BBS 2009). Women may be responsible for agricultural work as well as household and care duties. Thus outmigration has significant impacts on the family structure, family livelihood strategies, the gendered distribution of labor and income, agricultural production and food security within the family and across the region more generally. Particularly significant in the context of this chapter is the way these trends are shaping changes in agricultural production.

Changes in the agricultural workforce

While men are generally landholders and recognized farmers, women are becoming an increasingly significant part of the workforce in what some are recognizing as a feminization of agricultural work (Alston 2015; FAO 2013; Garikipati 2008; Gartaula, Niehof, and Visser 2010; Lastarria-Cornheil 2006). Women compose a vast percentage of agricultural workers – constituting 43 percent of the agricultural workforce worldwide (World Bank 2012; FAO 2013), over 50 percent in many Asian nations, and representing 70 percent of employed women in South Asia (FAO 2010). Thus food production is highly dependent on the efforts of women.

The outmigration of men and young people has changed the social relations of agriculture and the methods of production. Our respondents in Bangladesh noted that changing seasons and labor availability have led to a greater reliance on fertilizers and pesticides and to fewer crops being produced annually (Alston 2015). Landowners and fishermen may work away seasonally, coming back to plant and harvest crops, or fish during the appropriate seasons. In these instances there is an increased reliance on women for ongoing agricultural activities. Thus there are a greater number of female-headed households either permanently or during long periods of the year and a greater reliance on women for food production.

Impacts for women

While women are increasingly involved in outside labor, they also retain responsibility for household and care work and are subject to gendered divisions of labor and decision-making that result in time poverty and disempowerment within the household (Oxfam 2014). Women and girls are subject to customs that reinforce gender inequalities. Despite changing labor relations, Pinstrup-Anderson (2009) notes that who has access to food within the family is a gendered decision particularly during periods of seasonal hunger (Hyder et al. 2005). This was reinforced in our Bangladesh research. Of the 617 respondents to our quantitative survey, 76 percent of women and 48 percent of men noted that women would be expected to eat less when food is scarce (Alston 2015).

While women form a critical part of the agricultural workforce, the significance of their contributions is overshadowed by their inability to access assistance because of their lack of ownership of land and resources. The FAO (2013) suggests that globally, because women own less than 10 percent of land, they have very limited access to agricultural extension services (estimated to be 5 percent), and receive only 10 percent of total agricultural aid. Because of this, they argue that women's agricultural productivity may be

10 to 20 percent lower than current production levels. This is evident in our research, where women's access to extension services and large projects aimed at building commercialized agricultural products is limited.

In Bangladesh women own very little productive land and have little input to decision-making relating to agricultural production (Paris, Chowdhury, and Bose 2004). Only one percent of the 298 Bangladeshi women who completed our survey noted that they owned land (Alston 2015). By contrast, women in Lao PDR have greater legal and customary access to land (FAO 2011) and some ethnic groups support matrilineal inheritance practices (GRID and ILO 2006). However, because of the lack of legal recognition of traditional ownership, land tenure is becoming increasingly contentious in Lao PDR (FAO and MAF 2010). Women are reportedly finding it difficult to prove customary practices (World Bank 2009) and in some cases are being stripped of legal ownership because of a lack of adequate recording of their title (Daly, Osorio, and Park 2013).

In summary, while women form a significant proportion of agricultural producers/laborers, their access to land and resources is limited/threatened and their input to agricultural decisions is restricted. Nonetheless they are critically responsible for ensuring household food security, often compromising their own health in order to ensure this and constituting a majority of those who are food insecure (Ivers and Cullen 2011; WFP 2014). Developing empowerment strategies aimed at women would appear a critical strategy to address gender inequality and ultimately food insecurity.

Women's empowerment – strategies and practices

We argue that gender inequalities threaten food security in South Asia. Therefore the development of empowerment strategies for women requires a more detailed assessment of policies and strategies aimed at food production. These may reinforce inequalities by simply ignoring gendered patterns and strategies and unequal access to resources. Consequently we argue that gender mainstreaming of policies and practices relating to food production is essential to ensure they do not unintentionally cement gender inequalities. Gender mainstreaming demands attention to the impacts of all policies and practices to assess for unintended gendered consequences and therefore enables gender proofing, or positive actions for women, to ensure that women and men are treated equally and that outcomes do not create or reinforce gender inequalities. Gender mainstreaming and the gender proofing of policies and practices is a critical step in ensuring that women are supported to remain fully engaged in agriculture and in agricultural developments forming part of the modernization processes across South Asia.

A rationale for the introduction of gender mainstreaming and women's empowerment strategies is not hard to find. It is increasingly recognized across the world that gender sensitivity has positive social and economic benefits for women and men, providing the basis for stronger economic growth and healthier communities. International research confirms that the engagement of women significantly increases positive outcomes. For example the UN International Strategy for Disaster Reduction (2007, 9) notes that attention and resources directed *to local women's ... traditional cultural knowledge and expertise produced more efficient, relevant and cost-effective projects.*

In global discussions relating to the UN's Sustainable Development Goals 2015 and in regional negotiations concerning sustainable *climate-smart agriculture* (e.g.; ASEAN 2012; UN Women 2013), female empowerment is recognized as a significant factor in building resilience and enabling ongoing food security and is viewed as central to improving agricultural output. In Lao PDR and Bangladesh women have high levels of engagement in agricultural work. However, a failure to adopt gender mainstreaming processes has resulted in women's access to the infrastructure and services that facilitate engagement remaining limited. This occurs for a number of reasons, including the gender "blindness" in the delivery of policies and services and the unconditional acceptance of gender inequality practices as normative. There are additional peculiarities within countries including large-scale developments, language barriers, the geography and isolation of some areas, and cultural factors that further reinforce gender inequalities. Attending to women's empowerment requires a number of strategies and actions including recognizing the changing context in which agricultural production is taking place.

Recognizing context

Across South Asia, the process of food production is changing and recognizing the nuances of context is critical to effectively addressing women's empowerment. Our research in Bangladesh and Lao PDR allows a summation of overarching trends occurring across the region alerting as it does to the contextual issues in each area. This includes understanding the impact of geography, infrastructure development, access to markets, and climate variations. Also critical is the socio-political-cultural context that shape gender relations in unique ways. The rise of religious fundamentalism in some countries, including Bangladesh, has the potential to further and dramatically reduce women's freedoms and rights. Across Lao PDR there are a number of ethnic groups and a diverse range of religions that shape gender relations in markedly differing ways. The nuanced differences across the region differentially affect women and alert to the need for governments and transnational bodies to centralize and protect women's rights in the context of a rapid mobilization of religious fundamentalism and to shape responses consistent with the overarching need for human rights, gender equality, and for food security. This requires attentiveness to the socio-political contexts across South Asia and gender mainstreaming attention to all aspects of the enabling environment.

Enabling environment

The enabling environment refers to the factors that shape engagement with agriculture. Critically, women's engagement is affected by problematic access to extension services and agricultural assets, and the abilities needed to use these assets, including literacy, knowledge, information about markets, and social networks. Women's access to financial resources such as credit is also limited, often because they are not considered to be landowners and therefore not eligible.

In considering the barriers to women's equitable engagement in agricultural production in South Asia, Murray-Prior et al.'s (2014) work on the "enabling environment" is useful. They argue that maximum agricultural engagement is highly dependent on the enabling environment that surrounds production but is beyond the control of the small-scale producer. This includes the socio-economic and political factors that frame national agricultural production – policies, financial service delivery and agricultural services, business services, research and development and microfinance. We argue that if these operate in such a way that gender inequalities are reproduced then women are limited in their ability to fully participate and may never receive the support they need to protect against food insecurity. Without gender mainstreaming and with no regard for gender constraints or emerging trends relating to women's increased engagement in agriculture, food insecurity will inevitably increase.

In incorporating Murray-Prior et al.'s analysis of the enabling environment, we argue that this can be further differentiated into infrastructure and services. Thus enabling *infrastructure* includes agricultural assets such as land, livestock, tools and equipment, agricultural inputs, water, electricity, and other forms of energy. Enabling *services*, on the other hand, include education and training, extension services, access to financial resources including credit and business services. Education and literacy are also important enabling factors, as is knowledge and information about markets and other value chain components.

Enabling infrastructure

Equitable access to enabling infrastructure requires attention to policies relating to land and agricultural resource ownership, inheritance practices, legal endorsements of ownership, and women's access to services implicit in land ownership such as financial services and agricultural extension services. The practice of matrilineal inheritance in some areas of Lao PDR being undermined by the lack of legal recognition of these arrangements and the active undermining of the intent of inheritance through new legal arrangements is a good example of the way women's rights can be eroded when there is limited gender mainstreaming scrutiny. Women's increasing engagement in agricultural production and the rise in the numbers of FHH forces many into poverty because of their more limited access to enabling infrastructure.

Enabling services

Equally important are the services through which agricultural knowledge and the means to enable production are delivered. For example if the delivery of financial services, and agricultural extension and training, is linked to land ownership this limits the recognition of women as clients and reduces women's legitimacy. Equally important is the way knowledge is disseminated and to whom. Women are often excluded either because they are not viewed as clients or because the services are inaccessible and not sensitive to the limitations of household and care work. For women to have access, training and extension services should be delivered in local villages at times and locations appropriate for women. These are just some examples of the way the enabling environment can impact on women's engagement and ultimately undermine food security.

Conclusion

In this chapter we present insights from our research in South Asia – an area over-represented in statistics on poverty and food insecurity. We note the processes of modernization underway in these countries and the significant restructuring in agricultural production as countries move from small-scale subsistence agriculture to commercialized venture. We note also the changes in labor allocation as families become increasingly dependent on outmigration of family members to earn remittance income. The subsequent rise in the numbers of FHH is evident in South Asia and therefore there is an emerging reliance on women for agricultural production. We argue in this chapter that ongoing food security across South Asia is dependent on the introduction of empowerment strategies for women to build their skills and access to information to ensure that they are more fully engaged in agricultural development. Limited space means we have not addressed the more entrenched issue of the right to food and the insidious expectation that women and girls must restrict their food intake when food is scarce. This requires a more detailed analysis of gender inequalities and the rights of women and girls.

For the purposes of this more general attention to food security, we argue that critical to the empowerment of women is an understanding of the significant changes occurring across the region and an awareness of the growing reliance on women's labor for food production. We note that gender mainstreaming and gender proofing of policies and practices associated with food production in South Asia is essential as processes of modernization accelerate. A failure to gender mainstream agricultural policies and practices will result not only in ongoing food insecurity but also in a reduced capacity to build agricultural production and capacity. Improved rates of engagement and participation of women in agricultural developments will not only empower women, it will increase agricultural productivity, and positively impact on livelihoods by reducing poverty and hunger in South Asia.

Note

1 A more detailed analysis of food security is available in Alston, M and Akhter, B. *Gender and Food Security in Bangladesh: The Impact of Climate Change*, currently under review.

References

Ahmed, F.E. 2004. "The Rise of the Bangladesh Garment Industry: Globalization, Women Workers, and Voice." *NWSA Journal* 16 (2): 34–45.

Alston, M. 2015. *Women and Climate Change in Bangladesh*. London: Routledge.

Alston, M., and K. Whittenbury. 2015. *Facilitating Women's Engagement in the Agribusiness Value Chain in Lao PDR: Report to ACIAR*. Gender, Leadership and Social Sustainability Unit, Social Work Department, Monash University.

Alston, M., K. Whittenbury, A. Haynes, and N. Godden. 2014. "Are Climate Challenges Reinforcing Child and Forced Marriage and Dowry as Adaptation Strategies in the Context of Bangladesh?" *Women's Studies International Forum* 47: 137–44.

Asian Development Bank (ADB). 2013. *Gender Equality and Food Security: Women's Empowerment as a Tool Against Hunger*. Mandaluyong City: Asian Development Bank.

Association of Southeast Asian Nations (ASEAN). 2012. *Vientiane Declaration on Enhancing Gender Perspective and ASEAN Women's Partnership for Environmental Sustainability*. www.asean.org/images/2012/Social_cultural/ACW/Press_release/First%20draft%20of%20Vientiane_Declaration_of_AMMW_FINAL.pdf.

Australia. Department of Foreign Affairs and Trade (DFAT). 2015. *Countries, Economies and Regions*. www.dfat.gov.au/geo/Pages/countries-and-regions.aspx.

Bangladesh Bureau of Statistics. 2009. *Facts and Figures of Gender Compendium of Bangladesh 2009 (In Shortcut)* (online). www.bbs.gov.bd/WebTestApplication/userfiles/Image/SubjectMatterDataIndex/GSCompend_09.pdf.

Daley, E, M. Osorio, and C. Y. Park. 2013. "The Gender and Equity Implications of Land Related Investments on Land Access and Labour and Income: A Case Study of Selected Income-Generating Opportunities Agricultural Investments in Lao PDR." *FAO Report*. Rome: FAO.

De Schutter, Olivier. 2011. "The Right of Everyone to Enjoy the Benefits of Scientific Progress and the Right to Food: From Conflict to Complementarity." *Human Rights Quarterly* 33: 304–50.

———. 2013. *The Right to Food*. www.srfood.org.

Food and Agriculture Organization of the United Nations (FAO). 1996. *Rome Declaration on World Food Security and World Food Summit Plan of Action*. World Food Summit 13–17 November 1996. Rome.

———. 2011. *State of Food and Agriculture 2010–2011. Women in Agriculture: Closing the Gender Gap for Development*. Rome: FAO.

———. 2013. *The Female Face of Farming*. Rome: FAO. www.fao.org/gender/infographic/en/.

Food and Agriculture Organization of the United Nations (FAO) and Ministry of Agriculture and Forestry (MAF). 2010. *National Gender Profile of Agricultural Households, 2010 Report based on the Lao Expenditure and Consumption Surveys, National Agricultural Census and the National Population Census*. Vientiane, Lao PDR: FAO.

Food and Agriculture Organization of the United Nations, International Fund for Agricultural Development, and World Food Programme. 2014. *The State of Food Insecurity in the World: Strengthening the Enabling Environment for Food Security and Nutrition.* Rome: FAO.

Garikipati, S. 2008. "Agricultural Wage Work, Seasonal Migration and the Widening Gender Gap: Evidence from a Semi-arid Region of Andhra Pradesh." *The European Journal of Development Research* 20 (4): 629–48.

Gartaula, H. N., A. Niehof, and L. Visser. 2010. "Feminisation of Agriculture as an Effect of Male Out-migration: Unexpected Outcomes from Jhapa District, Eastern Nepal." *International Journal of Interdisciplinary Social Sciences* 5 (2), 565–78.

Gass, P., H. Hove, and J. E. Parry. 2011. *Review of Current and Planned Adaptation Action: East and Southeast Asia. Cambodia, China, Democratic People's Republic of Korea, Indonesia, Lao People's Democratic Republic, Malaysia, Mongolia, Myanmar, Philippines, Thailand, Timor-Leste and Viet Nam*, International Institute for Sustainable Development, Winnipeg.

GRID and ILO. 2006. *Gender Issues in Micro and Small Enterprises in the Lao PDR.* Vientiane: ILO.

Hyder, A. A., S. Maman, J. E. Nyoni, S. A. Khasiani, N. Teoh, Z. Premji, and S. Sohani. 2005. "The Pervasive Triad of Food Security, Gender Inequity and Women's Health: Exploratory Research from Sub-Saharan Africa." *African Health Sciences* 5 (4): 328–34. doi: 10.5555/afhs.2005.5.4.328.

Intergovernmental Panel on Climate Change. 2007. *Fourth Assessment Report: Climate Change 2007, Synthesis Report.* Geneva: IPCC.

———. 2013. *Fifth Assessment Report: Climate Change 2013, Synthesis Report.* Geneva: IPCC.

Ivers, L. C., and K. A. Cullen. 2011. "Food Insecurity: Special Considerations for Women." *American Journal of Clinical Nutrition* 94 (6): 1740S–1744S. doi:10.3945/ajcn.111.012617.

Khatun, F., and A. K. N. M. Islam. 2010. *Policy Agenda for Addressing Climate Change in Bangladesh: Copenhagen and Beyond.* Occasional Paper 88. Dhaka, Bangladesh: Centre for Policy Dialogue.

Lao PDR. 2010. *Strategy for Agricultural Development 2011–2020.* Vientiane: Ministry of Agriculture and Forestry.

Lastarria-Cornhiel, S. 2006. *Feminization of Agriculture: Trends and Driving Forces.* Santiago, Chile: Rimisp-Latin American Center for Rural Development.

Leung, P. S., S. Sethboonsarng, and A. Stefan. 2008. *Rice Contract Farming in Lao PDR: Moving from Subsistence to Commercial Agriculture.*, ADBI Institute Discussion Paper, No. 90. Toyko: Asia Development Bank Institute.

Murray-Prior, R, P. Batt, L. Hualda, S. Concepcion, and M. F. Rola-Runzen. 2014. "Increasing the economic role for smallholder farmers in the world market for horticultural food." In *Horticulture – Plants for People and Places, Vol. 3 Social horticulture*, edited by G. R. Dixon and D. E. Aldous, 1139–69. Dordrecht, The Netherlands: Springer.

National Institute of Population Research and Training (NIPORT), Mitra and Associates, and Macro International. 2009. *Bangladesh Demographic and Health Survey 2007.* Dhaka, Bangladesh and Calverton, MD, USA: National Institute of Population Research and Training, Mitra and Associates, and Macro International.

Oxfam. 2014. *Monitoring for Better Impact: Why the Asian Development Bank should monitor Food Security at Household and Individual Level.* Carlton, Victoria, Australia: Oxfam.

Paris, T. R., A. Chowdhury, and M. L. Bose. 2004. *Changing Women's Roles in Homestead Management: Mainstreaming Women in Rural Development.* CDP Occasional Papers Series, Paper 42. Dhaka: Centre for Policy Dialogue.

Phouxay, K. and A. Tollefsen. 2011. "Rural–Urban Migration, Economic Transition, and Status of Female Industrial Workers in Lao PDR." *Population, Place and Space* 17 (5): 421–34.

Pinstrup-Andersen, P. 2009. "Food Security: Definition and Measurement." *Food Security* 1 (1): 5–7.

SOFA, and C. Doss. 2010. *Role of Women in Agriculture.* Working Paper 11–02, Agricultural Development Economics Division. Rome: FAO.

Sudo, N., M. Sekiyama, C. Watanabe, M. H. Bokul, and R. Ohtsuka. 2004. "Gender Differences in Food and Energy Intake Among Adult Villagers in Northwestern Bangladesh: A Food Frequency Questionnaire Survey." *International Journal of Food Sciences and Nutrition* 55 (2): 499–509.

UN 2007. *Gender Perspective: Working Together for Disaster Risk Reduction Good Practices and Lessons Learned.* International Strategy for Disaster Reduction. Geneva: UN/ISDR.

———. 2010. *Human Development Report 2010, The Real Wealth of Nations: Pathways to Human Development.* New York: United Nations Development Programme. http://hdr.undp.org/sites/default/files/reports/270/hdr_2010_en_complete_reprint.pdf.

UN Secretary-General's High-level Panel on Global Sustainability. 2012. *Resilient People, Resilient Planet: A Future Worth Choosing.* www.un.org/gsp/sites/default/files/attachments/GSPReport_unformatted_30Jan.pdf.

UN Women. 2013. *A Stand-alone Goal on Achieving Gender Equality, Women's Rights and Women's Empowerment: Imperatives and Key Components: in the Context of the Post-2015 Framework and Sustainable Development Goals.* www.un-ngls.org/IMG/pdf/UN_Women_Note_on_Gender_Equality_Goal.pdf.

World Bank. 2009. *Vulnerability and Safety Nets in Lao PDR.* Washington: World Bank.

———. 2012. *Advancing Gender Equity for Food Security.* www.worldbank.org/en/news/feature/2012/10/03/advancing-gender-equity-food-security.

World Food Programme. 2014. *Women and Hunger: 10 Facts.* World Food Programme www.wfp.org/our-work/preventing-hunger/focus-women/women-hunger-facts.

Zimbabwe

6 "Livelihoods in a sack"

Gendered dimensions of sack potato farming among poor households in urban Zimbabwe

Manase Kudzai Chiweshe and
Kudzai MacMillan Muzanago

Introduction

This chapter provides an exploratory analysis of how sack potato production can increase food security for women living in urban areas. Urban agriculture in Zimbabwe started in the early 1950s as a survival strategy for poor African households under colonial rule (Mbida 1995). It has grown over the years and now an estimated ten percent of land in Harare is used for urban agriculture (Brazier 2012). Sack potato production provides another dimension to the increased importance of urban agriculture especially after the economic meltdown in Zimbabwe. Chiweshe, Chakona, and Helliker (2015) argue that women form the bulk of the agricultural workforce and are thus responsible for producing the bulk of the food in Zimbabwe. This exploratory study sought to provide an in-depth analysis into the emergence of sack potato farming as an alternative empowerment platform for urban women in Zimbabwe. It used qualitative methodologies and secondary literature to understand how sack potato farming has transformed the socio-economic livelihoods of the marginalized groups. The method started in Israel and the United States as a way of maximizing yields on limited spaces of land. In Zimbabwe, the method rose to prominence in 2013 and has since received a positive response amongst the marginalized groups such as women. This chapter shows that urban farming in the form of sack potato production can play an important part of food and income provision in urban households. It highlights how sack potato production has emerged as a way of promoting micro-economic enterprises among urban women.

Women are not homogeneous; they have differences in resources, knowledge, and power, hence different groups of women have different experiences. Within this chapter we outline how this sack potato project is affecting different types of women all living at the margins of an urban center. In a bid to socially and economically empower marginalized groups, the Zimbabwe government has adopted the sack potato farming method. A newspaper report in the Herald argues that

> the revolutionary way of growing potatoes in sacks was meant to significantly transform the lives of urban women who have embraced this method in a major way. A number of them are re-writing their stories through adoption of this lucrative way of growing potatoes as they take advantage of the pieces of land they obtained under land reform. The women, in a bid to fight poverty, have taken up the initiative to start self-sufficiency projects to grow potatoes in discarded sacks.
>
> (Mupangi 2013)

Women thus dominated the uptake of sack potato production in Zimbabwe with the promise of high yields and improved livelihoods. The experiences of women at Stoneridge Farm provide varied stories of success and failure.

Urban agriculture in a historical context

By 1995 more than 60 percent of Harare residents were involved in house gardening or on-plot cultivation, 83 percent of them cultivated food crops, while a further 23 percent kept livestock, of which 80 percent were chickens (Smith and Tevera 1997). An AGRITEX (2008) report estimates that in 2007, 25 percent of the maize produced in Zimbabwe was produced in and around the cities. Urban agriculture boosts the asset base of the urban poor, increasing income, alleviating poverty and including the urban poor and women into mainstream economic activities, thus reducing vulnerability and food insecurity (Mbiba 1995). Ngena (2012) argues that urban agriculture contributes significantly towards food security, waste management, income generation, health through nutrition, and improved environment. It also plays a major role in women's livelihood activities and thus has the potential of empowering vulnerable women. According to Kisner (2008), 60 percent of urban farming producers are women, which makes urban agriculture an important arena in promoting women's economic empowerment. Overall, agriculture is the mainstay of the Zimbabwean economy and women form the backbone of the sector providing the bulk of the labor yet deriving little benefit (Matondi, Chiweshe, and Mutopo 2013).

Zimbabwe, like many other African countries, is experiencing an increase in urban population. Food is one of the most difficult challenges facing urban populations and urban agriculture provides an alternative source of food. Urban agriculture is as old as urbanization in Africa. The increase in the number of urbanites has seen an increased demand in the area of settlement. Rapid urbanization has resulted in a decrease of open spaces suitable for urban agriculture. The adoption of sack potato farming has come as a panacea towards addressing the challenges of shortage of land because unlike other forms of farming, it requires small pieces of land, with lump sum returns. During the colonial period in Zimbabwe black workers who lived in urban centers preferred areas with open spaces which resembled their rural homes so that they could engage in agriculture (Yoshikuni 2007). Post-2000 Zimbabwe suffered a dilapidating socio-economic crisis characterized by high inflation, massive food shortages, and widespread hunger among the poor. Hadebe and Mpofu (2013) highlight how the crisis led to women facing challenges in providing meals for their families. Urban agriculture emerged as one of the plethora of survival strategies employed by women to ensure food security in poor urban households.

City by-laws prohibit farming on vacant municipal land (Banda 2014). This has led to increasing conflicts between urban farmers and municipalities over the years. Municipal authorities largely favor an approach of slashing grown crops on illegal land, leading to violent altercations with farmers who fear losing their crops. This is mainly because most land in urban spaces is earmarked for residential suburbs. The municipality and environmentalists also accuse urban farmers of causing environmental degradation and the siltation of the drainage systems, and this has seen local authorities slashing crops such as maize in the past. In an online news report, Mupangi (2013) notes that with the introduction of the sack potato, "farmers in the cities do not have to worry about that challenge since a single hectare of sack potatoes carries more plants than those planted in the ground," hence, one does not need vast pieces of land, since it can be practiced on one's backyard.

Methodological framework

The study utilized a qualitative research methodology that sought to offer an in-depth analysis of women's lived experiences. The study included ten women at Stoneridge Farm and two key informants who were purposively sampled to provide their life histories and experiences with sack potato farming. Stoneridge Farm is situated about 16 kilometers southwest of Harare and has more than 2,000 residential stands. It was chosen because it provides an interesting view into women surviving at the margins of the city. The people on the farm are mixture of working class and unemployed people, which provides insight into the dimensions of access and differences in levels of poverty. The farm is a relatively new settlement, with the residential stands still not legally recognized by the local government. We conducted a single group discussion with the ten women and then conducted life histories with them. Watson and Watson-Franke (1985, 2) state that a "life history is any retrospective account by the individual of his [*sic*] life in whole or part, in written or oral form, that has been elicited or prompted by another person." The life histories helped the researcher to know the different backgrounds of the women and how, when, and why they ventured into the sack potato production. According to Keyton (2001), collecting and analyzing life histories can provide a method for weaving meaning into everyday practices that appear as isolated events. It also provides insights into how participants make sense of their everyday lives.

Theoretical discussion

According to Van Veenhuizen (2006) and McFadden (1996), women in urban Zimbabwe, just like women in the rest of the Sub-Sahara African region, are traditionally viewed as being food providers and distributors within the family. Gendering food security requires a nuanced analysis of how the roles of men and women in African spaces are defined within household food provision. Household food provision is seen as the prerogative of women. Women's food insecurity and poverty lies in the structural inequalities that exist in the access and control of agricultural resources such as land, inputs such as fertilizers and the proceeds from their labor (IFAD 2008; Bhatasara 2011). Women in Zimbabwe have been marginalized from mainstream economic activities despite the fact that they are 52 percent of the population (Zimbizi 2007; Ministry of Women Affairs 2004). The dominance of women in urban agriculture extends from production to marketing.

Van Esterik (1999, 15) offers an explanation of the gendered nature of food security, arguing that

> women's special relationship with food is culturally constructed and not a natural division of labor. Women's identity and sense of self is often based on their ability to feed their families and others; food insecurity denies them this right. Thus the interpretation of food as a human right requires that food issues be analyzed from a gender perspective.

The value of women's activities in meeting food needs in difficult times and providing diverse diets has been under recognized. Women perform the bulk of food processing activities in the household, the informal economy, and the formal economy. The gender division of labor in households across Zimbabwe assigns cooking, processing, and meal preparation to women. Despite their overwhelming responsibility for labor in household food provision, women are less likely than men to have equal access to food in their households (Chakona 2012). A key gender issue at the household level is intra-household inequities in food access. In most societies, women play the primary role in translating available food into nutritional security for children and other family members. In addition, women also typically assume major responsibility for food preparation, cooking, and provision of water and sanitation within the household. Health care and water and sanitation services must consider gendered needs. Unequal gender relations in the household and in communities can seriously impinge on women's ability to meet the nutritional needs of their families (Behrman and Wolfe 1984; Ecker and Breisinger 2012; Glewwe 1999).

Access to food is a fundamental human right that is recognized under international statutes. As such the concept of food justice becomes important in understanding how vulnerable groups are impacted by lack of access. Food justice is an important concept to understand how communities should have the right to grow, sell, and eat healthy food. It is thus necessary to support food production within cities to ensure that communities are food secure especially among the poor. Connected to this is the concept of food sovereignty. To avoid the problems associated with food insecurity such as poverty and conflicts, communities need to work towards food sovereignty. Food sovereignty is a term coined by members of *Via Campesina* in 1996 to refer to a policy framework advocated by a number of farmers, peasants, pastoralists, fisherfolk, indigenous peoples, women, rural youth, and environmental organizations, namely the claimed right of peoples to define their own food, agriculture, livestock and fisheries systems, in contrast to having food largely subject to international market forces (Bobichand 2012). In Osuntogun's (1988) study of urban agriculture in Africa, the author observed that women play a very significant role in the farming operations of their communities. The women are involved in the bush clearing, land preparations, ploughing, hoeing, planting, and weeding (Osuntogun 1988).

Findings and discussion

Social differentiation of research participants

The study group is made up of ten women based in Harare. Table 6.1 contains key biographical information on the women. The names used in the table and throughout the paper are pseudonyms to protect participants and ensure privacy. The participants are from different socio-economic backgrounds; four of them are formally employed and six are in the informal sector. The four who are formally employed come from economically stable backgrounds and the other six are trying to earn a living through sack potato production. This shows that class does not necessarily preclude the decision to produce sack potatoes. Six of the study group members are married, three are divorced, and one is widowed. According to Moghadam (2005) feminization of poverty is more visible in female-headed households. However, at the same time, marriage limits the influence one has in the production of the potatoes; for example, married women cannot claim the land they are farming as theirs because they received the land under the names of their husbands, unlike single mothers who were given the land in their names. Therefore, the women all have limited livelihood options.

Gendered dimensions of sack potato farming

Most urban farmers are women, mainly because in most patriarchal societies they constitute the greatest number of those unemployed. Informal activities are common in places with a high rate of female unemployment and this is the case at Stoneridge Farm. Sack potato farming is viewed by most of the female interviewees as a way of reducing their dependency on their husbands. It enables women to bring something into their families' basic needs basket

Table 6.1 Demographic characteristics of participants

Group member	Age	Marital status	Educational qualification	Employment	Dependents
Mrs. Hungwe	41	Married	Ordinary Level	Not employed	4
Mrs. Chanda	63	Widowed	Not provided	Vendor	5
Mrs. Kupa	34	Married	A' Level	Employed	3
Mrs. Shava	52	Married	Not provided	Employed	6
Ms. Chisvo	42	Divorced	O' Level	Retrenched	2
Mrs. Changamire	58	Married	Bachelor's Degree	Employed	3
Ms. Chehanga	61	Divorced	Diploma	Employed	4
Mrs. Murwira	30	Married	O' Level	Not Employed	3
Mrs. Banda	62	Married	Standard six	Not Employed	5
Ms. Shumba	41	Divorced	O' Level	Not Employed	1

without using much land. Mrs. Kupa, who is a potato farmer at Stoneridge Farm, said

> although I am employed and my husband is employed and can afford a decent life, I just found it okay to venture into sack potato farming to enhance food security in my house and save the money for some other things. As a true African woman, I just felt it is one of my primary duties to provide a balanced diet for my three children and my husband and it gives me pride to know that I am living up to the expected standards, and since we got space to farm on I planted a few sacks which I know will be enough for my family.

Figure 6.1 shows Mrs. Shava's potatoes at her Stoneridge Farm homestead. She notes that sack potato farming has enabled her to be an active partner as food provision in her family. She harvested two ten kilogram packages from the seven sacks she planted last year. This yield was below her expectations because one sack is supposed to produce 12 to 15 kilograms if properly done. Mrs. Shava attributed the outcome to insufficient water; she was unable to give the potato sacks enough due to her employment schedule. However, this year she is expecting a better harvest since she is making full utilization of her weekends to take care of her crops. Although last year's produce was below her expectations, it gave Mrs. Shava a sense of pride to know that her family was feasting on something she produced with her own hands from miniature stage to harvesting, and above all her husband is now supporting her in sourcing the required chemicals and fertilizers.

For many of the women, participation in sack potato farming is driven by financial factors. Many view sack potato farming as the panacea to save them from hunger. This is aptly captured by Mrs. Chanda, who notes that

> farming is the only way I can enhance food security in my house since I am a widow with five orphans looking up to me. I have been farming

Figure 6.1 Sack potatoes nearing their maturity stage.
Source: the authors.

since the days I was living in Mbare, then I got resettled here in 2014. I joined sack potato production after seeing the benefits from those who started it earlier and after the M.P. [Member of Parliament] encouraged us to venture into it. Even though I farm at a small scale, the little I got from my first harvest played a pivotal role in bringing food on the family table. I am expecting a better harvest from the last time from the ones I have right now, because I received further knowledge from the ones who have better knowledge on how to farm them.

For women heading households, sack potato farming has emerged as an important source of food and money through trading potatoes on the roadside markets. Ms. Chisvo, who is divorced, noted that

> I started living here in 2005. Since I got retrenched in 2008 during the economic meltdown, I started to practice market gardening and producing tomatoes and other vegetables for sale to generate income for the up-keeping of my family. When I received news of the benefits in sack potato farming, I immediately ventured into it. I started with 100 sacks. I had a fair harvest, because I managed to raise $300, selling each potato sack at $10 each. This helped me a lot to raise the living standards of my two children who are still in school. This year I planted 350 sacks and I am expecting a bumper harvest, since I now have the technical know-how on how to realize a good harvest.

Sack potato farming thus offers spaces for women to ensure food production and also engage in semi-commercial agricultural ventures. Sack potato farming has enabled women to assume the role of breadwinners in their families and also to complement their husbands' incomes. It has also helped women to control the inflow and outflow of cash with limited male dominance, and has improved the livelihoods of some of the formerly marginalized groups, especially widows and single mothers.

Experiences of women with sack potato production

It is important to highlight that women involved in sack potato farming are not a homogenous group and thus their experiences of this activity are different. Experiences of women targeted in this study are mainly based on their socio-economic backgrounds. Whilst all the women tend to belong to lower-income classes, their access to income and level of poverty differs especially between those who are employed and unemployed. For example Mrs. Hungwe, who is unemployed, argues that, "For me being involved in sack potato production gives me a sense of worth and relevance. It is an important part of my life." Employed women tend to view the activity as a supplement and not the sole provider of income. This also determines the scale of the operations as unemployed women tended to have more crops and bigger projects. There have also been serious challenges in undertaking this venture. These challenges have led to many people quitting, as noted by Ms. Chisvo

> we were encouraged by our M.P. to venture into sack potato production. He came with people who gave us lectures on how to produce potatoes in sacks, and we were also given notes on how to produce them. This helped, but according to my own view this did not fully help, as most people are failing to harvest better harvests. Most people … who are into sack potato production in this area failed to produce expected harvests and

this has led to most people giving up this type of farming. Most people failed to buy the required chemicals, which led to their crop failure as a result of pest attack. Some of us we failed to buy the required fertilizers and we ended up using organic fertilizers, leading to poor harvests. From the 50 sacks of potatoes I had, I only managed to produce half of a ten-kilogram sack.

With sack potato production women face problems of accessing critical inputs such as fertilizers and chemicals. These challenges are similar to the perennial challenges facing rural women farmers. It is employed and married women who are mostly able to afford some fertilizers and chemicals.

It is thus clear that for poorer women, sack potato production is hampered by lack of financing. Women facing production challenges noted that the major factors behind their failure are a lack of knowledge and inputs. Some of the interviewees were told that potatoes do not require much watering, only to later realize that they actually require significant amounts of water. According to the respondents, this led to the failure of most farmers, because their potatoes wilted before flowering. Mrs. Shumba discussed some of the challenges related to knowledge of farming sack potatoes:

> most of us have the notes on how to farm the potatoes, but not all of us understand them and this has led to reduced production. When we first ventured into this type of farming, we had limited knowledge, but now we are making use of the agricultural experts in our area. In this area we make use of the Agricultural Officers at Waterfalls District Offices. They have proved to be very much helpful, and this has seen the improvement of our crops, and we are expecting better harvests this year.

The manuals were first produced in English and the instructions were confusing even though the women were all literate. The women were hoping that in the near future they will be able to access funds from different NGOs and other government organizations. One of the respondents noted that for most women, under such harsh economic conditions, the regular sources of capital have dried up. They have had to resort to the banks or the loan sharks, who want collateral and many of the women do not have it. The poorest women who are mainly unemployed and unmarried are finding it difficult to sustain sack potato activities. The program can thus entrench already existing class or income based inequalities.

According to the participants and the Member of Parliament for Harare South, sack potato farming is being viewed as a viable income-generating project if properly done. Some women such as Mrs. Changamire and Ms. Chehanga, who farmed the potatoes on a large scale, managed to realize a fair amount of profit. In 2012 they harvested a combined 3,450 sacks, with each sack producing about eight kilograms of harvested potatoes. They supplied the potatoes to a restaurant in town and some were being sold at the farm and other surrounding locations. These two participants managed to access a loan from the bank to start their project, and have since paid back the loan and accessed another one. This year, each reported planting close to 7,000 sacks and both were expecting a good harvest. The success of these two women in accessing loans can be attributed to their educational and employment backgrounds which provided them with knowledge and important networks. For unemployed and less educated women, accessing loans remains a major challenge. Mrs. Murwira, who is also doing sack potato farming as a business, said she has got 200 sacks and is expecting a good harvest and profits since the plants are healthy and developing well. She noted that the profits she will realize after selling her produce will take her a long way in supporting her family and complementing her husband's income. Mrs. Murwira's husband has been supportive and helps her financially to buy the required chemicals and fertilizers. Figure 6.2 shows part of Mrs. Murwira's potatoes.

The findings of this study challenge the generalizing tendencies of the existing literature, which posits that urban farming is a practice of the poor. The results also show that that even those who are formally employed and in the position to buy foodstuffs are engaging in potato sack growing. Mrs. Murwira noted that even though her husband is employed and can afford to buy foodstuffs, she just feels it right to complement her husband's income by putting the potatoes on the family's table. The findings also highlight how sack potato cultivates positive benefits for women through improving income and also works to increase social networks within communities. The women also highlighted the increasing numbers of men involved in agriculture in urban spaces due to the economic crisis which has affected Zimbabwe post 2000. There is thus increased competition for space with unemployed men who are seeing the success of some of the women as a threat to their masculinity.

Conclusion

This chapter provides an interesting narrative on the emergence of sack potato farming as an alternative urban agriculture activity. In the outskirts of urban Harare, women have embraced this activity, albeit with varying levels of success due to pre-existing income differences. The chapter has shown that women believe that sack potato farming is a sustainable initiative and can be a positive step towards employment creation, as women now have the opportunity to shift from the traditional roles in domestic and childcare work. Sack potato farming is environmentally friendly if practiced properly, as it does not degrade the soil. It requires small pieces of land, thus saving the environment from deforestation as there is no need to clear large tracts of land. The study has shown that traditional barriers to women's empowerment, such as access to credit and support, are also hampering the success of the project. It is also clear from the findings that female-headed households are among the most disadvantaged groups, which require deliberate assistance from policy makers.

Figure 6.2 Sack potato production at a commercial scale.
Source: the authors.

References

AGRITEX. 2008. *Second Round Crop and Livestock Assessment Report*. Harare: AGRITEX.

Banda, Ignatius. 2014. "Zimbabwe's Urban Farmers Combat Food Insecurity but it's Illegal." *Relief Web*, April 10. http://reliefweb.int/report/zimbabwe/zimbabwe-s-urban-farmers-combat-food-insecurity-it-s-illegal.

Behrman, Jere, and Barbara Wolfe. 1984. *The Social Benefits of Education*. Michigan: University of Michigan Press.

Bhatasara, Sandra. 2011. "Women Land and Poverty in Zimbabwe: Deconstructing the Impacts of the Fast Track Land Reform Program." *Journal of Sustainable Development in Africa* 13 (1): 316–30.

Bobichand, Rajkumar. 2012. *India, Food Sovereignty in Manipur*, http://viacampesina.org/en/index.php/main-issues-mainmenu-27/food-sovereignty-and-trade-mainmenu-38/1250-india-food-sovereignty-in-manipur.

Brazier, Anna. 2012, July 10. "Conflicts over Urban Agriculture in Harare Zimbabwe." *African Arguments*. http://africanarguments.org/2012/07/10/conflicts-over-urban-agriculture-in-harare-zimbabwe/.

Chakona, Loveness. 2012. "The Impact of the Fast Track Land Reform Programme on Women in Goromonzi District, Zimbabwe." MA Thesis, Rhodes University.

Chiweshe, Manase Kudzai, Loveness Chakona, and Kirk Helliker. 2015. "Patriarchy, Women, Land and Livelihoods on A1 Farms in Zimbabwe." *Journal of Asian and African Studies* 50 (6): 716–731. doi: 10.1177/0021909614541083.

Ecker, Olivier, and Clemens Breisinger. 2012. "The Food Security System: A New Conceptual Framework."*IFPRI Discussion Paper 01166* www10.iadb.org/intal/intalcdi/PE/2012/11073.pdf.

Glewwe, Paul. 1999. "Why Does Mother's Schooling Raise Child Health in Developing Countries?"*Journal of Human Resources* 34(1): 124–59.

Hadebe, Beth Lillie, and John Mpofu. 2013. "Empowering Women through Improved Food Security in Urban Centers: A Gender Survey in Bulawayo Urban Agriculture."*African Educational Research Journal* 1(1): 18–32.

IFAD. 2008. *The Gender in Agriculture Sourcebook*. Rome: IFAD.

Keyton, Joann. 2001. *Communication Research: Asking Questions, Finding Answers*. Mountain View, CA: Mayfield Publishing.

Kisner, Wendell. 2008. *A Species Based Environmental Ethic*. Alberta: Athabasca University Press.

Matondi, Prosper, Manase Kudzai Chiweshe, and Patience Mutopo. 2013. *Gender Scoping of the Agricultural Sector in Zimbabwe for Ministry of Agriculture*. Harare: FAO.

Mbiba, Beacon. 1995. *Urban Agriculture in Zimbabwe, Implications for Urban Management and Poverty*. Aldershot: Avebury.

McFadden, Partricia. 1996. "Fragmenting women's bodies–breast-feeding." *Southern African Feminist Review* 9 (6): 45–46.

Ministry of Women Affairs, Gender and Community Development, 2004. *National Gender Policy of the Republic of Zimbabwe*. Harare: Government of Zimbabwe Publications.

Moghadam, Valentine. 2005. "The 'Feminization of Poverty' and Women's Rights." *SHS Papers in Women's Studies/Gender Research No.2*. Paris: UNESCO.

Mupangi, Sarudzai. 2013. "When Potatoes Grow in Sacks." *The Herald*, November 15. www.herald.co.zw/when-potatoes-grow-in-sacks/.

Ngena, Tawanda. 2012. "Urban Farming-Curse or Blessing?" *The Herald*, December 4. www.herald.co.zw/urban-farming-curse-or-blessing/.

Osuntogun, Adeneyi. 1988. *Rural Women in Agricultural Development: A Nigerian Case Study*. Ibadan: Ibadan University Press.

Smith, David, and Daniel Tevera. 1997. "Socio-Economic Context for the Householder of Urban Agriculture in Harare, Zimbabwe." *Geographical Journal of Zimbabwe* 28: 25–38.

Van Esterik, Penny. 1999. "Right to Food; Right to Feed: Right to be Fed. The Intersection of Women's Rights and the Right to Food." *Agriculture and Human Values* 16: 225–32.

Van Veenhuizen, Rene. 2006. "Cities Farming for the Future." In *Cities Farming for the Future: Urban Agriculture for Green and Productive Cities*, edited by Rene Van Veenhuizen, 1–17. Cavite: International Institute of Rural Reconstruction.

Watson, Lawrence Craig, and Maria-Barbara Watson-Franke. 1985. *Interpreting Life Histories: An Anthropological Enquiry*. New Jersey: Rutgers University Press.

Yoshikuni, Tsuneo. 2007. *African Urban Experiences in Colonial Zimbabwe: A Social History of Harare before 1925*. Harare: Weaver Press.

Zimbizi, George. 2007. *Gender Scoping Report*. Harare: Joint Donor Steering Committee.

Burkina Faso

7 Diversifying the garden

A way to ensure food security and women's empowerment

Liette Vasseur

Introduction

The triangle of environment–gender–sustainable development has been studied from different angles over the years, mostly looking at sexual division of labor and feminization of poverty. Through the Millennium Development Goals, the critical role of women in moving forward has been underlined. But while there have been some improvements, gaps remain between men and women in terms of empowerment and their capacity to make decisions in relation to environmental issues and sustainable development. In rural communities of developing countries, two scenarios can occur. It is possible that the family stays together and the man travels to town only once in a while to sell produce. In these situations, little money comes back to the household, either because of low prices for the produce or the use of the gain by the men in town for luxuries or festivities. In addition, the sexual division of labor makes women, especially poor rural women, important contributors to agriculture, and often makes them solely responsible for the collection of firewood, fodder, and water. In the second scenario, the man of the household leaves the family for the city to find employment. In this circumstance, the woman is left with the children at home and must ensure that the household remains functional. In both cases, women are limited in providing for the family (mainly the children). With little or no financial means, they must rely on subsistence agriculture to feed the family. Very few women in those conditions can find work and provide through alternative means.

This sexual division of labor and therefore livelihood implies that women and men have different domains of knowledge on the use and management of natural resources, and different interests in these matters. However, women's knowledge about the environment is often more comprehensive because of the diversity of their tasks. Their main responsibility of sustaining the family makes women's knowledge an important issue in environment management and rehabilitation. This is critical for rural women who will most likely never have the opportunity to find a place in the labor market. There are many reasons for this challenge, including limited or no education and the distance between home and job location. Attempting to empower women in agricultural settings means finding new ways to ensure that they will benefit at several levels: health, family, education, environmental protection, and finance. All these components are associated with well-being, one of the bases for community sustainability.

In Africa, especially in West Africa, food insecurity and low agricultural productivity remain difficult problems that cannot be fixed through simple humanitarian aid (Sasson 2012). West Africa continues to have one the highest population growths in the world at 2.7 percent for the past 30 years (Hollinger and Staatz 2015). Considering that most people live in rural communities and from subsistence agriculture, economic wealth is limited and this is reflected by the high percentage of people, especially children, who are malnourished (Sasson 2012). Because of this situation, many developed countries have focused their aid efforts in improving the agricultural outcomes of West African countries. Unfortunately, these efforts have been met with limited success. Indeed, recently production is no longer increasing and, in some years, it cannot meet the demands of the local populations (FAO 2011). Many reasons have been suggested to explain the limited improvement in agricultural production in African countries.

For decades, western countries have been promoting industrial agriculture, new technologies and seeds. These may be readily available in western countries and result in important yields but this is not always the case in West African countries. Even with these technologies and recent expansion, yields are low and cannot satisfy all the needs (Challinor et al. 2007). Soils in Africa are considered old, weathered and low in nutrients, therefore are not favorable for high plant productivity (Lahmar et al. 2012). Since these soils are inorganic, water retention is also limited, exacerbating the situation (Bationo et al. 2007). The use of chemical fertilizers should remain constant to ensure production but this leads to other negative environmental impacts. In West Africa, Eswaran et al. (1997) suggest that only ten percent of the land has a good productive capacity, a large part being arid or desert conditions. The issue of climate change with changing annual rainfall patterns is certainly not helping the current situation (IPCC 2013).

For these reasons, new solutions must be proposed that will help mitigate these conditions and enhance the capacity of rural communities to maintain their livelihoods. These solutions must focus at least on alleviating the problems of low soil nutrient and organic matters and water retention. Solutions can rely on modern agriculture and biotechnology including the use of genetically modified crops, but other techniques may also play important roles such as drip irrigation and conservation agriculture. Interestingly when we look at conservation agriculture, several techniques are not new. In fact, some of these methods have been used in historical times but have been abandoned because of the lure of modern agriculture. Is it possible to introduce, or in some cases reintroduce, methods that can lead to more sustainable production? Can these techniques be solutions that can also help improve women's lives and empower them in the rural communities?

In this chapter, I examine some techniques that have been developed and are currently being promoted in rural China and several other countries, including a small case study in Burkina Faso. The objectives here are to (1) discuss the current challenges facing women in West Africa, with a case study in Burkina Faso, (2) examine some of the potential techniques that can become solutions to improve rural productivity and sustainability, and (3) describe an example in Burkina Faso where a simple agricultural alternative was used to improve production. Finally I will conclude by bringing together some of the lessons learned from these actions that may also become an effective way to empower women in rural African communities.

Women in rural communities of West Africa

In rural communities of Burkina Faso, women are central for household maintenance and subsistence agriculture. Women must also work with their husbands in the fields when needed, especially during the planting and harvest seasons. These observations originated from a survey which included a gender analysis of two rural communities in Burkina Faso.[1] In this section, I present these two communities, the situation of the women and how the use of a simple cropping diversification method has helped improve productivity in a school garden. Between 2008 and 2010, I made several visits to complete a gender analysis and complete practical training in environmental education and sustainable agriculture. In the following section, I explain the process and the case study in one of these two villages where it was possible to change the views of women in terms of sustainable agriculture.

The first rural community that I studied is in northern Burkina Faso. This community is close to Mali and has been stable for a long time in terms of population. In this community, I was able to meet several of the women who were willing to discuss various themes related to women and gender issues. While this is not the place to describe the complete analysis, a few points are worth mentioning in regards to the conditions of the women in this community and their roles in the agricultural sector. It is important to note that the concept of family for the women of this community is related to the children, the husband and gradually the grandchildren. Even after probing, the concept of a woman as a person never came up as an important component. This may be explained by the fact that in the Burkinabe culture, the tradition that the man "owns" his wife is strongly anchored. In fact, this is so fundamental that women cannot be independent. Independence means that they have nothing and are worth nothing.

When the work issue is discussed, I am told there are two components: feeding the family and attempting to find some revenue. Usually women try to work together to better provide for the families (mainly food and clothes). Daily tasks include sweeping the house, fetching water and firewood, cleaning the children, searching for and cooking food. They are the first up but not always the last to go to bed (depending on how tired they are). They also explain that they must contribute to crop production since if nothing is produced, there is a fight at home and they are blamed. Traditionally children also helped in the fields but education has become a priority for most families. Women believe that educated children will lead to better help in the future with more secure jobs than if they stay in the fields. They also mention that this is especially true for girls who are more reliable than boys once they have a job to help support the family. The concept of children has changed significantly in this community. The women explain that traditionally they used to have seven to eight children, but with education and slightly better access to health care, the average family has now only three or four children.

Most women complain, however, that they do not have opportunities to establish small businesses to either sell local produce or art craft (such as traditional fabric). They believe that acquiring supplemental income is a must to provide for the needs of the family (e.g., kids in school or a sick family member). Some of the women had entrepreneurial ideas such as building grain storage to keep the grain until the prices go up. However they state that this cannot be done without the approval of the husband. It is clear that women are limited in how they can expand their work outside of the house. It also means that most financial decisions are made by the husband, although women underline that for good financial management, it is the woman who must maintain the expenses. For school, the decisions are made differently with both men and women making the decision whether or not to sell more grain to pay for the school materials. Most women with children in school will be part of the mother committee, which takes care of the school ground. It is also this committee that will plan the school garden where vegetables are grown for the school canteen. Like education, this has become a priority in the community, and most women are highly involved.

Only a few women in the discussion group had some education. They admit that this is important if they want to start small businesses. Previous experiences have been unsuccessful as they did not know how to manage the funds and this led to a loss in revenues. Further probed on the challenge of starting a small business, they explain that if they are doing this, they must make enough money to pay for the supplemental employees that are required to replace them in the fields. Some of them believe that this is possible and get enough income to also cover the school supplies for their children (one of their main priorities). There have been over five technical assistance projects (from various countries, mainly European aid agencies) with the women of this village: two on grain grinders, one to build a water cistern, one on improved cooking stoves, and one to raise sheep. However none has been successful. Three major lessons can be extracted from these previous projects: no technical training was given to fix equipment, the advantage of some new techniques like the stoves was not explained, and there was a lack of profit.

The second community is located in the southern part of Burkina Faso near the Ghana border. The discussion follows the same pattern as in the first community but a few elements differ. For example, the concept of family is the same but women underline the importance of getting married to "own" a family for themselves. Their activities are similar to the first community, but during the rainy season (when cultures are most important), they must go to the fields to help with planting and feeding the workers. Farm animals (goat, sheep, chicken) are also under their responsibilities. In both communities, firewood has become more difficult to collect and they must go farther to get it. They tend to attempt the small business activities during the dry season when possible. This must be done in addition to the other daily activities, which do not vary. However business activity seems more important and lucrative in this community where they can sell condiments, shea butter, "doulo" (local fermented drink), small fruits, etc. These items usually represent extra income for the family. For a while, the women tried growing organic cotton but this was not lucrative enough to maintain. In previous years, the government bought the cotton readily but due to certification problems, they have stopped. Instead, women decided to try growing peanuts, despite fencing problems leaving the animals grazing on the plants. Most women have their own small gardens beside their home; this is in part due to a lack of water limiting the possibility of having a larger communal garden. The daily routine of these women is relatively the same as in the other village, although their small business using shea and cotton is an option that the other women do not have, considering their environment. Very few leisure activities are permitted to women who have families, due to their daily tasks; only during festivities are women able to meet, sing, and dance together.

In this community, tensions can be seen in different spheres. There is a hierarchy among women, which means that a few are talking more than others in the group. Similarly there are two types of families, those with both husband and wife working on the finances and those with the husband controlling everything, leaving nothing to the wife. In this case, the woman is left alone to find funds for school supplies, and have more control over activities, medications, etc. This disparity among families seems to add tension in other areas such as fetching water during the dry season. They explain that there may be some fights between families.

Humanitarian projects have included literacy from a UNESCO program. The women enjoyed it, but it was cancelled due to lack of funding. However they would like to have it back as they felt they saw "the light" (their own words). They want this knowledge to be able to expand their small businesses. The sale of the cotton in previous years has shown them that because of their lack of education, they were not paid the right price. The women also do not know how to invest and share the profits among themselves and possibly the rest of the community. Other international projects have been attempted. Similarly to the other community, improved stoves were introduced. In this case, women decided to modify them to make them more efficient for their needs. However, they still have to search for firewood. With deforestation, they now go to the National Park of Nazinga where they have the right to collect dead wood. Most other projects have been related to HIV-AIDS education.

Education is important for the women, as most never went to school. They do not differentiate girls and boys for schooling. The advantage of sending girls to school is that if they do not eat everything at the school lunch program, they bring it back to the family; the boys do not usually do this. The challenge is that schooling is only available in the village until grade six. To pursue studies, children must move to a larger town and this is often too expensive for the parents to pay. The women try to encourage the girls to be sent first, since an educated girl will bring back money to the parents. Contrary to the other community, the school canteen is abandoned and no school garden is produced. Women have no time to organize themselves to maintain the garden. Most women members of the committee work at keeping the property manageable, although the efforts are questionable.

In this village, the tradition has been to have up to 12 children per family. In the past decade, this number has been reduced to about five children. Some women complain that this is already too high because of the costs for education and health care. The women, most likely after being exposed to information during the literacy project, were also interested in contraception options. But they are faced with two challenges: lack of education (reading skills) and therefore they are unable to understand what they need to do, and having their husbands against it.

The gender analysis and the surveys done in these two communities have helped understand the women's burdens and their priorities, especially in regards to education of their children. In the first community, this was reflected by the importance that women gave to the school garden and their involvement in this activity. The fact that the second community had more options in terms of income may have influenced women's support for the school. Further discussion with members of these communities showed that a greater number of children were going, staying in, and graduating from school in the first community than in the second one where children were often needed in cotton fields.

Solutions for better production?

Finding solutions to food insecurity and empowering women in rural communities of West Africa like in Burkina Faso remains a challenge. For decades, humanitarian aid has focused on advancing agricultural technologies, equipment, training (mostly men), and industrialization of the agricultural system. In many cases, these measures have failed due to lack of long-term support. This is especially true for farm equipment that can be found in various fields that is unused due to mechanical failure. For women, most projects have focused on improved stoves, health education, and some specific types of agricultural systems thought to be beneficial for them. Most of the projects never took into account the existing burden on women in terms of their daily lives. In the long term, most of these activities were added to their workloads and by the end became unsustainable.

Empowering rural women in these conditions is difficult, as it is clear that adding new techniques or activities will continue to increase their workload while not necessarily empowering them to move forward with new strategies. In this case, it is important to find ways to improve their work in such a way that they first feel empowered and then capable over time to add other actions that can lead to greater access of what they need. In this case, the school garden became the entrance to enhancing their lives and empowering them in terms of understanding the benefits of sustainable agriculture, while not adding to their burden and not threatening the family (especially the men who may not want their wives adding external activities). This may be considered as a mild and low level of empowerment but my previous experience has shown that trying to move too fast often leads to denial from the men and greater risks for women.

The school garden represents a positive strategy to ensure that children have food during schooldays. It is well known that such a system is beneficial and helps retain children in school. The women usually involved in this activity believe in the education of their children and this is done in addition to their own household work. However, I rapidly learned that like for any other farming practices, techniques used are often dictated by the husbands or learned from what the men are doing. For example, if pesticides are used, women will also tend to use them, without necessarily understanding the impacts on health or even the reasons for their usage. The misuse of chemicals is in fact very frequent, leading to environmental contamination (especially the school well which is usually located close to the school and the garden) and health issues.

In this project, the main goal was to reduce chemical use and improve environmental conditions for the women and the children through the use of the strategy of diversification. In the next section I explain the principles of crop diversification and its benefits for humans and ecosystems.

Crop diversification as an alternative

In an industrialized agricultural system, with the increase of monoculture – that is the cultivation of one species in a large area – farmers have changed the biological diversity, structure, and function of these systems. This has led to the weakening of recovery mechanisms needed to respond to disturbances and sudden changes in environmental conditions (MacDougall et al. 2013). This includes not only events such as drought or heavy rainfall but also biotic factors such as insect pest outbreaks. Biodiversity plays an important role in buffering and enhancing ecosystem resilience in the face of changing environments. More diverse communities are less susceptible to stress than monocultures (Steudel et al. 2012). Low diversity in intensive agriculture increases the possibility of pests, weeds, and disease, while high diversity has been hypothesized to affect crop system functions through partitioning of resources (Theunissen 1997). In order to enhance resilience of agricultural systems, diversification therefore becomes a sustainable alternative (Lithourgidis et al. 2011; Steudel et al. 2012; Tuomisto et al. 2012). Sustainable agriculture includes techniques and practices such as polyculture, agroforestry, intercropping, etc. These practices can help maintain soil fertility through nutrient and water management while increasing productivity or yield, increasing diversity, and reducing pest incidence (Lithourgidis et al. 2011; Tuomisto et al. 2012).

In the case of Burkina Faso, small scale diversification at the plot level was promoted in the first village. Initially, during the first visit to the school garden, the women complained of many issues. First, most vegetables were infested by pests. Soil was drying very fast and water was often either limited or contaminated. It took some time to understand that the contamination came from the use (or in fact the overuse) of chemical fertilizers. This led to increasing nutrients in the water and the proliferation of algae and infestation of other pests and insects such as bees. The overuse of pesticides did not help in terms of soil contamination. By the end the production was poor and looking unhealthy. During this initial visit, a group of us discussed the issues and explained the reasons for low production, contamination, and infestation.

Through further dialogue, three solutions were encouraged. The first one was to reduce the use of pesticides and chemical fertilizers. Women understood very rapidly the concern related to the health of their children and this alone already helped convince them to accept this reduction (if not elimination). The second solution was that to compensate for the lack of nutrients in the soil, the easiest method would be to encourage the children coming to school to pick up feces from the goats. This might seem a simple task but it needed convincing the parents of the usefulness of this free manure. Indeed, goats are free to run everywhere in the community. It would be easy for them to collect and bring manure to the school for the garden. Finally the solution of plant diversification was explained. Because of the small size of the garden, it was suggested that they plant the various vegetables in a relatively random way (i.e., tomato, eggplant, onion, etc.), intermixed in the same plot and in relatively high density to reduce weeds.

The results were quite amazing after only one year. As shown in Figure 1, the mixture of cultivated plants was quite diverse. In general the plants were healthy with little infestation. Between rows, it was possible to see the feces of the goat, which led to two advantages: the addition of organic nutrients and the retention of water in the soil. The women explained that they did not need to water as often, which helped maintain the well over a longer time period during the dry season. The women were also feeling proud of their accomplishments. It was clear that the activities of environmental education and the adoption of the techniques had really improved the conditions for the women. It is important to note that, through one of our partners in Burkina Faso, we learned that the class that was present at the time of this work has now graduated. In total about 10 girls and 17 boys have successfully graduated and this represented the highest numbers of children graduating

Figure 7.1 Photo of the polyculture mixed school garden in the community in the northern region of Burkina Faso.

from this community ever. The main significance of this accomplishment is that more girls graduated than before, because they had access to food. Some mothers were proud because their girls usually brought back food at night if there was any left over. As a woman stated, "my daughter will be able to go in town, get higher education, and support us better than a boy as she will know better how to manage her money." In general, the women now expect to maintain these numbers over the years with greater coordination, mainly the women who have now the capacity to maintain a healthy environment for them and their children. Unfortunately in the second community, due to lack of coordination and involvement in the school garden, while solutions were suggested, nothing was initiated.

Linking crop diversification to food security and women's empowerment

Agricultural practices in developing countries have for a long time been taught to men, while the reality has been that, in many countries, women are responsible for subsistence agriculture, school gardens, and to some extent crop production for markets. Because of their roles, they are highly exposed to various contaminants as well as social and family pressures. Their burden is even greater if the husband is away finding work in the city. In most circumstances, because of lack of education, they only repeat practices that they were told either by the husband or extensionists.

Through this project, some environmental education sessions have been provided including the use of manure in school gardens. The women believe that these tools and pieces of information have helped them in many aspects. For example, they mentioned better understanding of the role of chemicals on their health and the health of their children. They also felt empowered in directly contributing to the success of the children in being in school and eventually graduating.

Sustainable agriculture can be one of the pivotal points that may help women in rural communities to be able first to achieve basic subsistence and from there some economic gain needed to add other items in the household. It is important, however, to understand their needs and their daily activities and obligations. Some techniques, when not planned with the burdens of women in mind, can be quite detrimental to their lives. This was found to be the case for techniques such as the strategy of rice intensification where manual weeding is required and usually relies on women for such tasks. In this case, in the long term, while this may help some environmental issues such as water conservation and help produce more rice, this is done on the backs of women who end up having even more to do at the end of the day. Such cases are not the best way to empower women. I critically argue that any strategy used to help women should also take into consideration their daily activities and the limitations that they may have due to culture and traditions. For a long time, gender and women's equality issues have been discussed with this framework and have led to few improvements. In fact, I have seen cases where the push for women's equality has led to tensions at the work place and in communities. This might have been the case in the second village where many health workers have been coming to discuss women's independence, especially regarding sexuality. This community has been over stressed by the arrivals of refugees from the Ivory Coast and the settlement of some former nomadic tribes.

At the same time, I argue that no one technique of agriculture is perfect in itself. In this case, it has worked and empowered women. This should always be contextually situated. There are several other practices that can be used to enhance sustainability. Among them, intercropping, polyculture, and cover crops are certainly promising. These strategies reduce the concerns related to monocultures by increasing diversification and reducing soil erosion, chemical pesticides, and fertilizers. Therefore, these strategies improve habitats for pest predators and soil organic matter and potentially fertility with the use of legume intercrops. Other additional techniques can also be integrated into a sustainable agriculture strategy, including integrated pest management and nutrient management with the addition of compost or other sources of nutrients. Once women have a good handle on some of these techniques they can also start experimenting and find ways to augment their income through more efficient production. This would come over time when they gain enough confidence to innovate in their own activities.

Interestingly, it is important to know that several of these solutions are in fact far from new. They were traditionally used in those countries, but with mechanization and industrialization of the agricultural sector they have been forgotten. Other barriers will have to be overcome to ensure sustainability of these actions. The failure to empower women in agriculture, especially in Africa, comes from diverse angles. At the national level, many countries have been lured and influenced by the economic gains promised by multi-national companies and access to international markets. This has pushed countries to promote, if not force, farmers to increase production and use specific seeds on large areas. This requires time investment from all family members, including women who have limited voice and agency on such enterprises. In many cases, this type of intensive agriculture relies heavily on synthetic chemical fertilizers and pesticides, and heavy equipment. Tensions in families increase when farmers are unable to afford or repay debts caused by such production. Women are often the target of violence from men in those circumstances.

Traditions and culture remain barriers for women's empowerment in rural communities of most developing countries. The lack or limited education of farmers in rural areas exacerbates the issue and solutions cannot be rapidly implemented. In fact, rapid interventions have often led to a backlash from communities and reduced success for the adoption of new techniques or practices. Demonstration projects and further research showing their potential can help persuade women to change their habits. In addition, there should be opportunities for women to share experiences and knowledge among themselves within communities and between them. It is important to remember that cultures and traditions are strongly anchored, like in rural communities of Burkina Faso, and expecting women to be rapidly independent and empowered with little education and capacities is utopic. Solutions must be realistic and incremental to be successful.

With men increasingly travelling to urban centers to work, women are becoming the main person caring for the farm. Women are more vulnerable to influences from outside and as most women are even less educated than men, their capacity to evaluate best practices remains limited. Encouraging women to go to school and gradually having a stronger network for agricultural practices can certainly void this knowledge gap. To get there, national policies and some of the rural traditions may have to be changed. In the meantime, finding ways to empower women at the local level through actions that are close to the heart may be the most effective way to encourage them in the long term.

Conclusion

Once I had a friend asking: how many generations do you need to remove poverty from a family? I would question the same in terms of women's empowerment. How many generations? In Burkina Faso, like many other countries, women are "owned" by their husbands and cannot own land. These traditions are deeply anchored and will not be changed over a generation. Persistence and incremental actions will best assist women in understanding their capabilities. One of the lessons learned from these two communities relates to the capacity of the women to work together to enhance their livelihoods and that of their children. If there is a will, women commit to their educative associations as volunteers. They then not only try to deal with the school facilities but also work with the school canteen for their children. This is where they can feel empowered, as they know that having successful children in education leads to better lives.

I strongly believe that diversification in the agricultural system may be one of the best ways to improve women's capacity to make decisions and see their own values for society. Further education, support, and attitudinal shifts from the men's side will also help contribute to this empowerment. But, this must be accomplished carefully in order to maintain sustainability not only economically or environmentally, but also culturally or at least socially.

Acknowledgments

This project was supported financially by the Canadian International Development Agency, under the University-Cooperation and Development (UPCD) Program (project entitled Management of the Ecosystems based on the Communities – towards a durable exploitation of the Resources in Burkina Faso, Université de Moncton).

Note

1 The gender analysis was conducted in 2009 by the author.

References

Bationo, A., J. Kihara, B. Vanlauwe, B. Waswa, and J. Kimetu. 2007. "Soil Organic Carbon Dynamics, Functions and Management in West African Agro-ecosystems." *Agricultural Systems* 94: 13–25.
Challinor, A., T. Wheeler, C. Garforth, P. Craufurd, and A. Kassam. 2007. "Assessing the Vulnerability of Food Crop Systems in Africa to Climate Change." *Climate Change* 83: 381–99.
Eswaran, H., R. Almaraz, E. van den Berg, and P. Reich. 1997. "An Assessment of the Soil Resources of Africa in Relation to Productivity." *Geoderma* 77: 1–18.
FAO (Food and Agriculture Organization of the United Nations). 2011. FAOSTAT database. http://faostat.fao.org/.
Hollinger, Frank, and John M. Staatz. 2015. "Agricultural Growth in West Africa: Market and Policy Drivers." Rome: African Development Bank and the Food and Agriculture Organization of the United Nations. www.fao.org/3/a-i4337e.pdf.

IPCC (Intergovernmental Panel on Climate Change). 2013. "Climate Change 2013: The Physical Science Basis." Summary for Policymakers. Working Group I Contribution to the IPCC Fifth Assessment Report. www.ipcc.ch/pdf/assessment-report/ar4/wg1/ar4-wg1-spm.pdf.

Lahmar R., B. A. Bationo, N. D. Lamso, Y. Guéro, and P. Tittonell. 2012. "Tailoring Conservation Agriculture Technologies to West Africa Semi-arid Zones: Building on Traditional Local Practices for Soil Restoration." *Field Crops Research* 132: 158–67.

Lithourgidis, A.S., Dordas, C.A., Damalas, and D.N. Vlachostergios. 2011. "Annual Intercrops: An Alternative Pathway for Sustainable C.A. Agriculture." *Australian Journal of Crop Science* 5: 396–410.

MacDougall, A.S., K.S. McCann, G. Gellner, and R. Turkington. 2013. "Diversity Loss with Persistent Human Disturbance Increases Vulnerability to Ecosystem Collapse." *Nature* 494: 86–89.

Sasson, Albert. 2012. "Food Security for Africa: An Urgent Global Challenge." *Agriculture & Food Security* 1: 2. doi:10.1186/2048-7010-1-2.

Steudel, B., A. Hector, T. Friedl, C. Lofke, M. Lorenz, M. Wesche, and M. Kessler. 2012. "Biodiversity Effects on Ecosystem Functioning Change along Environmental Stress Gradients." *Ecology Letters* 15: 1397–1405.

Theunissen, J. 1997. "Application of Intercropping in Organic Agriculture." *Entomological Research in Organic Agriculture* 15: 251–59.

Tuomisto, H. L., I. D. Hodge, P. Riordan, and D. W. Macdonald. 2012. "Does Organic Farming Reduce Environmental Impact? A Meta-analysis of European research." *Journal of Environmental Management* 112: 309–20.

India

8 Reviving and strengthening women's position and agency in ensuring household food security

The role of home gardens

Rengalakshmi Raj, E.D.I. Oliver King,
B. Raghini, S. Abubaker Siddick, Venkatesan
Gurumoorthy, and G. Kaleeswari

Introduction

Home gardens are unique agricultural spaces and one of the oldest production systems; however, they are highly neglected in agricultural development programs. Women's role, level of participation and responsibilities in home garden management varies across societies. In most cases women play a predominant role (Seeth et al. 1998; Talukder et al. 2000), whereas in others they perform a supportive role (Hoogerbrugge and Fresco 1993); this depends upon the purpose of managing the garden and kind of crops cultivated. In general the management of the home garden is labor intensive and needs continuous management and care. Issues related to women's time, mobility, responsibility for food and care needs of family members, and other household reproductive tasks makes it convenient for women to play an active role in home garden management.

Since home gardening is an agricultural activity associated with women it is determined by sociocultural norms (Mitchell and Hanstad 2004), and it has not received much research attention from either national or international institutions. Garí's (2003) study indicated that prevailing gender inequalities associated with garden management is the primary reason for limited technological improvements in productivity. This is also related to women's negative position in accessing productive resources and institutional linkages, in spite of the benefits of home gardens in addressing food security and nutritional values.

Of late, home gardens have been promoted as an agricultural development strategy to improve the food and nutritional security and livelihoods of rural poor households. However, since rural women are often the managers of the garden, could the home garden development strategy be used as a pathway to reduce gender-based disparities and empower women's position at the household level? Several studies have raised issues and suggested ways to ensure gender-equitable interventions in time use and sharing of benefits from gardens. Garí (2003) pointed out that when home gardens are used to generate income by selling the produce in the market, gender equality issues need to be addressed in sharing the benefits of income from sales in the market, considering the patriarchal social systems prevailing in many societies. A study by Marsh (1998) raised the issue of women's time when home garden activity is introduced, since women may have less time due to their engagement in their family farms as well as time-consuming reproductive domestic tasks like fuel wood collection, fetching water from far off places, and cooking. A 2004 study by Soumya in Kerala, India shows that women's involvement is higher in smaller plots compared to larger plots, and that men dominate decision-making and control as the value of a garden increases. This corroborates with the gendered pattern that women manage and engage in activities that are small in scale and have less market value when compared to men.

Previous studies have attempted to conduct gender analysis on existing home gardens with a biodiversity perspective. The study done by Perrault-Archambault and Coomes (2008) in the Amazon region revealed that the increase in species composition is related to age and sex of the person who manages the garden. The gardens managed by women are more diverse by 4.0 species than the gardens managed by men, and older managers' gardens have more species than those of younger managers (Perrault-Archambault and Coomes 2008). The authors estimated that an increase by ten years in age corresponds to a predicted increase of 1.40 species. Apart from sex and age, social and kin networks play an important role in managing the garden with diverse and more species. Perrault-Archambault (2005) reported that women use matrilineal kin networks to acquire planting material, such as seeds or cuttings and Perrault-Archambault and Coomes (2008) also described that older women develop stronger social networks and enrich their garden with more and diverse species. Similar observation of how social networks enhance the sharing of planting materials was reported by Coomes and Ban in 2004 at an Amazonian peasant village in Peru.

The theme of home gardens and gender has received little attention from research and developmental actions despite its recognized importance in determining food and nutritional security. Helen Keller International (HKI) initiated an intervention to improve home gardens' contribution in reducing nutritional problems in South Asian countries where women were the primary partners. Several researchers studied its impact; the study of Talukder et al. (2010) revealed that women's active participation in home garden initiatives enabled them to gain control over resources and income, which enhances their participation in household decision-making. Studies by de Pee and Bloem (2007) and HKI (2010) in Bangaladesh, observed that women's active participation in decision-making processes makes it possible for them to influence "overall household spending, food preparation, food choices and intra-household food allocation as well as care-seeking behavior of the women." Similarly, the study of Iannotti, Cunningham, and Ruel (2009) reported that women's participation in small household decisions has increased from 14 percent to 50 percent, which suggests a change in the intra-household power dynamics.

Hillenbrand (2010, 416), who studied the initiative from a gender per-spective, argued that the "small household decisions" women make are within the acceptable female domain of decision-making in Bangladesh, rather than challenging the power relations. She further added that since the model deliberately does not contest existing gender norms or patriarchal power structures, it was possible to upscale the intervention to many house-holds. Iannotti, Cunningham, and Ruel (2009, 6) concluded that although such food security programs support women's culturally acceptable role, the opportunity helps them to build their bargaining power and become "more productive in their traditional role". However Wilson-Moore's (1989) study in Bangaladesh clearly pointed out that the success of wom-en's performance in homestead gardens may not be sufficient to positively influence their socio-economic status. The main reason she cited was that the income generated out of the activity is directly handled by men, since women's mobility and participation in public space is culturally restricted among Muslim and Hindu communities.

Nonetheless, HKI interventions evolved strategies to address the gen-der disparities by understanding women producers' capabilities, needs, and rights. One such intervention was the introduction of collective marketing, which allowed women to have strategic control over the businesses and gain access to income and take decisions to use it (Hillenbrand 2010). The other most important intervention was critical engagement with women's partners, sensitizing them on unequal norms without directly challenging the power structures; this process required complex skills from the facilitators' end (Reid 2004). The above review of research on gender and home gardens clearly shows that through the interventions women become stronger in their tradi-tional role and participate in household decision-making, but this may not be sufficient to bring desired changes in gender relations at the household level or beyond. In the following sections, the authors share their experiences in addressing these issues.

Background of the study site

The study was conducted in Kolli Hills, which is the tail end of Eastern Ghats in South India, administratively located in Nammakkal district of Tamil Nadu state in India. The total geographical area of the hills is 28,293 hectares, of which forest occupies 44 percent and agricultural activities take place in 51.6 percent. The forests are both deciduous and dry deciduous. The hills are inhabited by *Malayali* tribal communities. They are descended from early migrants from the plains at the beginning of the sixteenth century (Thurston and Rangachari 1909).

The main occupation of the men and women is agriculture, combined with cattle herding and pig rearing, and working as laborers in coffee plantations or migration to other districts/states as wage laborers. Little millet and Italian millet are the common small millet species cultivated on terraced beds (mid slope) as well as rocky terrain (highest slope) under rain-fed conditions. Of the total workers in the area, 88 percent are cultivators (of whom 90 percent are small and marginal holders), 7 percent are agricultural laborers and 5 percent are other workers. Small millets, grain legumes, and wild yams supplemented with rice served as their staple food in the past and this has shifted to rice-based food systems in the recent past. The traditional agriculture of *Malayali* people has been undergoing changes during the last three decades, due to the introduction of cash crops such as tapioca, coffee, and pineapple (Rengalakshmi 2004). Consequently, their diets have changed from small millet to what is the main staple today, rice. Small millets are rich in micro nutrients and proteins, and rich in fibre when compared to rice. Agricultural intensification driven by the assured market for tapioca, lack of market for small millets, less supportive government policies, erratic climatic factors, drudgery in processing of millets, and decline in per capita land availability are other important factors speeding up the erosion of diversity of millets. The introduction of rice in the Public Distribution System (PDS) and Noon Meals Program in schools has begun to have an impact on culinary preferences. In addition, the menace of wild animals and changes in cultural values and lifestyles has reduced the preference for millets (Rengalakshmi 2004).

Gender issues and gaps associated with nutrition

Earlier studies (Vedavalli et al. 1999; Rengalakshmi 2004) on *Malayali* people's traditional diet indicated that greater emphasis was given to cereals and pulses than to vegetables (except greens) and fruits. It was common that they cooked grain legumes like French bean and lablab (*semmochai, karumochai, and avaraimochai*) at least thrice a week. Pork was a special delight, fish was unheard of, and seasonal hunting of wild animals (wild boars and other small animals) supplemented their protein intake. Even in the case of vegetables, mostly green leafy vegetables, tubers/rhizomes/roots harvested or collected either from cultivated fields or forests were the major ones and within this, the species diversity varied according to the seasonal availability.

In the past, women were largely involved in collection of wild species of greens and frequently consumed greens in their diet (twice weekly). Women played a predominant role in mixed cropping systems as well as millet cultivation to ensure household food needs. Thus they had more control and agency over their household food security in terms of availability and access and had control over resources including associated traditional knowledge and planting materials. The experiential knowledge acquired by the women from their gendered roles and responsibility in ensuring household food security gave them an important role in decision-making at the household level.

Since the 1990s changes in the cropping system (i.e., mono-cropping of cassava), have reduced the options of cultivating other crops. This has led to changes in diet and eating habits, with reduced availability and access at the household level. The change from self-sufficient and subsistence systems to a focus on the commercial economy consequently increased the household dependency on external markets for food, especially vegetables and rice from the public distribution system. However, in terms of affordability, many women and men informants pointed out that their household budget does not allow them to spend money on pulses and vegetables.

Apart from the affordability and negative nutritional outcomes among household members, especially children and women, the changes in food systems have weakened the position of women by reducing the availability and access to diversified food products, and women now have a very limited role in ensuring household food security and voice in decision-making. Women's control of food systems is particularly weak among younger women (younger than 25 to 30 years old) due to the changes in gender roles, responsibilities, and knowledge, which ultimately changed the gender relations between women and men. In other words, changes to food systems have restricted the women's role and voice in ensuring household food security. Also, it is common that men go to the market (weekly local market) to sell fruits or any other produce from their farm and at the end purchase vegetables for a week's time. Women do not involve themselves, and they accept whatever men purchase. If there is any special need, women request men to buy it. According to women participants, changes in the cropping system, restricted mobility, reproductive domestic roles, and limited control over economic resources have reduced their access to market. Commonly purchased vegetables are mostly potato, onion, tomato, and some seasonal vegetables. Ultimately reduction in dietary diversity, especially greens and tubers, and shift of food habits from millet to rice-based foods with reduced consumption of grain legumes led to negative nutritional outcomes among the household members especially among women and children. Apart from these external factors, cultural norms play an important role in ensuring equitable sharing of food among household members. Generally men and children eat first and then women eat at the end and usually get the leftover portions of the food.

This chapter describes a set of interventions focused on reviving and strengthening the culturally accepted role of women in ensuring household food security by adopting diverse strategies from 2010–2014 in Kolli Hills. The intervention was carried out as a part of a Canadian International Food Security Research Fund supported research project on Alleviating Poverty and Malnutrition in Agro-biodiversity Hotspots by M. S. Swaminathan Research Foundation. The overall goal of the project was to demonstrate innovative and integrated interventions in small farm agriculture to achieve increased income and improved food and nutritional security of 4,000 poor farmers at individual, household, and community levels from three different field sites in India. Kolli Hills was one of the sites in which 1,000 households were targeted in Vallapur nadu panchayat; from them, 570 households were involved in home garden based initiatives.

Research process and design

In Kolli Hills keeping a homestead agricultural space near the habitation is a traditional practice, but they are largely used to plant perennial fruit tree species with very few vegetable species. This is done for economic reasons rather than to meet household nutrition. Though the space is available it receives little social recognition at the village level and does not get any support from agricultural or horticultural departments. Keeping traditional values in line, attempts have been made to introduce vegetable species with multiple strategies to improve the structure, cultivation practices, and crop diversity for a higher productivity in nutrition, income, and labor management. The division of labor clearly indicated that women play a primary role in maintaining the home garden, and hence developmental actions were planned to strengthen women's role in home gardening as well as household nutrition. The project was done in such a manner that it does not increase women's labor, by involving other household members in sharing the labor demands. The production is targeted to provide a variety of vegetables for consumption by the family members; on the other hand, excess production was shared with other households or sold in market.

Initially, a detailed situational analysis was carried out using both qualitative and quantitative methods to understand the food- and nutrition-related practices and challenges. In order to understand the gendered consumption pattern as well as overall dietary diversity, pre- and post-consumption surveys were conducted to ascertain the changes. In relation to nutrition, issues related to inadequate calorie consumption (energy) and hidden hunger (i.e., malnutrition issues), were focused with due importance to maternal and child nutrition. Focus group discussions were also conducted with women and men to understand changes in local food systems and gender roles, particularly changes in gendered access to assets, division of labor, and decision-making at household and community levels. This was supplemented by key informant discussions with men and women of different age categories and participant observation on different occasions. Care was taken to mobilize the women and men of the household and sensitize men and other family members to create household-level ownership of the garden. Such sensitization programs enabled the participation of men in the garden management activities like soil preparation, fencing, and watering. Field-level women staff were appointed to mobilize, coordinate the training programs, and provide context-specific technical inputs. Following this awareness, participatory experimentation and technical training on home garden management, cultivation techniques, and hygienic ways of cooking vegetables were conducted.

Capacity programs were organized to strengthen the knowledge, skill, and capacity of women on various garden management technologies, as well as on health and nutritional aspects. The programs enabled women to take a lead role and responsibility in managing the garden, which provided an opportunity for them to take decisions related to design and planning of the garden,

Table 8.1 Annual plan of nutritional garden to ensure year-round availability of vegetables

Tomato	Jan–Mar
Radish	Apr–May
Cowpea/beans	Jun–Sep
Bhendi	Oct–Dec
Bhendi	Jan–Apr
Radish	May–Jun
Chilli	Jun–Oct
Onion	Jun–Oct (intercrop)
Cabbage/beet	Nov–Jan
Greens	Dec–Feb
Tomato	Mar–Jun
Onion	Jul–Sep
Beetroot/radish	Oct–Nov
Cluster beans	Jan–Apr
Greens	Apr–May
Brinjal	Jun–Dec
Dolichos/f. bean	Dec–Jan
Onion	Feb–May
Tomato	May–Aug
Greens	Sep–Nov
Bhendi	Feb–May
Brinjal	Jun–Oct
Cauliflower/beans	Oct–Jan
Cluster bean	Apr–Aug
Bhendi	Dec–Jan
Tomato	Aug–Nov
Cabbage/beans	Dec–Feb
Radish	Mar–Apr
Tomato	Nov–Feb
Chillies	May–Nov

when to plant and what to plant, decisions regarding agronomic practices like choice of crops and varieties, spacing, weeding, watering, pest and disease management, harvesting, and how to use the harvested produce (e.g., own use, share with neighbors and relatives, sales). The gardens have both perennials and annuals, with a diverse mix of green leafy vegetables, fruit and other locally grown vegetable species and tubers to meet family nutritional needs with provision for composting and water saving through organic mulch application (Table 8.1).

During demonstrations and garden visits, discussion of gender roles and different agronomic and management practices of the garden were done with family members, especially husbands, elder members of the family, and children. The activity supported the women to seek labor support and involve family members in the intervention. Most importantly, based on the gendered need assessment, nutritional literacy programs were organized periodically along with demonstrations. Simultaneously interventions were focused on behavioral change aspects, in which women, men, and children were involved specifically on the need to have equal food distribution among members especially for women and girl children.

Both quantitative and qualitative methods were used to document the changes after the intervention. A survey was conducted among 115 households using a structured questionnaire, and four focus groups were held with women and men separately. It was supplemented with field and participant observation and interviews with six key women members. All the surveyed households belong to the *Malayali* community, and 94 percent of them are smallholders having land in middle and upper slopes of the hills; the remaining six percent have a small piece of land (average of 0.08 ha) only. The composition of the age group of the participants was: 46 percent between 18–30 years of age, 38 percent between 31–45 years, and 16 percent over 45 years.

The success of nutritional gardens is apparent from the level of participation and subsequent increases in vegetable consumption and nutritional awareness among women members. The consumption survey clearly showed that the average vegetable consumption increased from 46 kg to 107 kg per household per year, and especially vegetable intake frequency as well as quantity has increased. One of the most significant changes in the attitude as well as practice was equitable distribution of food among members of the family and ensuring that women get adequate food and vegetables. There has been a shift in eating behavior at the household level; 42 percent of the households expressed that at least at dinner time, all the household members eat together. The average savings were ₹120 to ₹480 per month depending upon the family size through reduced purchase of vegetables from market. Vegetables from the garden were largely used by the households for their own consumption as well as sharing with kin and friends, and only 12 percent of the households reported that they sold excess vegetables in the market. The analysis further indicates that in those households located near to weekly market places, women are being involved in marketing the products, otherwise it is difficult due to the geographical distance in this hilly terrain.

Regarding outcomes related to the position or status of women in household food security, women expressed that the whole process helped them to gain intangible benefits like self-esteem and confidence, satisfaction in taking the lead role in garden management, recognition from family members, especially husband and in-laws, and increased control over the garden and harvested products. Women have increased access to homestead vegetable production with a corresponding increase in decisions about food preparation and use of harvested products.

In regard to workload, although women accept an increase in responsibility, they seek the support of male members of the family and children to support them on weeding, watering, and fencing, and through this they increase household ownership of the garden's management. Altogether, the intervention helped to revive and strengthen women's traditionally accepted gender role in ensuring household food needs (restricted to vegetables only), but at the same time it enabled them to improve their negotiation skills to participate in decisions related to gardening at the initial level and slowly in other domains.

Strategies to revive women's position and agency in household food systems

As discussed previously, the intervention resulted in significant direct outcomes on dietary diversity, saving of income, and women's increased role in household food-related decisions. The women's active participation in the home garden management resulted in further changes, which are described below.

Creating space for women to participate

The main strategy of the intervention was ensuring women as primary participants in the intervention. The intervention provided an opportunity for them to think, understand its importance and relevance, and negotiate with other household members to have a garden with their choice of species. This process was done with the consensus of men in the households, which helped women to freely participate in the program and interact with outsiders without any difficulties, and it ensured the cooperation of men in the intervention. The success of the intervention is evident from the fact that the suggested model of home garden was adopted by 570 households during the last two years (2013–2014), of which 12 percent are landless households but have a backyard for vegetable cultivation, and remaining members are landed small farm holding households. The average age of women who participated in the program was 38 years, with a ranges from 22 to 56. They established gardens in their homesteads with an average size of 40 m^2. The average number of species cultivated in a garden is 18, including the greens, whereas non-participating households have only an average of 4 species in their gardens.

Enhancing women's knowledge and skill to act on the new role

Necessary training, as well as awareness and exposure to outside places and successful cases, provided women with confidence to practice and manage the garden. Based on the need assessment, training was organized and 1,050 trainee days were completed on nutrition education and the key themes discussed included common nutritional disorders, nutritional profile of the vegetables cultivated, the importance of balanced food, and ways to improve the nutrient absorption. The new knowledge acquired through training programs on nutrition and its relation to health aspects further resulted in increased care of the garden as well as consumption of green leafy vegetables, other vegetables, and millets, along with essential nutritional actions such as wearing footwear to prevent infectious disease and consumption of iron tablets and de-worming to reduce the nutritional leakage. Adoption of nutritional gardens was about 65 percent for households that were exposed to nutrition awareness compared to 15 percent for households that were not exposed. This enhanced knowledge enabled women to appropriately care for and sustain nutritional gardens with nutritionally rich species, such as diverse green leafy vegetables in cases of families with anaemic members. The proportion of participants aware of iron rich foods rose from 30 percent to 90 percent, and the proportion aware of anaemia rose from 5 percent to 75 percent. Nutritional awareness also proved to be an important factor in uptake of the nutritional garden activity.

Gaining recognition and respect for special knowledge

In the context of the decline in the value placed on women's knowledge of wild green leafy vegetables and small millets, due to reduced use at the household level, the role of women in household nutrition has been largely restricted to cooking, a physical activity determined by men's decisions about which vegetables to buy. The intervention provided space and opportunity for women to revive and establish their recognition and position at the household level in deciding the food according to nutritional values, and to use the new knowledge they gained through the interventions. One woman, Ms. Dhanam, Olayaru, Kolli Hills expressed that "our role was restricted to the physical task of cooking in the kitchen and extending labor to agriculture but now the new knowledge and skill provided a space and household members are recognizing and consulting us in any discussion."

Opportunity to strengthen social networks among women and kin groups

The sharing of vegetables among households was repeatedly expressed as an important community value for the households. Of the participating households, 92 percent expressed that they shared vegetables with neighbors and relatives. Ms. Jeyammal, Manjalpatti, Kolli Hills, one of the women in the meeting, expressed that "now we consider the garden as an important asset to the households to build and nurture the relationships." The *Malayali* community places high value on sharing the available vegetables, food, and seeds or other planting material from their fields with kin groups and neighbors. Such community-level food sharing practices had been culturally promoted among *Malayalis* until 2000, and a typical example is group hunting of wild animals and sharing of products like tubers, pumpkin, lablab, greens, etc. The intervention helped to strengthen these horizontal networks, trust, and shared values between neighbors and kin groups. They value these as significant positive outcomes of the home garden practice in the context of increasing nuclear families and cash crop oriented agriculture systems. Apart from both material and nutritional values for women, their active participation in the garden helped them to strengthen their social networks and relationships with neighbors and kin groups through sharing the seeds or planting materials and harvested produce as well as through meetings and visits to the gardens. Other than these activities, women's daily social life in Kolli Hills is largely restricted to their home and field spaces. The age of the women involved in home garden management is an important variable, as it has implications for the structure and species diversity among households. The gardens maintained by older women are more diverse by six species than gardens managed by younger women. The acquired knowledge as well as experience in managing the garden along with family members' support (especially children) may be the major reasons. Apart from this, as the women become older their social network is broader, which helps them to source and share planting materials among network members.

Women's voice and the wellbeing of girl children

Women's empowerment from home garden management is also helping women to proactively initiate actions and participate in decision-making related to the health, education, and marriage of girl children. Of the women participating in the intervention, 24 percent expressed that they played a key role in the discussion as well as making decisions related to the marriage of female children in the household. Furthermore, 68 percent of the women expressed that they monitored the health of girl children and insisted that girls consume iron rich foods to overcome the anemia prevalent among adolescent girls.

Change in the perception of stereotypical gender roles

Amongst the 26 percent of households aged 20–30 years for whom gardening is a new experience, women often reported that men see their masculine role as restricted to the productive and community domains. The time use study indicated that, on average, one hour of extra labor time in a day is needed to manage the garden. Considering women's triple burden of work (i.e., productive, reproductive, and care work), the participation of men, children, and other elders is necessary to share the additional home garden work which is now stereotypically considered women's work. The intervention process set an example for women to seek support from household members, especially from men, which is a significant change in women's mindset and perception on similar stereotyped tasks. Although initially men saw gardening as women's work, sensitization programs helped them to come forward to share the workload of women, especially in areas such as preparing the land, fencing the area, and watering the plants. In 44 percent of the households women stated that they had the support of men in fencing and watering the plants, and 72 percent of the members expressed that all the household members including children were involved in managing the garden.

From the study it is evident that the involvement of women in home garden development raises the issue of reinforcing the traditional food-caring roles of women while enhancing their active participation and decision-making in household food systems. This leads to development of women's 'power within'; that is, gaining personal strength to address gender issues. Women's increased agency in household food decision-making is evident from their participation in the intervention, which has helped them to access information on seeds, plant protection inputs, and new home-gardening schemes; decide how much area to be allocated and what species to be cultivated and when; participate in training and capacity building programs; join the local level groups and participate in the collective's meetings; and take decisions on household food systems.

It could be argued that one of the major negative outcomes of the introduced home gardening model is decreasing value for women's traditional ecological and ethno-botanical knowledge about different wild species, since the intervention is directly reducing their dependence on wild species of green leafy vegetables and other wild species in their diet. But according to the participants, home garden intervention is not the reason for this reduction and there are other larger factors contributing to this; the important ones are changes in the cropping systems as well as environment. Ms. Muthammal from Keel Sengadu, Kolli Hills, one of the women participants, aged 53, shared that "earlier when I go to work daily on the evening I come with a bunch of mixed wild greens but now due to tapioca and silver oak trees in the hill slopes and terraces, the availability of such diverse species are less, also the common spaces (field bunds, common area between fields etc) are invaded by *parthenium* and *lantana* species, hence we are not getting preferred species and adequate quantity for cooking and also in frequency."

Conclusion

The life and livelihoods of *Malayali* tribal communities have undergone social, economic, and political transformations during the last two decades. Traditionally among *Malayali* communities in Kolli Hills, women played a key role in ensuring household food and nutritional security. They actively participated in decisions related to selection of food crops (grain and legumes) and area under cultivation. Simultaneously they planned and sowed vegetable crops and stored grain legumes required for the family, which were produced largely in mixed cropping systems. Women acquired experiential knowledge, which provided an opportunity for women to play the lead role in taking decisions on food choices and had greater agency over food systems. This position of women gave space and opportunity to have equitable gender relations at household level, though men played a dominant role at community level governance.

However, in the recent past, macro-level changes in social, economic, and policy spheres have led to changes in the *Malayalis'* lives, livelihood and consequently on food practices and systems. The degree of dependence on traditional food systems and sources, associated knowledge, practices, and attitudes are largely influenced by education, changes in the cropping system from subsistence to commercial orientation, and age, as well as mobility and transport services, networks, and linkages. Interventions to enhance home garden activity, such as the intervention described in this chapter, have increased women's control over foods consumed in the household, increased their self-efficacy for nutritional garden management, decreased reliance on the market to obtain food, and promoted knowledge of positive health outcomes associated with home grown vegetables. It is expected that the improved status and agency of women in household food systems may lead them to participate in decision-making and gain control in other household resources in the long run. As stated by Wilson-Moore (1989) and Hillenbrand (2010), changes in women's position and status in household food systems may not directly transform overall unequal power relations, but they provide opportunities for women to negotiate and participate in decisions; according to *Malayali* women, this is a positive step to challenge the current context of their declining position and voices.

Acknowledgments

The authors sincerely acknowledge and are grateful for the financial support provided by the International Development Research Centre under Agriculture and Food Security Program – Canadian International Food Security Research Fund. They are thankful to Prof. M. S. Swaminathan, Founder Chairman, Dr. Ajay Parida, Executive Director for their constant inputs, motivation and encouragement. Most importantly the authors respect and appreciate the cooperation and participation of women and men farmers, who constantly shared their time, views and experiences for this valuable learning.

References

Coomes, Oliver T., and Natalie Ban. 2004. "Cultivated Plant Diversity in Home Gardens of an Amazonian Peasant Village, Northeastern Peru." *Economic Botany* 58 (3): 420–34.
de Pee, Saskia, and Martin W. Bloem. 2007. "The Bioavailability of (pro) Vitamin A Carotenoids and Maximizing the Contribution of Homestead Food Production to Combating Vitamin A Deficiency." *International Journal for Vitamin and Nutrition Research* 77: 182–92.
Garí, Joseph A. 2003. "Agro-biodiversity Strategies to Combat Food Insecurity and HIV/AIDS Impact in Rural Africa." In *Advancing Grassroots Responses for Nutrition, Health and Livelihoods.* Preliminary ed., Rome: FAO Population and Development Service.
Helen Keller International (HKI). 2010. "Homestead Food Production Model Contributes to Improved Household Food Security, Nutrition and Female

Empowerment – Experience from Scaling-up Programs in Asia (Bangladesh, Cambodia, Nepal and Philippines)." *Nutrition Bulletin* 8 (1): 1–8.

Hillenbrand, Emily. 2010. "Transforming Gender in Homestead Production." *Gender and Development* 18 (3): 411–25.

Hoogerbrugge, Inge, and Louise O. Fresco. 1993. "Homegarden Systems: Agricultural Characteristics and Challenges." Gatekeeper Series, 39. London, UK: International Institute for Environment and Development.

Iannotti, Lora, Kenda Cunningham, and Marie Ruel. 2009. "Improving Diet Quality and Micronutrient Nutrition: Homestead Food Production in Bangladesh." IFPRI (International Food Policy Research Institute) Discussion Paper No. 928, International Food Policy Research Institute, Washington, DC.

Marsh, Robin. 1994. "Household Food Security through Home Gardening: Evidence from Bangladesh and Central America." In *Adapting Social Science to the Changing Focus of International Agricultural Research*, edited by S. K. Ehui, J. Lynam, and I. Okike, 158–172. Addis Ababa, Ethiopia: ILRI (International Livestock Research Institute).

Mitchell, Robert, and Tim Hanstad. 2004. "Small Home Garden Plots and Sustainable Livelihoods for the Poor." Livelihood Support Programme Working Paper 11, Rome: United Nations Food and Agriculture Organization.

Perrault-Archambault, Mathilde. 2005. "Who Manages Home Garden Agrobiodiversity? Patterns of Species Distribution, Planting Material Flow and Knowledge. Transmission along the Corrientes River of the Peruvian Amazon." Master's thesis, McGill University.

Perrault-Archambault, Mathilde, and Oliver T. Coomes. 2008. "Distribution of Agro-biodiversity in Home Gardens along the Corrientes River, Peruvian Amazon." *Economic Botany* 62 (2): 109–26.

Reid, Elizabeth. 2004. "Transformational Development and the Wellbeing of Women." *Development Bulletin* 64: 16–20.

Rengalakshmi, Raj. 2004. "Conservation Biology of Little Millet (*Panicum sumatrense* rothex roem. A schultz) Landraces of Kolli Hills, South India." PhD diss., University of Madras.

Seeth, Harm tho, Sergei Chachnov, Alexander Surinov, and Joachim Von Braun. 1998. "Russian Poverty: Muddling through Economic Transition with Garden Plots." *World Development* 26 (9): 1611–24.

Soumya, Mohan. 2004. "An Assessment of the Ecological and Socioeconomic Benefits Provided by Home Gardens: A Case Study of Kerala, India." PhD diss., University of Florida.

Talukder, Aminuzzaman, Saskia de Pee, Abu Taher, Andrew Hall, Regina Moench-Pfanner, and Martin W. Bloem. 2000. "Increasing the Production and Consumption of Vitamin A–rich Fruits and Vegetables: Lessons Learned in Taking the Bangladesh Homestead Gardening Programme to a National Scale." *Food and Nutrition Bulletin* 21 (2): 165–72.

Talukder, A., N. J. Haselow, A. K. Osei, E. Villate, D. Reario, H. Kroeun, L. SokHoing, A. Uddin, S. Dhungel, and V. Quinn. 2010. "Homestead Food Production Model Contributes to Improved Household Food Security and Nutrition Status of Young Children and Women in Poor Populations: Lessons Learned from Scaling-up Programs in Asia (Bangladesh, Cambodia, Nepal and Philippines)." *Field Action Science Reports* Special Issue 1. http://factsreports.revues.org/404.

Thurston, Edgar, and K. Rangachari, eds. 1909. *Castes and Tribes of Southern India.* Vol. 6 (K to M). New Delhi: Cosmo Publications.

Vedavalli, Linga Reddy, R. Rengalakshmi, E. D. Israel Oliver King, and K. Balasubramaian. 1999. "Biodiversity, Under-Utilized Crops and Socio-cultural Dimensions in an Historical Perspective." Paper presented at Consultative Workshop on Enlarging the Basis of Food Security: Role of Under-Utilized species, In proceedings of a workshop, M. S. Swaminathan Research Foundation, Chennai, India, February 17–19, 1999: 20–26.

Wilson-Moore, Margo. 1989. "Women's Work in Homestead Gardens: Subsistence, Patriarchy and Status in Northwest Bangladesh." *Urban Anthropology* 18 (3–4): 281–97.

Part III

Women's empowerment in policy and finance

Tanzania

9 Improving agricultural land security for women

Assessing the FAO's Voluntary Guidelines on land tenure

Andrea M. Collins

Introduction

Following the global food and fuel crises of 2007–2008 and the subsequent rise in large-scale land acquisitions, or "land grabs," several global initiatives have emerged to advise governments, investors, and activists on how to ensure agricultural land rights for the world's rural populations. International NGOs (INGOs) likewise call for greater recognition of customary land use, as well as the rights of women to control land (Geary 2012). Given the influx of corporate interest in agricultural land in sub-Saharan Africa and South America, a common refrain has been to promote the formal recognition of heretofore considered "informal" land tenure and the usufruct land rights of women. Regional and global actors alike have begun enshrining these principles in global recommendations and agreements. The African Union, the World Bank, and the FAO have all introduced principles or recommendations for stronger land governance in countries targeted for large-scale investment.

None of these global initiatives have earned as much praise as the Voluntary Guidelines on the Responsible Governance of Tenure of Land, Fisheries and Forests (henceforth, "Voluntary Guidelines"). Adopted by the FAO's Committee for World Food Security (CFS) in 2012, the Voluntary Guidelines provide a set of principles and 26 clauses outlining best practices for protecting the land tenure of populations around the world. Supported by INGOs, and earning commitments from major corporations like PepsiCo and Coca-Cola, the Voluntary Guidelines are poised to become the standard set of recommendations for ensuring land tenure security (FAO 2014). However, several questions remain about the viability of the Voluntary Guidelines for promoting gender equality in access to and control of land. Mentions of gender equality are mainstreamed throughout the final version of the document, but what do they mean? What evidence is there to suggest these approaches will be effective?

This chapter assesses both the Voluntary Guidelines and its accompanying Technical Guide on their recommendations to improve women's access to and control over agricultural land. By comparing these recommendations to the realities on the ground in Tanzania – a country with a widely celebrated legal framework that recognizes both customary land tenure and women's land rights – this chapter highlights the promises and pitfalls of the Voluntary Guidelines. This chapter also shows where policy implementers, researchers, and activists need to focus their efforts to ensure women can protect their rights to agricultural land. While there are gaps in the general recommendations of Voluntary Guidelines, the Technical Guide provides clear paths to gender-sensitive land tenure reforms and addresses complicated implementation issues. By relying heavily on feminist expertise, the Technical Guide advances several steps to navigate issues facing gender equality advocates. Yet questions linger about who will undertake such reforms, and who is willing to pay for them.

The chapter proceeds by first illustrating why the Voluntary Guidelines have earned such widespread praise and stand out amidst similar global initiatives. However, when contrasted with the challenges facing states undertaking such reforms, the need for a more nuanced approach to gender-equitable land reforms is evident. This chapter demonstrates this gap by looking more closely at Tanzania's land reform efforts and the challenges faced by women's rights advocates. Finally, the chapter shows how the Technical Guide addresses many of these issues in ways that speak to the challenges of implementation. The Technical Guide, in providing thoughtful steps to overcome patriarchal practices, fills in the gaps of the high-level Voluntary Guidelines, but also reveals the distance between international agreements and the actual steps that need to be taken.

Why do the voluntary guidelines stand out?

The development of the Voluntary Guidelines involved a series of regional and topical consultations, in addition to state-to-state negotiations within the CFS itself. Major state players in global agricultural trade – including Brazil, China, and a contingent of African states – were active in the process (Seufert 2013). Regional consultations in Brazil, Burkina Faso, Ethiopia, Jordan, Namibia, Panama, Romania, the Russian Federation, Samoa, and Vietnam allowed rural social movements to participate and frame their own ideas about the Guidelines (Kropiwnicka 2012). The consultative process also welcomed the participation of academics, private sector representatives, and civil society organizations (CSOs), including some of the most marginalized groups affected by land tenure insecurity (McKeon 2013). A zero draft of the Guidelines was made available in April 2011 for web-based consultation with the general global public. Following a first draft based on these inputs and several rounds of consultations, the Voluntary Guidelines were endorsed by the CFS in May 2012. Though transnational corporations and civil society organizations acted as observers throughout the process, only member states voted on the final approval of the guidelines.

In many ways, the CFS' development of the Voluntary Guidelines fulfills important criteria of inclusive global decision-making. A common refrain on the part of scholars is that global governance initiatives often fall short of liberal democratic ideals of legitimacy and transparency, failing to listen to key stakeholders, providing too prominent a role for powerful transnational corporations, and reducing opportunities for accountability (Bexell, Tallberg, and Uhlin 2010). Yet CFS consultations were inclusive and transparent, with experts providing topic specific input on issues such as gender equality and indigenous rights. Other stakeholders were able to observe and participate in dialogues, but were not given a vote. The consultative framework has been celebrated as highly democratic for an international initiative, earning it a high level of legitimacy among academics and INGOs such as FIAN International and Oxfam (Geary 2012; Seufert 2013). Yet despite this commitment to participatory decision-making, not all organizations have embraced the Voluntary Guidelines. For instance, the INGO GRAIN faults the CFS for being insufficiently critical of agricultural investment and has pointed to the unlikelihood of corrupt and dysfunctional governments enacting a voluntary code of conduct (GRAIN 2012).

Indeed, though the development of the Voluntary Guidelines has been widely praised, the content of the Guidelines also needs to be assessed. The final document is comprehensive, including provisions for advancing gender equality as well as seeking protection for customary and traditional practices. Rather than singularly including women as untapped productive resources, efforts to include gender in the Voluntary Guidelines are focused on bringing women into land ownership and governance and anticipating the gendered impacts of land reforms in several clauses. The CFS clearly made efforts to mainstream gender throughout the document, making mention of gender sensitivity several times with reference to participation, consultation, negotiation and transparency. By mainstreaming gender throughout the document, this vision of land reform contextualizes land governance within social, political and economic relations and the potential for power imbalances.

Yet despite the sheer number of issues the Voluntary Guidelines address, there are significant gaps. The Guidelines lack important definitions and concrete steps to achieve the goals laid out. Specifically, despite recognizing the dual challenges of accepting women's rights to land and protecting customary land tenure, the Voluntary Guidelines offer only a single clause that hints at the possible tensions between these two goals. Section 9.6 encourages states to adapt frameworks to recognize the tenure systems of indigenous peoples and other communities with customary tenure systems. It follows, "[w]here constitutional or legal reforms strengthen the rights of women and place them in conflict with custom, all parties should cooperate to accommodate such changes in the customary tenure systems" (FAO 2012, sec. 9.6). Thus, although many clauses include references to "gender-sensitivity," there is little to no clear direction on how to address these issues in practice.

As the following section demonstrates, these are not problems with straightforward or easy solutions. Literature abounds on the tensions between recognizing customary tenure while promoting gender equality in land rights and access (Whitehead and Tsikata 2003; Englert and Daley 2008). Moreover, as the case of Tanzania demonstrates, even where states make careful efforts to introduce both gender equality measures and legal reforms to recognize customary tenure, there are often problems with implementation. While the Voluntary Guidelines fulfill several democratic criteria as a set of governance recommendations, they do not address in detail the real challenges of land tenure reform, especially with reference to gender.

Gender and customary practices

Tanzania's land reform efforts have earned much global praise and are an oft-cited case for the FAO and the World Bank. In 1999, Tanzania introduced the Land Act and the Village Land Act, which together reshaped Tanzania's land governance framework. Recognizing the realities of legal pluralism in rural Tanzania, the Act introduced Certificates of Customary Rights of Occupancy (CCROs), which permit rural villages to govern and allocate land to villagers based on local customary practices. The Land Acts also enshrine CCROs as being legally equal to Granted Rights of Occupancy, which are similar to individual land titles in most Western countries. In doing so, the Tanzanian government sought to protect customary land rights and ensure that these rights were protected by the force of law. At the same time, the Land Act and Village Land Act also promote women's rights to own land. Building upon previous legislation that mandates women's representation on local Village Councils, the Land Acts likewise require women's participation on Village Land Councils. Moreover, the Land Acts promote spousal co-registration on CCROs to further protect women's claims on land in the event of widowhood or divorce.

The World Bank and several global experts on land reform have thus praised Tanzania as a best-case scenario for land reform. In passing land laws that recognize the co-existence of statutory and customary land rights and also advance women's interests in land ownership, access, and governance, Tanzania is certainly deserving of accolades. Yet in the 15 years since the passage of the Land Acts, many observers have been disappointed in implementation efforts and the realities of reforming land governance in rural communities. It is clear that the problems of legal pluralism run far deeper than simply recognizing the legitimacy of customary tenure.[1] As feminist advocates in Tanzania have argued, recognition of customary tenure can reinforce customary forms of discrimination against women, undermining their statutory rights to land. These tensions are complex, in some cases pitting rural land rights advocates against urban-based feminist legal advocates (Tsikata 2003). Yet some analysts are optimistic that there are solutions to be had in existing customary practices, however difficult they may be to achieve (Mbilinyi 2012; Koda 2000). As seen above, however, there appear to be few concrete solutions to these problems offered in the Voluntary Guidelines.

Overcoming discriminatory practices in customary institutions

Though many feminist legal advocates in Tanzania continue to support the Land Acts as written, they note that there has been little government effort to support their implementation and address widespread practices of gender discrimination. By enhancing the power of local authorities to invoke customary practices and failing to provide supplemental training or awareness-raising about the laws, some observers suggest that Land Acts have reified gendered power structures in customary land governance. Though the Land Acts attempt to improve the representation of women in local decision-making and increase the registration or co-registration of women's land and property, customary attitudes about the role of women in social, economic, and political life combine with the lack of implementation to prevent effective change.

The majority of rural communities in Tanzania follow patrilocal and patrilineal customary practices regarding land and property. Only about 20 percent of communities in Tanzania are matrilineal, though even in these communities land may be transferred between male family members and patriarchal practices are sometimes adopted under new land registration practices (Hilhorst 2000). In patrilocal communities, a woman typically remains with her father's family until marriage, at which point she moves into the community of her husband. For this reason, women are often viewed as transitory members of their communities and as a threat to land held by the community (Tripp 2004). This view of women as transitory within patrilocal communities – whether as a daughter or as a wife – presents a serious challenge to promoting women's individual rights to own and control land. Insofar as land is seen as a communal good, giving control of land to someone "in transit" proves to be a serious obstacle. For the providers of legal aid in Tanzania, the strength of customary law undermines their efforts to protect women's rights to land through co-registration of land and other property (Women's Land Rights Advocacy Officer, personal interview, June 26, 2013). Both inheritance and joint registration of land or property are viewed negatively through the lens of customs in which women are viewed as only temporary members of the family or community.

Participation and governance

These patriarchal practices further influence local land governance. Local governance institutions described in the Land Acts and other legislation are supposed to be participatory and community-based, particularly the Village Council, Village Land Council, and the Village Assembly. Yet marginalized groups, particularly women whose household responsibilities restrict their ability to attend, continue to be excluded from these meetings. Village Assembly meetings are held during parts of the day when women and younger people cannot attend and have physical layouts that typically reinforce existing hierarchies: "There's the high table where the village leaders sit, and you often have the men who sit close, youth, and, right at the back, you might have the women who attend. So the women are further, cut away from where the real power is," (INGO Governance Specialist, personal interview, June 13, 2013, Dar es Salaam). Local NGOs also report the prevalence of gender bias in the "traditional" values that shape the decisions of judges, land officials, and local councilors: "Indeed, customary practices in the study sites are adhered to by some Village Land Councils and Ward Land Tribunals … These organs were required to be at the forefront in disallowing traditions and customs that impinge on the rights of rural women to land ownership"(WLAC 2010, 30).

Women elected to Village Councils or Village Land Councils are also not provided training regarding their roles or the roles of the councils in the structure of governance. According to many interviewees, particularly field workers for NGOs and INGOs, this is a significant problem, raising serious doubts about government efforts to improve gender equality in participation and local governance. Where women are included in local governance, it appears that they are there strictly to meet legal requirements and are not informed about their roles or equipped with the training to be effective representatives.

> Once they [women in councils] are appointed, they are not given any training to build their capacity, to understand why they are there. So you'll find that they are just there as a matter of numbers … [A]nd members of those councils … were not given any training when they were appointed, so they were just working on their experience and the culture and whatever existed there before.
>
> (Women's Legal Advocate, personal interview,
> June 18, 2013, Dar es Salaam)

Given the power vested in village bodies, the marginalization of women limits discussions on land that affect the entire community. Where village land use or sales infringe on land used by women for subsistence farming, water, and firewood, village decisions on land can have serious unanticipated impacts on the population at large. For example, in Tanzania, several instances of land transfers to foreign investors have highlighted how lost land access impacted women's abilities to fulfill household roles and support the community more broadly (ActionAid 2010). Without additional training, the perception is that women are present only to be counted and not to participate in a meaningful way.

Efforts to address gender inequalities

As a result of these obstacles, many NGO projects operating in rural areas focus on awareness of women's land rights and improving women's participation in local governance, both of which challenge the practices of patrilineal and patrilocal communities in rural Tanzania. An INGO officer explained how their organization has had to transform their efforts to register CCROs to include extensive training on gender equality, as, without it, the co-registering of CCROs had led to little changes in the lives of women: "Just because you get a land certificate doesn't mean you have any say ... Learning from that was that we needed to do a lot more than just a few sessions on rights to land and women's rights, on trying to change attitudes about power and control of resources" (INGO Officer, personal interview, June 25, 2013, Dar es Salaam). Civil society organizations have also taken on their own efforts to provide public education on land rights, gender equality, and political participation, including the recording of music about gender empowerment, plays for public performance, and TV and radio programming (Nkya 2008; TAWLA n.d.). Moreover, among the most prominent NGOs and INGOs there appear to be new efforts to include men in addressing these issues. Concern Worldwide, an Ireland-based INGO, reports increasing its attention to gender equality in its programming related to local governance and land ownership, in particular, recruiting men as peer educators and advocates of gender equality (Concern Worldwide 2013). All of these efforts underscore the need to enhance women's capacity to participate in local governance and exercise the rights afforded under the Land Acts.

Although these organizations note that the government is cooperative with their programs, there remains disappointment with government priorities. Pedersen and Haule (2013) report that the decentralization of land governance has reduced the sense of responsibility in the Ministry for Lands, Housing and Human Settlements Development and it appears that little effort has been made by the government to incorporate those lessons internalized by NGOs. Government efforts to force or rush equal gender participation and representation into land management faces stiff opposition from both community members and implementers themselves. For example, the World Bank and Ministry for Lands-led Business Environment Strengthening for Tanzania (BEST) Program imposed requirements for addressing gender inequality after projects were already underway. This earned criticism from officials who viewed the promotion of gender equality in land rights as forcing something that is unnatural (Pedersen and Haule 2013).

This resistance reveals the challenges of introducing reforms without close attention to local obstacles. Though CCRO implementation did involve telling villagers that women had equal rights to land under the law and that joint registration was an option, joint titling was not the default option, despite this being the preference described in the Land Acts (Pedersen and Haule 2013). As Pedersen and Haule (2013) suggest, it appears that the primary goal was to achieve high numbers of issued CCROs, rather than attention to who was receiving them and improving women's access to land rights.

In sum, the Tanzanian case illustrates the major obstacles in implementing land reforms that both protect customary practices while also encouraging gender equality in land ownership and access. These are delicate challenges that require expertise and long-term political and financial commitments, as well as partnerships between government and civil society groups. As the following section shows, the Technical Guides offer some solutions to address the very real problems that neither the Voluntary Guidelines nor existing government efforts have explored beyond general platitudes.

Policies for implementation – looking at the Voluntary Guidelines and the Technical Guide

The Technical Guide is a product of the FAO's consultation processes affiliated with the Voluntary Guidelines. Elizabeth Daley, a world-renowned expert on gender and land issues, led a team tasked with developing the Guide. A preliminary document was released in 2011 and indicated where supports are needed to improve women's access to land via information and legal resources as well as changing modes of local governance in favor of gender-equitable land access (Daley and Park 2011). Many of these themes are found in the final version of the Technical Guide, released in 2013. Though the Technical Guide does not have the same endorsement as the Voluntary Guidelines, it does provide more specific and actionable details on what gender equality looks like in practice and what policy-makers and implementers need to be aware of.

The Technical Guide itself is a 120-page document that is broken down into five modules providing "mechanisms, strategies and actions that can be adopted to improve gender equity in the processes, institutions and activities of land tenure governance" (FAO 2013, 4). The modules are presented in a logical sequence – policy-making, legal issues, institutions, technical issues, and "getting the message across" – but were designed such that any module might be used independently (FAO 2013, 7). These modules draw not only from existing literatures on gender and land, but on the experiences of those undertaking reforms. While the Technical Guide notes the importance of gender analysis in identifying how gender relations affect people of different social groups (age, wealth, caste, race, ethnicity, religion), it acknowledges that the Guide cannot address all of these issues in detail and still be broadly applicable. The Technical Guide nonetheless offers details to suggest how gender relations do shape access to land under different conditions. The next sections of this chapter highlight the major themes and strategies offered by the Technical Guide, with special attention to how these strategies apply to the Tanzanian case.

Policy-making

The Guide begins by focusing on gender-equitable participation in policy-making, noting how "power differences between women and men ... often create hierarchies that determine who participates in policy-making, affecting the likelihood of gender-equitable processes and outcomes" (FAO 2013, 11). Here, the Guide argues that gender-equitable policy-making cannot occur without gender-equitable participation and consultation, and acknowledges the social obstacles to such participation. As we have seen above, efforts to improve gender equality in local participation are constrained by long-standing social practices. Everything from the timing and organization of meetings to possible threats of violence shape the experiences of those participating in meetings, and power hierarchies fall squarely along gender lines. In order to understand and address these challenges, the Technical Guide recommends a five-pronged approach, and though the approach is couched in rather technical terms, they do capture the critical factors in effectively implementing land reforms.

The Guide first recommends a *Context Analysis*, which includes not only the local environmental or commercial pressures on land, but also the role of family laws in controlling land, gender inequalities in knowledge or resource access, and colonial legacies. The Guide provides broad continental examples of such analysis in Africa and Asia, and closes with a checklist of questions to be asked, including: "Do cultural and social norms require that participatory processes be separate for women and men, and for other groups? ... Is it locally acceptable for women and men to mix openly in public meetings?" (FAO 2013, 14).

Following this initial analysis, the Guide recommends *advocacy* to convince audiences – policy-makers, local populations, and researchers – of the value of gender-equitable policy-making. The Guide also recommends *sensitization and training* on gender and land issues, making an important distinction between simply examining women's land issues and looking at gender relations more broadly. Lastly, the guide recommends creating a *stakeholder dialogue*, including government, the private sector, civil society, and international organizations, and taking a *long-term approach*. Each set of stakeholders has its own action checklist – for example, civil society is tasked with training staff on gender-sensitive policies, campaigning for change, and monitoring implementation. The module concludes with a summary of the key messages, and suggestions for the kinds of indicators advocates may want to use in their advocacy (FAO 2013).

Legal pluralism

The Technical Guide provides a substantive discussion of legal pluralism and its prevalence in several regions throughout the world. It recognizes that, where land tenure reforms fail to understand the role of customary tenure and family law in perpetuating gender inequalities, these reforms will have limited effects. Thus, at the forefront of the legal issues identified is a list of measures in order to promote gender equality in land inheritance, including legal reforms – such as those that already exist in Tanzania, Uganda, and Kenya – but also recommends that advocates "organize public sensitization and awareness-raising sessions on existing laws, so that people – especially women – know about the laws that protect them," "[t]rain customary authorities on statutory inheritance laws," "help women to use customary laws to negotiate their land rights," and "[p]romote community discussions on: marriage and inheritance practices, friction between these practices and statutory law, and possible solutions for aligning the two" (FAO 2013, 32).

Local land institutions

The third module addresses the challenges of reforming institutions, including local land institutions. The module recognizes the trend towards decentralizing land governance and highlights the opportunities and challenges therein. As we have seen above, land reforms like those in Tanzania can greatly democratize land governance, but can also stifle claims women make on their local institutions. The Technical Guide recognizes these tensions, which the Voluntary Guidelines do not enumerate; the Guidelines only note that states should place responsibilities for governance at levels that are the most effective for service delivery (FAO 2012, clause 5.6). In order to address these problems, the third module recommends not only introducing gender quotas, but also sensitizing members on the importance of gender equality. Perhaps most importantly, the Guide advises an incremental and collaborative approach to reforming customary institutions. Recognizing the challenges that often exist between protecting customary land tenure and promoting gender equality, the Guide recommends "[identifying] customary practices, processes and institutions that support gender-equitable land tenure governance" and supporting customary leaders in adapting to new governance processes (FAO 2013, 58). The Guide also specifically warns against assuming that customary leaders are against change.

Capacity building

Further echoing the recommendations of experts in Tanzania, the Technical Guide also includes several recommendations in order to boost the capacity of both women as participants in institutions, and the general capacity of institutions themselves. Thus, the recommendations balance between specific training for women in public speaking and debating, but also that institutions adapt to fit the needs of women: including time commitments, mobility restrictions, cultural norms, and the provision of childcare (FAO 2013). The Guide further recommends addressing the gender imbalance in land administration and technical positions, urging that advocates look to promote women's employment and establish mentoring relationships.

Implementation

The module on Technical Issues is largely concerned with the obstacles to implementing laws and policies. It points to several issues that have been implicit in earlier discussions: disparities in literacy and education rates;

cultural norms that restrict public participation; and finding ways to address gender discrimination. Moreover, the module suggests that when it comes to implementing land reforms or administration projects, these projects have many opportunities to exclude gender from the conversation, such as when governments attempt to register household land. As seen in the Tanzanian case, even where land was supposed to be co-registered between spouses, in some cases, government and international donor sponsored efforts failed to do so.

Communication

Much of the work of NGO groups in Tanzania has gone into communicating changes to land laws and the Technical Guide explains the role of communication in sensitizing community members to gender equity measures. Interestingly, the Guide connects its Communication module to the Voluntary Guidelines recommendations on transparency, but details a far more arduous task than suggested by the Guidelines. The Guide advises not only sensitizing men and women to these changes, but also providing training to the media, asking men and women to consider society's imposition of masculine and feminine roles, and using "culturally appropriate mechanisms" in order to identify and resolve conflicts (FAO 2013, 92). Effective communication also requires context analysis to design strategies that will reach people through these media. More specifically, this requires attention to how gender difference affects media consumption – will women be able to gain access to print materials and be able to read them (FAO 2013)?

The Tecmhnical Guide thus provides essential details that the Voluntary Guidelines do not offer. Though the Voluntary Guidelines meet standards for consultation and inclusiveness, they do not fully address the challenges of gender-equitable land reform. Yet as the Technical Guide demonstrates, this is not for lack of understanding on the part of the experts contracted to develop the guide. Rather, the drafters of the Technical Guide ably draw upon academic and practical expertise in order to draft a guide that actually aligns with concerns on the ground. The Guide benefits from being written in fairly plain language, expressing complex relationships and governance structures with clarity and precision. It distills issues that have specific local incarnations in way that is generalizable and offers checklists of actionable items for policy-makers and advocates to follow. Moreover, it navigates complicated discussions of the divides between customary tenure and gender equality and advances recommendations that require nuance and commitment on the part of policy-makers and advocates. These recommendations move beyond the dichotomous view that gender equality and customary tenure must be in tension with each other. By viewing customary governance as fluid and looking for customary rules that promote gender equality, the Technical Guide offers a thoughtful take on the opportunities for change that are available.

This is not to suggest that the Technical Guide is a perfect solution to addressing gender inequalities in land. While the Technical Guide begins its discussion of policy reform by noting that it must be long-term, the Guide ultimately does not reinforce this point. For those interested in seeing these measures and guidelines become a reality, there must be sustained commitment to these actions and the push for gender equality. Moreover, the comprehensiveness of the Guide suggests how costly committing these reforms will be. For the Technical Guide to be effective, it thus needs to be matched by long-term commitments and funding on the part of state leaders, international organizations, and global donors.

Conclusion

Without the Technical Guide, the Voluntary Guidelines are a well-meaning but ill-defined project for furthering gender equality in land tenure. Though the Voluntary Guidelines reflect a gender mainstreaming strategy, and indicate where gender-sensitive initiatives should be considered, there are no clear strategies for implementation. Moreover, the Guidelines provide only a cursory indication of the challenges of balancing customary land tenure with gender equality measures. In the absence of the Technical Guide, the Voluntary Guidelines gloss over some of the difficulties and realities of land governance and reform, especially where attempting to balance between gender equality and protecting customary modes of land tenure. Only when accompanied by a more detailed description of these challenges as well as specific goals and measures are the Voluntary Guidelines a useful governance framework.

The detail and nuance that the Technical Guide achieves is precisely that which is missing from high-level global agreements like the Voluntary Guidelines. There may be a benefit in taking such an approach: where agreement on gender-sensitive measures between states or stakeholders is difficult, it may make more sense to entrust policy-makers to treat gender as a serious technical matter. Yet, as the Tanzanian context illustrates, implementing gender-sensitive land reform also requires high-level political commitment on the part of state leaders and treating gender as a technical matter may make gender equality a less pressing concern. The Technical Guide introduces important ideas and suggestions to resolve conflicts, but these remain tangential concerns in global fora. The language in the Voluntary Guidelines is thus vague and avoids the more complicated issues at hand. Advocates of gender equality in land and agriculture need to think seriously about the limits of viewing gender as a technical policy-related issue rather than a broader ideological one worthy of being discussed at the global level.

Without the political commitments of political leaders, and the financial commitments that might come as a result, implementation efforts will be short-lived or punted to civil society organizations to take on. The reality is that many countries are able to attract investment based on the ease of which arable land can be alienated for commercial use. Measures to protect local land rights, strengthen democratic practices, and promote gender equality are unlikely to be high priorities for states dependent on their commercial agricultural output. The work of civil society organizations can be effective, but these organizations lack the financial resources of states and institutions such as the World Bank. The Technical Guide neglects to reinforce the message that reform is necessarily a long-term project, one that requires political commitment and adequate financial resources. Without changing mindsets at the level of global decision-making, the well-crafted messaging and strategies of the Technical Guide may well be lost.

Note

1 There have also been several notable challenges in the legal frameworks of the Land Acts as well (Collins 2014). From a gendered perspective, however, the tensions between customary tenure and statutory gender equality measures present the most challenging set of issues.

References

ActionAid. 2010. *Implications of Biofuels Production on Food Security in Tanzania.* Dar es Salaam: ActionAid Tanzania.

Bexell, Magdalena, Jonas Tallberg, and Anders Uhlin. 2010. "Democracy in Global Governance: The Promises and Pitfalls of Transnational Actors." *Global Governance: A Review of Multilateralism and International Organizations* 16 (1): 81–101.

Collins, Andrea M. 2014. "Reconsidering Gender in the Multi-Level Governance of Land in East Africa: Governing the 'Global Land Grab'?" PhD diss., Queen's University.

Concern Worldwide. 2013. *Tanzania Programme Plan 2013.* Dar es Salaam: Concern Worldwide.

Daley, Elizabeth, and Clara Mi-young Park. 2011. *Governing Land for Women and Men: Gender and Voluntary Guidelines on Responsible Governance of Tenure of Land and Other Natural Resources.* Rome: Food and Agriculture Organization.

Englert, Birgit, and Elizabeth Daley, eds. 2008. *Women's Land Rights and Privatization in Eastern Africa.* Suffolk: James Currey.

Food and Agriculture Organization of the United Nations (FAO). 2012. *Voluntary Guidelines on the Responsible Governance of Tenure of Land, Fisheries and Forests in the Context of National Food Security.* Rome: FAO.

———. 2013. *Governing Land for Women and Men: A Technical Guide to Support the Achievement of Responsible Gender-Equitable Governance of Land Tenure.* Rome: FAO.

———. 2014. "Cola Giants Back Voluntary Guidelines on Land Tenure." *Food and Agriculture Organization of the United Nations.* www.fao.org/news/story/en/item/224619/icode/.

Geary, Kate. 2012. *'Our Land, Our Lives': Time Out on the Global Land Rush.* Oxfam International. http://policy-practice.oxfam.org.uk/publications/our-land-our-lives-time-out-on-the-global-land-rush-246731.

GRAIN. 2012. "Responsible Farmland Investing? Current Efforts to Regulate Land Grabs Will Make Things Worse." *GRAIN*. www.grain.org/article/entries/4564-responsible-farmland-investing-current-efforts-to-regulate-land-grabs-will-make-things-worse.

Hilhorst, Thea. 2000. "Women's Land Rights: Current Developments in Sub-Saharan Africa." In *Evolving Land Rights, Policy and Tenure in Africa*, edited by Camilla Toulmin and Julian Quan, 181–96. London: IIED with DFID and NRI.

Koda, Bertha. 2000. "The Gender Dimension of Land Rights: Case Study of Msindo Village, Same District.," Ph.D. diss., University of Dar es Salaam.

Kropiwnicka, Magdalena. 2012. *A Brief Introduction to the "Voluntary Guidelines on the Responsible Governance of Tenure of Land, Fisheries and Forests in the Context of National Food Security."* Brussels: ActionAid, International Food Security Network and the European Commission.

Mbilinyi, Marjorie. 2012. "Struggles Over Land and Livelihoods in African Agriculture." *Development* 55 (3): 390–92.

McKeon, Nora. 2013. "'One Does Not Sell the Land Upon Which the People Walk': Land Grabbing, Transnational Rural Social Movements, and Global Governance." *Globalizations* 10 (1): 105–22.

Nkya, Ananilea. 2008. "TAMWA Programs for Social Transformation." In *20 Years of Tanzania Media Women's Association (TAMWA): Moving the Agenda for Social Transformation in Tanzania*, edited by Elieshi Lema, Dar es Salaam: TAMWA. 55–154.

Pedersen, Rasmus Hundsbaek, and Scholastica Haule. 2013. *Women, Donors and Land Administration: The Tanzania Case*. Danish Institute for International Studies (DIIS). http://pure.diis.dk/ws/files/55977/WP2013_19_Hundsbaek_Haule_Tanzania_Recom_Wwb.pdf.

Seufert, Philip. 2013. "The FAO Voluntary Guidelines on the Responsible Governance of Tenure of Land, Fisheries and Forests." *Globalizations* 10 (1): 181–86.

TAWLA (Tanzania Women Lawyers Association). (n.d.). *Research Report on Land Cases*. Dar es Salaam: Martisayi Investments Company Limited.

Tripp, Aili Mari. 2004. "Women's Movements, Customary Law and Land Rights in Africa: The Case of Uganda." *African Studies Quarterly* 7 (4): 1–19.

Tsikata, Dzodzi. 2003. "Securing Women's Interests Within Land Tenure Reforms: Recent Debates in Tanzania." *Journal of Agrarian Change* 3 (1–2): 149–83.

Whitehead, Ann, and Dzodzi Tsikata. "Policy Discourses on Women's Land Rights in Sub-Saharan Africa: The Implications of the Re-Turn to the Customary." *Journal of Agrarian Change* 3 (1–2): 67–112.

Women's Legal Aid Centre (WLAC). 2010. *Assessing Rural Women's Land Ownership Ten Years After the Enactment of the Land Laws*. Dar es Salaam: Women's Legal Aid Centre.

Tanzania

10 Addressing challenges of rural women

A focus on Tanzania

Godbertha Kinyondo

Introduction

The economy and agriculture sector performance

Tanzania's economy has been growing at least 6 percent per annum and shows a number of positive economic trends (e.g., decreasing inflation rates below the authority's target of 5 percent, an improving business climate, and strengthened infrastructure). However, it has been projected that growth rates of 8 percent would be needed to begin to redress poverty levels. About 60 percent of the women in Tanzania are estimated to live in poverty despite hard work (URT 2015). Addressing gender constraints is therefore a key component of unlocking Tanzania's economic growth and the government's pro-poor agricultural growth policy holds promise for improving the lives of women across the country. The manifesto of the ruling party, Chama Cha Mapinduzi (CCM), calls for the implementation of women-related initiatives, such as providing credit schemes for women, developing a Women's Bank, and reviewing inheritance laws and other laws suppressing women (Selbervik 2006).

Agriculture (crops, hunting, forestry, livestock, and fishing) provides 95 percent of the food consumed in the country and employs 75 percent of the labor force. This sector accounts for about 50 percent of the national income and represents 75 percent of merchandise exports. In addition, it provides 65 percent of the raw materials required by Tanzania's industries. Of the 44 million hectares of land suitable for agriculture, however, only 23 percent (10.2 million hectares) is utilized. Real agricultural growth is approximately 4.4 percent (URT 2011), which is below the Poverty Reduction Strategy Paper (MKUKUTA II) target of 6 to 8 percent and the Comprehensive Africa Agricultural Development Plan (CAADP) benchmark of 6 percent (URT 2011). CAADP's major objective is to revive African agriculture in order to reduce rural poverty and ensure food security. Inefficient technology and sole dependence on rain-fed agricultural production systems result in poor land and labor productivity.

Women in agriculture

In Tanzania women form an integral part of the society and of agriculture in particular. According to the 2012 Census, women are 51.3 percent (23,058,933) of Tanzania's population of 44,928,923 inhabitants. Women represent 53.3 percent (12,281,013) of the 23,466,616 workforce population between the ages of 15 and 64. Women of reproductive age number 10,905,117 or 47.3 percent of the total female population in Tanzania (URT NBS 2012, 46).

There are more than six million out of 9,276,997 households engaged in agriculture in Tanzania. As shown in Table 10.1 below, the vast majority of these households are based on the mainland and in the rural areas. However, 15 percent of households engaged in agriculture are located in urban areas (URT NBS 2013).

In Dar es Salaam, the commercial city of 4,364,541 residents, urban agriculture has been practiced since the 1970s and was encouraged under President Julius Nyerere's call for self-sufficiency. Vegetable gardening is the most common enterprise, followed by dairy and poultry. In 2000 it was estimated that 650 hectares of open space in Dar es Salaam were being used for vegetable production, mostly by women cultivators (Foeken, Sofer, and Mlozi 2004). A 2003 study by Hoogland found that there were 34,700 households farming in the city (quoted in Schmidt 2011). Urban agriculture is conducted in other cities as well, where the necessary conditions such as access to land, seeds, and water, and feed and medication for livestock, are generally available. The motivation often is to supplement other income sources and provide food for family consumption. However, a study conducted in Mbeya and Morogoro cities found that more than one-half engaged in agriculture do so because it is their "tradition" (quoted in Foeken, Sofer, and Mlozi 2004, 19).

Nevertheless, the bulk of agriculture production occurs in rural areas by smallholders with less than three hectares of land. An agriculture census conducted in 2007–2008 found that 98 percent of agricultural production is conducted by smallholders who rely on rain-fed agriculture (URT NBS 2010). Table 10.2 shows that maize is the predominant staple and cash crop grown by households in Tanzania, followed by cassava, paddy rice, and banana.

Table 10.3 shows that poultry and cattle are the most common livestock enterprises for both male- and female-headed households. In male-headed households, women often are responsible for caring for chickens and the collection of eggs, unless it is a large enterprise.

Finally, female-headed households appear to have far more dependents than male-headed households, as shown in Table 10.4 below. This can both be an advantage in that there is additional labor available if the dependents are able to care for the crops and livestock, but this also creates the need to feed, educate, and provide health care for them.

Furthermore, the large number of dependents may result in children being engaged in work around the house or in the fields that involve excessive hours that can jeopardize their attendance or performance in school, known as "time-related child labor." Nearly one-fifth of rural children in Tanzania are engaged in time-related child labor (REPOA 2010).

Table 10.1 Households engaged in agriculture by location

Mainland	5,962,091	
Zanzibar	121,748	
Combined	6,083,839	
	Rural (%)	**Urban (%)**
Mainland	85.10	14.90
Zanzibar	78.60	21.40
Combined	84.90	15.10

Source: NBS Census 2012.

Table 10.2 Households engaged in agriculture by crop

	Total	*Rural*	*Urban*
Total households	9,276,997	6,192,303	3,084,635
Households engaged in agriculture	6,083,839	5,168,218	915,621
Household grows maize	5,404,117	4,661,761	742,356
Household grows paddy	1,789,258	1,525,040	264,218
Household grows cassava	2,516,261	2,232,076	284,185
Household grows banana	1,605,152	1,455,378	149,774
Household grows other crops	4,723,475	4,181,020	542,455

Source: NBS Census 2012.

Table 10.3 Raising of livestock

	Cattle	*Goats*	*Sheep*	*Poultry*
Male headed	18,134,087	11,006,420	3,097,811	27,238,756
Female headed	5,971,721	3,972,920	1,292,416	9,239,976

Source: NBS Census 2012.

Table 10.4 Size of households

	Households	*Size*
Female headed	3,098,792	7.4
Male headed	6,178,205	3.5
Total	9,276,997	

Source: NBS Census 2012.

Key challenges for rural women

Policy development and implementation

The Government of Tanzania (GOT) participates in formulation of both international and national gender policies. The Tanzanian 1977 constitution prohibits various forms of discrimination, but unfortunately overlooks discrimination based on gender. The GOT has ratified the Convention on the Elimination of All Forms of Discrimination against Women (CEDAW). Tanzania is signatory to the Platform for Action and Beijing Declaration developed by the Fourth World Conference on Women held in China in 1995. The country is also part of regional and sub-regional policies, such as the Southern Africa Development Community (SADC) Declaration on Gender and Development and the African Charter of Human and Peoples Rights of 1981 (TGNP 2006). The country's National Strategy for Growth and Reduction of Poverty (URT 2010) comprises goals and targets on gender equity and equality and women's empowerment centering on education, health, employment, and land ownership. A Gender Development Policy was published in 2000 and a National Strategy for Gender Development was issued in 2005. Subsequently, individuals with gender expertise, called Gender Focal Points (GFP), were assigned to government ministries, agencies, and local government authorities to ensure that gender issues are taken into account in designing and implementing projects and programs (URT 2005). In practice, the GFP is an individual who has other core responsibilities and takes on the "extra" responsibility for the review of gender issues (GAD Consult 2012).

Policy may be well formulated but its implementation may often be deficient. Mattee (2007) describes the policy implementation process in Tanzania:

> The implementation of policy is often influenced by politics, internal dynamics of the implementing institutions, as well as their structural positioning. Individuals also have a key role on either catalyzing or inhibiting institutional change, which means that policy engagement must also focus on micro-politics of how decisions are made within an organization and the consensus required for different kinds of actions. Often, trusted and sympathetic individuals are key to effective communication and learning processes. (3)

Furthermore, often only during policy implementation does it become apparent that there is a lack of policy coherence, lack of funding, or an insufficient legal framework to advance the policy. Amongst other policies, land ownership illustrates this well.

Land ownership

Many countries in Africa have laws and customary practices that restrict women's access to land (Poku and Mdee 2011). In Tanzania, the 1999 Land

Act and 1999 Village Land Act contain provisions that give women rights and access to land equal to men. Tanzania's legislation is considered by some observers as the most progressive and elaborate legislation in East Africa (Benschop 2002; Maoulidi 2004). For example, a married couple should equally own any land. If there is a need to sell the land, the legislation requires both married individuals to give consent and it also provides inheritance rights to women. However, the legislation also permits customary or religious laws to take precedence. In some cases, customary law expects widows, mainly those who did not bear children, to return to their parents' family, thus losing all rights and access to the land that she shared equally with her husband. In other instances, widows may be granted access to the family land only until the children reach adulthood. In practice, the less-equitable customary law and religious rules and practices continue to take precedence over the progressive provisions in the legislation (Kempster 2011). With women being main agricultural producers, this is economically destructive on the local and national levels.

Having no guaranteed right to decide on the use and possible sale of family land, either as a widow or in marriage, is detrimental to women and communities where they work and live. Mbilinyi and Shechambo (2009) cite research by Kitunga that this provides opportunity for foreign investors and corrupt governments to strip women of their most valuable economic resource. They further observe that research conducted by Kihacha in Ngorongoro and Njombe districts from 1998–2002 found that more than half of the villages lacked food security throughout the year (quoted in Mbilinyi and Shechambo 2009). The main reason given by farmers and animal keepers was that food security has a direct link with access to and control over land. The study proposes greater participatory decision-making concerning the use of land and other resources at the home, community, and national levels. The extent of this limitation and its impact is more serious for women farmers because of their diminished role in decision-making and rights over a large resource such as land. Land is an important asset that serves as collateral, which is required to access capital from financial institutions. Precedence of customary laws over national laws is worrisome given that the percentage of land owned under customary law is about 69.3 percent (URT NBS 2013). Women farmers face a number of other constraints in maintaining and expanding their livelihood, such as limited access to credit, inadequate agricultural extension services, insufficient information about crop prices, and lack of improved technology.

Credit

Cooperatives have operated in Tanzania as key institutions for farmers since independence in 1961, providing support for inputs and marketing. However, it was not until 1997 that the first Cooperative Development Policy was published, which established a membership framework based on international cooperative standards. The Cooperative Societies Act of 2003 provided the legal basis and impetus for the formation of Village Community Banks (VICOBA) and Savings and Credit Co-operative Societies (SACCOS), which are two of the most popular and important microfinance institutions in rural Tanzania (Ahlén 2012). By 2009 Village Community Banks (VICOBA) had spread to 19 out of 25 regions in Tanzania, with approximately 56,280 members. With VICOBA, soft loans must be repaid after three months for the first loan and six months for the second loan. Capital for the VICOBA is mobilized through loans from other financial institutions and shares from members. Although numerous operational challenges were evident, a 2014 study of selected VICOBA concluded that they have helped in empowering women, who often are the majority members and owners of the banks (Bakari, Magesa, and Akidda 2014).

SACCOS are financial organizations owned and operated on a not-for-profit basis by their members. The 1997 directive from the central government requires establishing revolving "Women and Youth Development Funds," to which the local councils are expected to contribute 10 percent of their own collected revenues to SACCOS that are formed by youth and women. In 2009, SACCOS had some 726,000 members, of whom about 600,000 were saving with SACCOS and 440,000 were borrowing from SACCOS. About 345,000 of those borrowing and saving with SACCOS did also have a bank account (IFAD 2011). The International Fund for Agricultural Development (IFAD) also found that female membership is above 40 percent, with women taking important leadership roles, even political roles in the community after having served as SACCOS leaders (IFAD 2011).

On the other hand, Maleko et al. (2013) report that women represent 33 percent of SACCOS membership and are often subjected to domination by men in decision-making. They also observe that many SACCOS require collateral, most commonly land, which cannot be provided by most rural women. For this reason, informal groups, which do not apply such pre-conditions for loan applications, are increasingly becoming popular among rural women.

A survey by Finscope (2007) shows that 89 percent of the population above 16 years of age has no access to formal or semi-formal financial institutions in Tanzania. Informal financial associations, therefore, fill this gap and provide access to funds for emergencies. This has now become a critical tool in empowering women, as this segment of the society lacks, or has limited access to, banking services due to legal procedures and socio-cultural attitudes towards them. While financial need is one motivation for membership in these groups, the exchange of ideas and information and building social ties are valued equally as much. Maleko et al. (2013) cite studies that demonstrate how women are particularly empowered by informal savings associations. These informal arrangements are scheduled around women's time constraints so that they can fully participate.

The author made similar observations during a visit in the Katoma Ward in northwestern Tanzania. Katoma Ward comprises three villages with a population of over 9,000 people, Lukindo (4,221), Kashenge (2,864), and Irogero (2,338). The author observed that farmer groups can help individual farmers improve access to crop processing technology (i.e., banana chips, cassava chips, banana wine, palm oil processing, etc.); funding (i.e., VICOBA, family, friends, moneylenders); crops marketing (through ward crops marketing groups); fish production (participation in village fish ponds); and livestock farming (through collaboration with dairy groups). As informal groups, farmers get together to strategize and carry out planned activities. Women also are forming informal groups to assist each other, including during events such as weddings, sicknesses, and funerals. A small amount of money, and in-kind contributions such as beans and firewood, are collected on a monthly basis complemented by donations of banana at the time of the event. Similarly, groups of farmers, mostly men who own banana farms, sell brewing bananas at public auctions and the funds are collected and saved as a group. At an annual event, the funds are redistributed according to the contributions by each individual. Villagers sometimes conduct *Harambees* to enable them to contribute to local schools and health centers, and assist relatives or vulnerable groups in their respective communities. These informal financial and social schemes are designed to fit the situations of very busy rural men and women.

Time constraints

Women spend time taking care of children, the sick, and the elderly, visiting the sick and bereaved, and searching for firewood and water, which leaves little time for them to engage in paid economic activities. On average, women in rural sub-Saharan Africa spend between 0.9 and 2.2 hours per day transporting water and firewood; they travel, on average, between 1 km and 5 km per day on foot for 2.5 hours, while carrying a load of about 20 kg (Blackden and Wodon 2006). In an analysis of the time use patterns of 10,465 working age women and men, including those involved in agriculture, Floro and Komatsu (2011) found that the time spent in unpaid work activities by men does not vary greatly and remains at lower levels than women across labor force categories. Women's hours of unpaid work ranged between 245 and 406 minutes daily on average, while men's hours of unpaid work ranged from 136 to 200 minutes. Bardasi and Wodon (2009) observe that, because African women often have to work long hours for domestic chores and the collection of water and wood, apart from working in the fields or in other labor market activities, they are much more time-poor than men. Most men realize that women are overworked but few men assist their wives in domestic chores because they run the risk of ridicule from the other men and the community at large.

Due to the fact that the Tanzanian government is not able to fully meet the needs of the citizens, mainly those in the rural areas, the informal networks and financial associations will likely persist in the near future. GOT revenue and expenditure have been increasing; for example, total revenue in 2005 was TShs

3,248 billion and in 2012 climbed to about TShs 10,765 billion and although impressive, domestic revenue collection is not sufficient to cover all government programs. Therefore, the Government still receives funds from external donors. Dependency on external financing obstructs autonomy and many times leads the country to become vulnerable to financial shocks (Policy Forum 2011). Foreign aid inflows to Tanzania are increasingly being substituted by non-concessional borrowing, and domestic borrowing. Unfortunately, these modes expose the country to high cost of debt, interest rate risks and the possibility of crowding out the private sector. Insufficient government budget has negative implications on services delivery to the communities, which increasingly have to care for themselves. Indeed, this affects women more, as the amount of services provided at home through unpaid care labor rises. The 2011–2012 Tanzanian Household Budget Survey (URT NBS 2014) reports that access to safe drinking water is more prevalent in urban areas: about 74 percent of urban households have access to safe drinking water as compared to about 40 percent of their rural counterparts. There has been improvement in health delivery, with 70 percent of the households living within six kilometers of primary health for both urban and rural areas. Moreover, the country has experienced a drop of maternal deaths per 100,000 live births from 529 (1991) to 454 (2012), although this is still not an acceptable rate. However, these health facilities are poorly equipped in terms of qualified health workers, equipment, and medicines. Given continued poor service delivery of public goods and services, women farmers will still be trapped in the web of time poverty.

Development efforts

To accelerate development, the GOT has subscribed to a development model known as Big Results Now (BRN). Adopted from Malaysia, BRN started in the 2013–2014 fiscal year in six priority areas – energy and natural gas, agriculture, water, education, transport, mobilization of resources and later in 2014–2015, health was incorporated into the BRN process. The process identifies ambitious three-year targets that can accelerate development and hold sector Ministers accountable for achievements. While education and health sectors have established targets that are to explicitly benefit women, the agriculture BRN plan focuses on large commercial farming and rice irrigation schemes that will largely benefit men. For example, the already poor extension services to women farmers might deteriorate further given the tendency of such services to favor large-scale farmers, who are mostly men (Peterman, Behrman, and Quisumbing 2010).

There have been efforts by Civil Society Organizations (CSOs) and donors to ease the burden of women farmers in various ways. The success story of the Chololo village project in Dodoma region is a good example. The project has enabled the community to adopt, test, and evaluate varieties of alternative energy technologies, including energy-saving cooking stoves and low-cost domestic biogas plants. The project has imparted skills to women to enable them to construct energy-saving stoves and conducted community sensitization to allow wide adoption. Groups of other women are engaged in agricultural and non-agricultural activities such as production of seedlings, growing fruits, fish ponds, bee-keeping, and making leather products (Kinalilo 2014). A United States Agency for International Development (USAID) funded project has enabled female members to develop prototypes of technologies that will help them do their work more efficiently using locally sourced materials. Technologies involved include a palm oil extracting machine, a peanut sheller, a rice thresher, and a rice winnower (Aris 2014). However, these are donor-funded projects that often lack sustainability after donor funding ceases.

Groups such as Mtandao wa Vikundi vya Wakulima Tanzania (MVIWATA), the largest farmer-led network with national coverage in Tanzania, link local farmers' groups to enhance farmer representation and advocacy. Women play a large role in the organization as leaders and beneficiaries of training and other support. Through training on leadership and communication they are capable of defending their members' interests and building partnerships with service providers.

Prominent women's organizations in Tanzania utilize workshops, campaigns, and training to bring gender and social equality to the awareness of women and the public at large. They work towards establishing inheritable property rights for women and inform women of their legal rights to property. For example, the Tanzania Gender Networking Programme (TNGP) campaign for land of marginalized communities and women has led to increased food availability and environment management awareness (Mbilinyi and Shechambo 2009). A policy change for gender equality in agriculture requires the support of organizations such as TNGP and importantly must include the involvement of both men and women. Women will comfortably realize leadership roles in agriculture simply if male counterparts such as husbands, fathers, uncles, and other relatives accept, appreciate, and support their assuming these roles.

Women have been able to diversify into non-agricultural activities such as operating shops, trading in clothes, handicrafts, food sales, tailoring, and providing mobile money banking services such as M-Pesa and Tigo Pesa. Some women have been able to move from informal to more formal businesses. For example, utilizing indigenous technology and available raw materials have enabled a viable business in the neighboring country of Rwanda. The woman-owned Rwandese basket weaving project currently employs over 3,200 women in Rwanda. The growing business has formed a joint venture with an American company, FairWinds Trading, Inc., a marketing and trade company importing African crafts. FairWinds Trading supplies woven baskets to the prestigious American store, Macy's. The business has benefited from the Trade and Development Act of 2000 passed by the US Congress, known as the African Growth and Opportunity Act (AGOA). AGOA extends duty-free and quota-free access to over 6,400 products from Sub-Saharan Africa (SSA) into the US market.

Any policy designed to help farmers must take into account issues of gender equity and equality. Households are viewed as being cooperative enterprises (McElroy and Horney 1981); that is, they follow the Unitary Model (UM), which posits that a household is a single entity where house properties are shared as the whole family. Seguino (2012) argues that macro-level policies that varyingly affect men or women also affect power dynamics within the household, changing the degree of gender equality in the performance of labor and in access to resources. This supports an alternate view that households exhibit conflict and competition for resources with outcomes influenced by the relative power of household adults. Often a woman has no say whatsoever on the income gained by the partner. Thomas (1992) and Elson and Cagatay (2000) highlight the need to utilize a model that takes into account asymmetric power relations and the conflict of preferences between partners in the household. Sen (1983) proposes that the relationship between men and women in a household should be conceptualized as consisting of both cooperation and conflict. Scholars have argued that the relationship between men and women in a household must be examined more closely if the time constraints and other impediments to women's productivity are to be adequately understood.

Conclusion

Despite the overwhelming evidence about the central role of women in agriculture over decades of research, progress toward removing constraints that inhibit their economic advancement has been slow. Nevertheless, microfinance initiatives, such as those described here, have allowed women to access funds and mutual support, making it possible for them to seek other income avenues in addition to agriculture. Ample credit should be augmented with access to information to enable women to share information related to social and economic issues and access to technologies that ease their heavy workloads. The introduction of productive non-farm activities further enables them to improve their households' welfare. The Government budget must be gender proactive to ensure provision of agricultural resources and other services that will ease mostly women's time on non-paid activities. The CSO watchdog role must be enhanced to bring to light impediments and solutions for women farmers.

References

Ahlén, Marie. 2012. "Rural Member-Based Microfinance Institutions – A Field Study Assessing the Impacts of SACCOS and VICOBA in Babati District, Tanzania." Stockholm: Södertörn University. http://sh.diva-portal.org/smash/record.jsf?pid= diva2:544512.

Aris, Giselle. 2014. "Want to Empower Women in Agriculture? Use technology." *USAID Impact Blog*, March 6. blog.usaid.gov/2014/03/want-to-empower-women-in-agriculture-use-technology/.

Bakari, V., R. Magesa, and S. Akidda. 2014. "Mushrooming Village Community Banks in Tanzania: Is it Really Making a Difference?" *International Journal of Innovation and Scientific Research* 6 (2): 127–35. www.issr-journals.org/links/papers.php?journal=ijisr&application=pdf&article=IJISR-14-133-04.

Bardasi, Elena, and Quentin Wodon. 2009. "Working Long Hours and Having No Choice: Time Poverty in Guinea." Policy Research Working Paper 4961, Washington, DC: The World Bank. https://openknowledge.worldbank.org/bitstream/handle/10986/4156/WPS4961.pdf?sequence=1.

Benschop, Marjolien. 2002. "Rights and Reality: Are Women's Equal Rights to Land, Housing and Property Implemented in East Africa?" Nairobi: UN-Habitat. http://landwise.landesa.org/record/353.

Blackden, C. Mark, and Quentin Wodon, eds. 2006. "Gender, Time Use, and Poverty in Sub-Saharan Africa." Working Paper No. 73, Washington, DC: The World Bank. http://siteresources.worldbank.org/INTAFRREGTOPGENDER/Resources/gender_time_use_pov.pdf.

Elson, Diane, and Nilufer Cagatay. 2000. "The Social Content of Macroeconomic Policies." *World Development* 28 (7): 1347–64. http://dx.doi.org.proxy.library.brocku.ca/10.1016/S0305-750X(00)00021-8.

Finscope. 2007. *FinScope E-Book*. Dar-es-Salaam: Financial Services Deepening Trust. www.tccia.com/tccia/wp-content/uploads/2011/07/english-finscope2006.pdf.

Floro, Maria S., and Hitomi Komatsu. Forthcoming. "Labor Force Participation, Gender and Work in South Africa: What Can Time Use Data Reveal?" *Feminist Economics Special Issue on Unpaid Work, Time Use, Poverty and Public Policy*, vol. 2. www.american.edu/cas/economics/pdf/upload/2011–2.pdf.

Foeken, Dick, Michael Sofer, and Malongo Mlozi. 2004. "Urban Agriculture in Tanzania: Issues of Sustainability." Research Report 74. Leiden: African Studies Centre. https://openaccess.leidenuniv.nl/bitstream/handle/1887/4678/ASC-1241504-003.pdf?sequence=1.

Forum CC. 2014. "Chololo EcoVillage: A Model of Good Practice in Climate Change Adaptation and Mitigation." www.forumcc.org/Chololo.

GAD Consult. 2012. "A Needs Assessment of the Gender Focal Point System." *GAD Consult* (blog). October 3. http://gadconsult.blogspot.com/2012/10/needs-assessment-of-gender-focal-points.html.

IFAD (International Fund for Agricultural Development). 2011. "Rural Financial Services Programme and Agricultural Marketing Systems Development Programme: Interim Evaluation." Rome: IFAD. www.ifad.org/evaluation/public_html/eksyst/doc/prj/region/pf/tanzania/rfsp.htm.

Kempster, Erin. 2011. "Gender and Land Rights Debate in Tanzania." *Focus on Land in Africa*. www.focusonland.com/countries/gender-and-land-rights-debate-in-tanzania/.

Kinalilo, Deogratias. 2014. "The Role of Gender and Policies in Addressing Climate Change: The Case of Tanzania." Master's thesis, Bradford University.

Maleko, G. N., Basili S. A. Liheta, Deogratius Aikaruwa, Angelina Lukas, and Gerald A. Sumari. 2013. "Women Participation in Microfinance Institutions of Tanzania: The Case of Savings and Credit Co-operative Societies (SACCOS)." *Journal of Business Administration and Education* 4 (2): 139–75.

Maoulidi, Salma. 2004. "Critical Analysis of Land Laws – A Study." Dar es Salaam: Land Rights Research Institute (Haki Ardhi). www.hakiardhi.org/index.php?option=com_docman&task=doc_download&gid=72&Itemid=80.

Mattee, Amon Z. 2007. "Study on Options for Pastoralists to Secure their Livelihoods: Current Policy Making Processes in Tanzania." Arusha: Community Research and Development Services.

Mbilinyi, Marjorie, and Gloria Shechambo. 2009. "Struggles over Land Reform in Tanzania: Experiences of Tanzania Gender Networking Programme and Feminist Activist Coalition." *Feminist Africa: Land, Labour and Gendered Livelihoods*, no. 12: 95–103. http://agi.ac.za/journal/feminist-africa-issue-12-2009-land-labour-and-gendered-livelihoods.

McElroy, Marjorie B., and Mary Jane Horney. 1981. "Nash Bargained Household Decisions: Toward a Generalization of the Theory of Demand." *International Economic Review* 22: 333–49.

Peterman, Amber, Julia Behrman, and Agnes Quisumbing. 2010. "A Review of Empirical Evidence on Gender Differences in Nonland Agricultural Inputs, Technology, and Services in Developing Countries." IFPRI (International Food Policy Research Institute) Discussion Paper no. 00975, Washington, DC. www.ifpri.org/sites/default/files/publications/ifpridp00975.pdf.

Poku, Nana K., and Anna Mdee. 2011. *Politics in Africa: A New Introduction*. London: Zed Books.

Policy Forum. 2011. "Dependency on Foreign Aid: How the Situation Could be Saved: An Analysis of Tanzania's Budget 2010–2011." *Policy Forum*. www.policyforum-tz.org/files/RevenueEnglish.pdf.

REPOA (Research on Poverty Alleviation). 2010. "Tanzania Gender Indicators: Booklet 2010." Dar es Salaam: REPOA.

Schmidt, Stephan. 2011. "Urban Agriculture in Dar es Salaam, Tanzania." In *Food Policy for Developing Countries: Case Studies*, edited by Per Pinstrup-Andersen and Fuzhi Cheng. Ithaca, NY: Cornell University. http://cip.cornell.edu/dns.gfs/1297701745.

Seguino, Stephanie. 2013. "From Micro-level Gender Relations to the Macro Economy and Back Again: Theory and Policy." In *Handbook of Research on Gender and Economic Life*, edited by Deborah Figart and Tonia Warnecke, 325–44. Cheltenham, UK: Edward Elgar.

Selbervik, Hilde. 2006. "PRSP in Tanzania: Do Mkukuta and the CCM Election Manifesto Pull in the Same Direction?" Bergen: Chr Michelsen Institute.

Sen, Amartya. 1983. "Economics and the Family" *Asian Development Review* 1 (2): 14–26.

TGNP (Tanzania Gender Networking Program). 2006. "Gender Mainstreaming in Development Policies and Programs." Presentation, Policy Dialogue Seminar, Economic Research and Social Foundation, Dar es Salaam. www.tanzaniagateway.org/docs/gendermainstreamingindevelopmentpolicies.ppt.

Thomas, D. 1992. "The Distribution of Income and Expenditure in the Household." Paper presented at IFPRI-World Bank Conference on Intrahousehold Resource Allocation – Policies and Research Methods, Washington, DC.

URT (United Republic of Tanzania). 2008. *National Strategy for Gender Development*. Dar es Salaam: Ministry of Community Development, Gender and Children. www.mcdgc.go.tz/data/Tanzania_National_Strategy_for_Gender_Development.pdf.

———. 2010. *National Strategy for Growth and Reduction of Poverty II*. Dar es Salaam: Ministry of Finance and Economic Affairs. www.mof.go.tz/index.php?option=com_content&view=article&id=784:national-strategy-for-growth-and-reduction-of-poverty-ii-report-nsgrp-ii&catid=71:poverty-monitoring.

———. 2011. *Tanzania Agriculture and Food Security Investment Plan (TAFSIP) 2011–12 to 2020–21: Main Document.* www.google.co.tz/#q=Tanzania+Agricultu re+and+Food+Security+Investment+Plan+(TAFSIP)+2011%E2%80%9012+to+ 2020%E2%80%9021.

———. 2015. "Economic Empowerment of Women and Poverty Eradication." Dar es Salaam: Ministry of Community Development, Gender and Children. Accessed May1. www.mcdgc.go.tz/index.php/issues/economic_empowerment_of_women_ and_poverty_eradication/.

URT. NBS (National Bureau of Statistics). 2010. *National Sample Census of Agriculture 2007–2008 Preliminary Report.* Dar es Salaam: Ministry of Finance. www.nbs.go.tz/nbs/takwimu/Agr2007-08/Preliminary_Report_2007-08_Tanzania_ Agric_Census.zip.

———. 2012. *Statistics for Development.* 2012 Census Database. Dar es Salaam: NBS. www.nbs.go.tz/.

———. 2013. *Tanzania in Figures 2012.* Dar es Salaam: Ministry of Finance. www.nbs. go.tz/nbs/takwimu/references/Tanzania_in_figures2012.pdf.

———. 2014. "Household Budget Survey 2011–12." Dar es Salaam: NBS. www.nbs. go.tz/nbs/index.php?option=com_content&view=category&id=54&Itemid=153.

Kenya

11 Can sustainability be enGENDERed through informal microfinance?

A case study of the Kamba merry-go-rounds in Ukambani, Eastern Province, Kenya

Carlyn James

Leaving the market town of Kola that sits off the main highway leading into Ukambani, we snaked upward along the unpaved trails into Watema, shielding our mouths from the dust with our scarves. It was early morning during the dry season and we passed women carrying fruits and vegetables uphill, children playing in the grass, and young men leading donkeys up from the river. I was traveling on the back of a pikipiki (motorbike, used as a taxi) to the weekly meeting of Watema Farmers Self-Help Group, a mixed sex self-help group that was dedicated primarily to learning innovative agricultural techniques.

After about 20 minutes of traveling uphill, we stopped. The group meeting began shortly thereafter, once everyone had filed into a large shaded spot located at the southwest corner of the property belonging to the group's president. The normal proceedings included roll call, a report from each member about any progress on his/her farm, and various exchanges of farming advice. The major topic this week was about how to prepare one's farm for fertilizer. After the meeting, I stayed behind to watch the portion of the day's events in which an economic anthropologist might find particular interest. The men of the group either left or hung around to have a drink while the women of the group huddled in closer and prepared to carry out their weekly exchange of money.

One man stayed behind to conduct the post-meeting meeting. He sat comfortably with a notebook and pencil, calling each woman by name. In turn, each woman quietly provided a contribution – a relatively meager amount of Ksh40 (USD$0.45) – once her name was called. The man would record each woman's contribution, after which the money would be counted and neatly stacked by the woman sitting to the right of the man.

As it was explained to me, this accumulation of funds was a relatively new initiative that the women of Watema Farmers Self-Help Group spearheaded as a way of making additional use of the time they spent together each week. When asked, the men seemed disinterested in the idea, saying that it was mostly "a women's thing." Many of them stood by or left to work on the farm while the women stayed behind to participate. After the contributions were all made, the group waited patiently for the next directive.

After the contributions were all collected, the man tore a piece of paper from the notebook and began further tearing that into small thumbnail-sized scraps of paper which were then crumpled up and loosely collected into a pile in the dirt in front of him. Before crumpling up each scrap of paper, the man had quickly scrawled a simple "no" on each scrap of paper except for one. When called by name, each member took a turn walking up to the pile and selecting one of the scraps of paper. The air of the meeting was relatively somber, with members modestly walking up to the pile and returning to their seat with as little disturbance as possible. I watched as the woman sitting next to me took her turn. She reached down, grabbed a scrap, and casually returned to her seat to the left of me. She opened up the scrap of paper discreetly. Having been distracted by watching the other members taking their scraps, I leaned over to ask her what the paper said. Three letters and one big smile.

At first glance, this lottery-style draw, the habitual social interactions between group members and the respectful tone of the proceedings may seem like a relatively standard state of affairs. Just like any other club or organizational meeting, the leader of the group took attendance (via contributions) and a record was kept of everyone's participation. The air of the meeting was kept orderly and focused and everyone appeared diligent when it came to offering their monetary contributions. Still, what might be considered exceptional about these women's weekly meetings? A closer look reveals the material and non-material complexities of this money-sharing group. The women are shown contributing Ksh40 each, which is then amassed and doled out to one member (the lucky "yes" recipient) in the form of a loan. The group then gives the debtor a certain amount of time to repay the loan with interest, restoring the group "pot" but with a small profit for the group to enjoy at the end of the loan cycle. The group "pot" is then rotated to another member, who also repays it with interest, and so forth.

Though there are certain accountability measures in place to ensure that the money is repaid in a timely manner and that the same group member is not given a loan twice in a row, the basic mechanics of the group lending structure remain relatively simple. Most prominently, this group represents a powerful method for these women to *make money out of their own money*. Upon receiving the "yes," the woman pictured in Figure 11.1 explained to me the plans she had for the loan, including paying her son's school fees and remodeling her home. She discussed how she came to the group each week because it afforded her the opportunity to financially contribute to the welfare of her household. It was never certain that she would receive the money – in fact, it was very improbable – but in the meantime, she kept a mental schedule

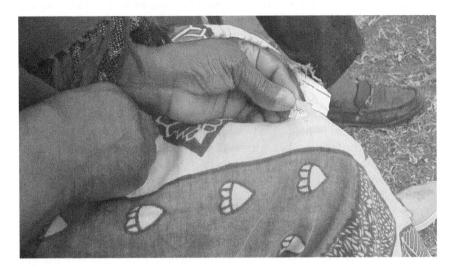

Figure 11.1 A woman from the Watema Farmers Self-Help Group randomly selected the slip of paper that reads "yes," indicating that she will receive the pooled contributions from this week's merry-go-round.

of which financial priorities were most pressing. School fees were her first priority, not only because she valued her child's education but because she indicated that the deadline for school fees was fast approaching. It became clear in our brief discussion that this woman dedicated a fair amount of time to financial planning, mostly revolving around the needs of the household. While for her the school fees deadline seemed swiftly approaching, I was left impressed with her long-term perspective and capacity to save since the deadline was in fact six months away.

Introduction

The anecdote above situates our discussion in the semi-arid midlands of Ukambani, the expansive territory of the Wákámbá (Kamba) people three hours southwest of Kenya's bustling capital city of Nairobi. Ukambani ("Kamba land") is characterized by low annual rainfall and long dry seasons. In spite of the harsh conditions that typify these semi-arid midlands, most of the Kamba rely on smallholder agriculture for their primary livelihood. With simultaneous goals of subsistence and profit-making, farmers combine food crop and livestock production under conditions of moderate land use intensity (Kenya, Ministry of Agriculture, 2006). Farmers in Ukambani may also pick up casual work in the off-season and many times the compensation for casual work is in the form of bulk crops that are kept in dry storage (e.g., beans, grains) or an unspoken understanding of returning the favor in the indeterminate future. Women are most commonly seen working the farm, running stalls in the town center, or engaging in artisanal income-generating activities such as basket and rope weaving.

With scarce rainfall leading to uncertain harvests and poor infrastructure making mobility difficult, agricultural finance is considered a high-risk game for both debtors and lenders in this area. As a result, only some Kamba smallholders transact through formal, registered financial institutions.[1] For the majority of Kamba smallholders who lack literal (i.e., physical) or figurative access to such commercial lenders, sustaining one's livelihood is sometimes best done through means that circumvent formal, bureaucratic, state-regulated institutions. Transactions which meet this description can come in many different forms – whether through peer-to-peer borrowing/ lending, group-based money-sharing like in the anecdote above, or otherwise. The ethnographic scene presented above is representative of the way in which smallholder women, in particular, manage their finances from day-to-day. In fact, smallholder women are statistically more likely to be involved in informal, interpersonal microfinance than smallholder men (Schreiner 2001; Xaba et al. 2002). Much of the research presented in this chapter is dedicated to answering the question of *why* this is so. In doing so, this chapter challenges some of the more commonly accepted narratives in how financial institutions market to women, which presume that they are primarily interested in borrowing funds to support income-generating activities. The women whose stories are woven together in this chapter present an ethnographic portrait of the lived experiences and socially embedded interactions Kamba women have with financial management, financial planning, and financial decision-making. More broadly, in the midst of dominant development narratives that champion "women's empowerment through microfinance" and Kenya's long-term development plan, Vision 2030,[2] which prioritizes the same, this research provides local, alternative perspectives on the way gender interacts with other aspects of people's identity to influence the way they approach finance.

The chapter relies primarily on 35 household interviews, several focus group discussions, and several interactive exercises (May to August 2013). Interactive exercises included PhotoVoice (using participant-produced photographs as a projective interviewing tool) and Financial Transaction Diaries (asking participants to keep daily journals of financial transactions). This analysis employs an ethnographic perspective on credit, but is also informed by discussions of credit in other disciplines (e.g., credit as part of the domestic economy and Marxist understandings of credit as helping to reproduce the household). The ethnographic perspective allows for a rich and nuanced understanding of the ways smallholder farmers conceptually engage with the world.

Reason and rationality in informal microfinance

Like many places in the world, the concept of traditional or informal finance is not new to Africa. Savings and credit groups have operated for centuries as *susu* in Ghana, "chit funds" in India, *tandas* in Mexico, *arisan* in Indonesia, and more (Anderson 1966; Bortei-Doku and Aryeetey 1995; Bouman 1995; Kurtz and Showman 1978). In every model, there is an effort to pool value-bearing resources (usually cash) from numerous sources into a "pot" from which each member can draw.[3] Usually, there is some mechanism for ensuring that the pot grows larger each time a member withdraws – in short, accruing interest. The term *micro* refers to the relatively small amounts of money contributed and/or lent in informal group-based lending, as well as the marginal gains made on returned loans with interest. This kind of structure nods to Marx's famous accusation regarding the commodification of money since the group is in fact "making money out of money" (Marx [1867] 1976, 155).[4] In the same way, this structure counters Peruvian development economist Hernando de Soto's remark that "money does not earn money" by showing that these groups do in fact generate wealth using none other than internal social pressure (de Soto 2003, 64). In Makueni County, it is very rare to meet a farmer who is not involved in at least one self-help group.[5] The Kamba have a long history of using rotating, cooperative group structures to share and lend out resources. Even in the pre-monetized economy (i.e., largely precolonial times), Kamba farmers used the same group lending structures to lend their time to working each other's farms, to collect resources for a community event (e.g., a funeral), and more. This research confines itself to the group-based lending structure (e.g., the aforementioned Watema Farmers Self-Help Group), since these groups appear to be permanent fixtures in the financial landscape of Ukambani.

A ride on the merry-go-round: informal finance among Kenyan farmers

Informal microfinance is much more multifarious than formal lending,[6] being delivered through savings/credit clubs, deposit collectors, interpersonal reciprocal lending, and more. Apart from the enormous amount of largely undocumented interpersonal micro-lending, the most prominent form of micro-lending in Kenya occurs within the group setting, particularly using a "merry-go-round" or "table banking" structure (refer to Table 11.1 for more details). Group-based informal microfinance in the Kenyan context may also be provided in more traditional bank-like settings, such as through unregistered village banks, accumulating savings and credit associations (ASCAs, common in Uganda), and financial services associations.

In conversations with Kamba farmers, it was clear that informal microfinance is generally considered to be convenient (i.e., low transaction costs), appealing (i.e., social benefits of working with friends/neighbors), and flexible. Most of the farmers I spoke with do not necessarily even leave their farm unless they have the intention of purchasing certain specialty or non-farm food items (e.g., sugar for tea, milk), making the transaction costs associated with banking at an institution even higher. Such transaction costs can include loss of time spent on the farm or in the household, loss of time due to risky

Table 11.1 Informal group lending structures

Classification in the literature	Local term	Mechanics	Average loan size
Rotating Savings and Credit Association (ROSCA)	"merry-go-round" or chama	Each member agrees to contribute a fixed amount at each meeting. The contributions are pooled and each member is loaned the entirety of the pool on a rotating schedule.	Ksh 150 per contribution
Accumulating Savings and Credit Association (ASCA)	"table banking"	Each member contributes a certain amount of money at each meeting. The money is pooled and accumulated at each meeting, and serves as a revolving fund. Members take short- or long-term loans as they repay previous loans at low-interest rates to build on the group's revolving fund.	Ksh 20 per contribution
Women's group (for monetary or other exchange)	Mwethiya	This term may be used for any women's group in Ukambani.	N/A
Any other self-help group that has not gathered for the purpose of monetary exchange	(referred to by group name)	Regular meetings (weekly, monthly, annually) for the purpose of knowledge exchange, advice sharing, skill building, entertainment/performance rehearsal, etc.	N/A

travel on unpaved roads through remote areas, and more. Flexibility refers to both the personalized nature of informal lending (i.e., no matter where one is, one can seek out someone to borrow from) but also to the capacity of informal banking to adapt repayment schedules and loan sizes according to individual need. For this reason, I argue that informal group lending models lend themselves more easily to innovation and resilience when faced with new challenges. This is precisely what makes them an important method for contributing to the sustainability of one's livelihood and household. While low levels of access to formal credit are often portrayed as a constraint on the smallholder livelihood system, this ethnography highlights the relevance, adaptability, and cost-effectiveness of informal group lending (Binswanger and Sillers 1983; Freeman, Ehui, and Jabbar 1998).

Informal microfinance has been framed thus far as a practice of convenience, a method for smallholders to access credit on their own terms and in their own time. In contrast to commercial banking institutions, however, informal microfinance also serves as a space where farmers find avenues for community leadership opportunities, exchange personalized advice, and build solidarity in times of environmental distress. As one farmer explained, "We do not get up and leave just because it is a bad season. These [credit/savings] groups are the way we stick together." While these groups often operate according to certain capitalist principles regarding profit maximization (by charging interest on loans), they are generally very cooperative in nature. Methods of peer-to-peer accountability are in place, including fines for being late, social pressures to avoid defaulting, etc.

The profit group members seek is not always about immediate returns nor is it necessarily in the form of cash. Talking to a Kamba friend who is involved in several groups, I asked him if accumulating more personal wealth was a primary incentive to join groups. He replied, "No, all money is ours," showcasing the Kamba understanding that money is a communal entity. This is not to say that no one is gaining from these groups, since we know that these groups certainly pull in a hefty profit through charging interest on loans and fining members for tardiness. Still, with the money not being owned by any individual group member, the group members remain indebted to one another, keeping the social relationships that comprise the group alive and active. An active group is an asset to the community, since it serves as a place of support and assistance for credit needs, advice, quality social time, and skill building. More broadly, the logic underlying informal group lending is that relying on others when it comes to money-sharing enhances the likelihood of repayment and profit, contrary to Western ideologies that regard debtors as atomized, entrepreneurial individuals. Professor Mary Kinyanjui at the University of Nairobi has written extensively on the topic of communalism and cooperative work ethic in Kenyan culture. In her book, *Vyama, Institutions of Hope: Ordinary People's Market Coordination and Society Organisation*, Kinyanjui (2012) also summons John S. Mbiti's famous writings on *ubuntu*[7] as a core value of African social life. Mbiti famously writes of the Bantu term *ubuntu* that it generally implies a sense of "because I am, we are; and because we are, I am" (Mbiti 1990, 106). This aligns with Kinyanjui's (2012) writings on Kamba culture where people generally feel a sense of obligation to "pull together" in times of need. Note that the term *mwethiya* in Kikamba, which means "pull together," was also historically used for rotating credit groups.[8] Cultural themes of mutual assistance and self-help underline the strength of interpersonal creditor-debtor relations in enhancing the resilience and sustainability of smallholder livelihoods.

Women as "agents of progress"

Shifting away from the realm of informal finance, it is worth balancing our conversation on gender and informal finance by understanding the characterization of women in rural finance. Many of Kenya's microfinance institutions target women directly, encouraging a group lending structure that seems to appeal much more to women than to men. In Bangladesh, research has shown how microfinance can have an impact on gender relations within the household, as women are able to better support the family through their earnings (Yunus 2007). At the same time, conflicting reports of women's financial "empowerment" through microloans have shown that in some instances, microfinance actually increases a woman's bargaining power within the household to the extent that a private engagement with money reads as dishonest and therefore results in increased domestic violence against women (Johnson 2004). One Kamba woman explained it to me in this way: "Sometimes women have drunkard husbands or are afraid their husbands will steal the money they get from these groups, so they ask [the group] to buy something and give it to them." This is to say that merry-go-round groups are willing to give out a loan to a member in the form of material/supplies as a way of ensuring the money is directed exactly where it was intended. The recipient then repays the group in cash, as he/she would any other time. Formal institutions refer to this as "in-kind" lending, and some institutions (e.g., the Kenyan bank K-Rep) are beginning to incorporate in-kind loans into their operations.

Although Kamba women overall confirm that they control less income than men in Ukambani, it appears that they are consulted in the household decision-making process about consumption. Still, women expressed frustration that they do not have direct control over money – if women did receive small amounts of money from peers or groups, some preferred to handle their money in secret, away from their husbands, to secure it against theft. Men in Makueni generally reported that the money they received from petty trading and the selling of agricultural products first came to them, and then they would give it to their wives in the form of petty cash for luxury food items and other basic grocery items (e.g., sugar for tea, *unga* flour, diapers). Sometimes, wives reported having to ask their husbands for money for basic items and other times, wives were given relatively small allowances of cash regularly. From the formal financial sector's perspective in Ukambani, microfinance connotes a clientele composed mostly of rural women. From the perspective of local farmers, women are clearly much more involved in informal group lending than in any other mechanism of accessing credit and savings. Women tend to be more "unbanked"[9] than men by far, and they tend to interact with and control less income than men overall. In part, this contributes to the dominance of women in informal group lending where microloans are the norm and most actors occupy the same low-income level. Still, many women do turn to microfinance institutions as a way of accessing money when in need. Sometimes they do so in shareholder group settings. Therefore, any discussion on the intersection of microfinance, in/formality, and poverty must include a gendered perspective.

When considering the effects of in/formal microfinance as a development tool, Akin and Robbins (1999) encouraged policymakers and researchers to make important distinctions between actors' "transactions for personal gain and those aimed at social reproduction," since not all debt relations are created equal (Guyer 2004, 20). Certainly along gendered lines, interactions with debt differ because women and men have dissimilar seasonal credit needs. Consistent with Susan Johnson's (2004) work in Central Kenya, this study has found that women tend to operate in smaller-sized amounts of money and have more frequent credit needs since they are focused more on the needs of the household. Men, on the other hand, tend to desire larger-sized loans and live their financial lives more seasonally according to the needs of the farm. Bearing this in mind, many microfinance institutions market their products and services directly to women, but this elides the number of obstacles that prevent women farmers from actually turning to formal microfinance institutions in a time of need. Among these are prohibitively high interest rates, individualistic/private loans that do not offer the social benefits that informal groups might, additional processing and legal fees, and the general "fear" of dispossession and public shaming. Women's focus on supporting the domestic economy more directly than they do the family's income-generating activities is one of many ways of bolstering the integrity of the entire smallholder livelihood system.

While visiting a middle-aged couple who lived nearby my host family's house in Nthangu, I asked about a vibrant, stately painting the man had completed, which was hanging on the main wall of their living room. The painting depicted a market scene, buyers casually walking by and eager female vendors presenting their vegetables to them. The sights and sounds of any local market in Kenya offer a cross section into everyday social life, including the way gender roles play out publically. The man – a retired public servant who took up a variety of different hobbies, of which painting was one – said that it was his favorite among all the paintings he had ever done. He said that the painting depicted Wote Town's weekly market day, a rich social event where people come to do their grocery shopping at the Southern edge of town. I asked the couple about why markets were dominated by female vendors. "You know women, it's their social day. If they sell everything, they stay. If they go home, the cows are waiting, the husbands are waiting, etc." The two of them laughed, indicating that when women are home, they are expected to keep the household in motion. For smallholders, the domestic economy is inalienably linked to their livelihood practice. If women are expected to maintain the household, then it is perhaps unsurprising that most of the credit women seek is not for income-generating activities. This is a highly important finding if only because microfinance institutions so often market their loan products as being intended for small-scale enterprise or income-generating activities only. The point here is simply that the female contribution to the household is, of course, central to the reproduction of the household as a whole and therefore contributes to the sustainability of the family and its livelihood. Understanding the worldview of Kamba women can make way for a conversation about how policymaking and regulatory decisions can better target the lived priorities of smallholder women.

Johnson (2004) reports that among the Kikuyu of Central Kenya, large-scale household assets were generally considered to be a male responsibility. Men typically harbored desires for new plots of land, expansions of the *boma* (homestead), bicycles or cars, etc. Because men tend to control the resources that produce the most income, they are more likely to be in a position to put forth certain collateral as a guarantee for a loan. Women technically lack this kind of ownership, though it is clear that women do have a strong custodial presence over certain items and spaces within the household. Johnson's findings tend to be consistent with what we see in Ukambani, where men are more likely to save money for large-scale household assets while women concentrate on small-scale items for the household. I found that when women know they are soon to receive money (say, as a microloan from a group), they immediately begin making plans to purchase smaller-scale assets for inside the household, such as plastic chairs, non-farm food items (e.g., sugar for tea), luxury food items (e.g., specialty meats), and *sufuriyas* (pots and pans). One woman even told me, smiling, "Women have plans; men don't." For both men and women, certain items were seen more as long-term investments and were thus considered to be objects of general desire for the household as a whole, such as a dairy cow or school fees. As it relates to income, women's income streams tend to occur in smaller increments and much more frequently. This is why, as Johnson (2004) suggests, women tend to be much more actively involved in the informal sector that allows for loan sizes and repayment schedules to be much more flexible due to the highly personalized nature of group lending.

After sharing a bowl of *githeri* (bean dish) for lunch at her home in Nthangu, Makueni County, a Kamba woman told me how exploited she felt by banks and other formal institutions. "Banks take advantage of women. Men will just beat them up if they misuse their money!" she said, chuckling. According to this woman, microfinance institutions[10] often involve lengthy contracts with terminology women do not always understand. The multitude of fees becomes a maze and a burden. "You pay 1,000 for the contract, 500 for a lawyer to stamp it, and the interest is too high. After all that, you find yourself working for the bank!" Women are less likely than men to be literate, especially in the rural areas, and there is a sense that the bureaucratized nature of formal banking emphasizes these disparities. Most traditional banks (i.e., excluding microfinancial institutions that specifically target women, such as Faula or K-Rep) require a husband's signature even if the loan is requested by a woman. One of my host family's neighbors explained one afternoon, chuckling as she placed two steaming cups of chai on the table in front of us, "You see, at the end of the day, women in Africa don't own anything." While women were targeted as "agents of progress" by banks and microfinance institutions, they felt taken advantage of by them. It was rare to come across a woman who had taken a loan from a microfinance institution individually; instead, most women took loans from microfinance institutions as part of a group.

Fear and trust in informal microfinance: obstacles or opportunities?

Fear and trust are central issues in understanding informal microfinance as a strategy for sustainability among smallholder women. This is not to imply that fear and trust are foils of one another, nor are they mutually exclusive when it comes to informal microfinance. Instead, it is my intention to discuss these two concepts in turn, as they arose quite commonly during my conversations with smallholder farmers. While the need for financial assistance is evident, farmers consistently expressed suspicion and reluctance as it relates to taking loans from formal financial institutions. Farmers often used the word "fear" to discuss both disaffection with banking institutions and the concern that defaulting on a loan would result in material dispossession. However, this pervasive fear of non-repayment seems unreasonable considering that informal microfinance is characterized by near-100 percent repayment rate that characterizes the informal credit/savings activity in which these smallholders are involved. As such, I interrogate the concept of *fear* – how it is produced, how it is industriously circulated and/or personally experienced, and how it functions to promote certain habits.

Most of the conversations in which a sentiment of fear or distrust arose were driven by questions surrounding loans from formal institutions. Commonly, farmers would indicate that peers of theirs had taken loans and were not able to repay them in full, therefore resulting in someone from the bank or microfinance institution coming onto their land and taking one of their major assets. Often, this was farm equipment, but some of the more dramatic stories involved taking iron sheets directly off of the roof of someone's home or actually evicting someone off of their land. One person even said that a neighbor had her front door taken off the hinges and hauled away as a result of defaulting. Most of the time, these stories revolved around women who took loans independently of their husbands through one of the microfinance institutions that targeted women (e.g., Kenya Women's Finance Trust). When asked what circumstances caused the woman to default, many people were unsure but often indicated that she somehow got ahead of herself by not telling her husband and probably lacked "a plan" for the money. This stands in contrast to the conversations I had with women about money in which every woman had shorter-term and longer-term plans in mind for the next loan she was set to receive. Both women and men relayed these stories of defaulting to me and while each story was different, the basic elements were always similar and the women remained anonymous or unknown, causing me to suspect that the stories were not all based in truth.

While fear was repeated during my interviews, it seemed that "fear" itself was used as a blanket term to categorize disenchantment on several fronts. First, as mentioned, fear seems to refer to a general disenchantment with the institutional constraints of formal banking. This can involve a sense of distrust, intimidation, a lack of belonging or entitlement in the formal sector space, or exasperation with the associated transaction costs of formal banking. More than that, "fear" appears to be underlined by a sense of doubt as it relates to farmers' ability to repay. Offering a major asset for collateral on a loan places the asset(s) in a tenuous, intermediate state of ownership between the lender and the debtor. Farmers were very uncomfortable with this, assuming that there was a high probability that they would not be able to properly repay the debt on time.

Even considering the farmers' protestations of fear, their doubt about their ability to repay loans may have nothing at all to do with reliability. Considering the low default rates in the informal sector, it would be an analytical mistake to assume that repayment in the formal sector speaks directly to one's character or trustworthiness. Instead, I would argue that the loans offered in the formal sector come with repayment schedules that are much less flexible than those in the informal sector. Moreover, these loans are generally larger sums of money than the farmers need or are accustomed to managing. This makes one's capacity to repay appear very limited. Several microfinance institutions actually measure one's "ability to repay" during the loan application period and they do so using a single metric: household income. For smallholder farmers, the levels of income are relatively low and they are therefore categorized as less reliable than other higher income populations. I would argue that because farmers enter credit/debt relations based on material and non-material wealth, their income cannot always be measured through cash.

It is clear that farmers do not want to put forth their major assets when applying for loans, because it throws their ownership of said assets into doubt. In my conversation with the Manager of the local African Financial Corporation (AFC[11]) branch, he expressed that collateral was seen as a "threat" by farmers in Makueni County. With the threat of collateral and doubts of repayment looming over farmers, I began to interrogate the intimacy with which people experienced these issues. In Ukambani, the confiscation of a major piece of one's property is a very public gesture that carries immense amounts of shame and guilt. When shame is incurred by a woman, however, it is perhaps even more devastating to her reputation than it would be to that of a man because women are not traditionally in control of their own money. Husbands reported consulting their wives as to how to spend the money, but the husbands also generally admitted to having more immediate access to cash-on-demand (that which results from farm income) than the wives had. For this reason, women found comfort in being able to attend merry-go-round and other groups to access cash when they needed it. In general, men seemed to support women's involvement in these groups because they saw that women were benefiting socially and were able to contribute to the well-being of the household. They were also considered very useful outlets for emergency credit needs.

Dispossession is clearly at the heart of the "fear" these farmers have expressed, but also because it relates to what I suggest is a more salient cultural theme: trust. Following Keith Hart (2000), my research demonstrates that trust is not the same as reliance. Similar to Hart's (2000) definition, I argue that trust implies a reliance on another person such that risk is mitigated. Trust potentially involves assured reliance, confidence, and/or faith. In my interviews with farmers, there was certainly evidence of mistrust when it came to formal loans. I would argue that this increases risk because the debt relationship the farmer has with the banking institution is not rooted in other social commitments, leaving the farmer either less compelled to comply or intimidated by the power dynamic that exists between an impersonal, formal institutional creditor and an individual debtor. My neighbor in Nthangu who complained of transaction costs that made her feel like she was "working for the bank," considered banks to be synonymous with "corruption."

In my interviews with farmers, it was clear that deciphering what is a rumour and what reflects an actual experience requires extensive probing. Following psychoanalyst Heinz Kohut, anthropologist Clifford Geertz developed a way of scaling experience according to one's "distance" from an experience. From Geertz's point of view, "experience is both *of* something (an intrusion from the external world) and *in* something (an internalization by reflection)" (Geertz 1974, 30). The anthropological project, therefore, is "experience-distant" in which the anthropologist tries to describe the native's first-hand experience using a conceptual framework. I have unpacked the concept of fear as it was described to me and reinterpreted it within an "experience-distant" framework. For the farmers themselves, however, there is no element of abstraction about the experiences of confiscation faced by their peers. The farmers who expressed fear were serious and intentional about their preference to avoid the formal sector, and thus there was a sense that fear was rooted in lived experience, even if the dispossession happened to the interviewee's neighbor and not to the interviewee. Examining the gendered aspects of dispossession is important in Ukambani, where these groups represent relatively more accessible, more comfortable, and more cost-effective places for women to access money used to buy small household assets and non-farm/luxury food items. While women may not have the same social obligations to a formal institution that they would have towards a peer, being dispossessed by an institution carries the same weight of public shaming that we see in the informal sector. Because women typically do not possess large sums of money, defaulting on a loan results in intense cynicism by men and sometimes women. The stories of dispossession which were used to exemplify why farmers "feared" bank loans almost always involved a woman not telling her husband she had taken a loan, and defaulting because she "didn't have a plan" to repay or "had problems" and could not repay. While most individual loans that women might take from an institution require a husband's signature, the women in the stories were taking loans from microfinance institutions through shareholder groups. The idea of planning is often mentioned in these groups, and the decision to join a money-sharing group signals to the public that they have decided to organize themselves financially. Sara S. Berry (1993) echoes Kenyan sociologist Enos Njeru (1978) to explain that these groups provide a channel for people to negotiate local resources but also to publicly display themselves as financially capable people, "People have different motives for contributing in *harambee* (fundraiser) meetings, including dramatization of one's social status" (Njeru, 1978, 34). It follows, then, that men fear bank loans because they, too, do not want to risk the shaming and loss of status that comes along with dispossession. Formal and informal loans represent a very high-risk game, though participating in the informal sector is a way of making more inroads toward establishing oneself as a leader and as financially viable. Fear of the formal sector creates a distance between farmers and the formal banking sector such that informal banking is by far the social norm.

Conclusion

The provision of small-scale financial services, microfinance, has been championed as a major social and economic development tool that could help lift small-scale farmers out of dire financial straits. Since the boom of microfinance in the 1990s, it has become part of the *lingua franca* of the global development industry. Still, in a region like East Africa where awareness of the microfinance industry is strong, micro-financial products and services have yet to become a fixed part of people's financial lives. In Kenya, formal microfinance seems to be available and accessible in theory, but in practice most people turn to informal means. Despite its popularity in the more concentrated urban areas of the country, formal microfinance has followed the pattern of the major commercial banking institutions by failing to serve the largest employment sector, the rural agricultural sector. It is for this reason that most producers are not involved in the formal economy at all, but instead turn to friends, family, and other members of their social network to ensure that their daily financial needs are met.

Rather than isolating gender as a separate topic of discussion (Karim 2011), this chapter has integrated gender throughout the discussion. Gender is thus positioned as an analytical category that shapes how informal microfinance operates as a strategy for smallholder livelihood sustainability in the Kenyan context. When it comes to the way smallholders access credit/savings products and services, gender represents a layer of social life that may be pronounced in certain situations. It is clear from informal and formal interviews with women farmers in Ukambani that very few of them conceptualized their farms as a business, but rather as a way of life. Those farmers who did perceive their farm as a business or an incubator for some larger goal were typically men. This illustrates how gender influences financial planning.

A March 2014 (2b) article, "Ease Access to Credit for Women," in one of Kenya's largest newspapers, *The Standard*, reported that more than 1.4 million Kenyans relied exclusively on "family and friends" for loans, and this was deemed wholesale as "unsettling." Existing financial inclusion policies relegate transactions made outside of the framework of formal calculations and documentation to the shadows. That is, informal banking is dismissed as a subversive market, a lesser option, or a "last resort" alternative to formal banking. This is not to make any sweeping moralizing statements about what is the best or right option for smallholder farmers, but, rather, the ethnographic evidence presented in this chapter exposes the important efficiencies and intricacies of the informal sector for developing a strategy for sustainability. This creates a space for the discussion of how to best meet the credit needs of smallholders who are already more active informally than they are through institutional or formal means, whether through policy channels or otherwise.

Women farmers in Ukambani were less likely than men to perceive their farm as a business. Because elements like physical proximity and social networks play important roles in informal finance, key tenets of classic economic models (e.g., approaching one's farm in an entrepreneurial way, seeking income maximization, etc.) do not apply. Still, when women farmers seek out credit to finance their lives and the lives of their household, it is clear that they seem to value highly the structural elements of formal banking such as incentives, regulation, and enforcement which are classically geared toward entrepreneurs.

Policymakers have entered the conversation on global microfinance largely in their efforts to build a legal and regulatory environment that allows for innovation, while maintaining standards of efficiency, accountability, and transparency. Underlining the argument in this chapter is the idea that widening the conversation on microfinance can actually allow the industry to become more contextualized, more localized, and ideally, much more effective on the ground level. The informal economy of East Africa has long been central to the livelihood of smallholder farmers, and gender is an invaluable piece of the puzzle. Creating a way forward means understanding informal microfinance as a strategy for sustainability, that is, how it is central to farmers' ability to innovate, respond to threats, and plan for the future.

Notes

1 The various challenges associated with commercial banking institutions will be a topic of discussion later in this chapter.
2 Kenya's Vision 2030 is a development plan covering the period 2008–2030. Among the many policies are provisions for greater employment among youth, gender equity, and economic growth in all sectors.
3 For further reading on an anthropological interpretation of "value," see David Graeber, (2001) *Toward an Anthropological Theory of Value: The False Coin of Our Own Dream* (Basingstoke: Palgrave).
4 In *Das Kapital* (1867,155) Marx famously wrote, "money begets money." Benjamin Franklin (1748) and others also expressed this sentiment in their work on capitalism.
5 "Self-help group" is the broadest term both in the literature and in local Kamba use, which suffices to encompass not only credit/savings groups, but also groups that exchange non-cash media.
6 There is not space here to discuss the spectrum of institutions considered "formal," but in general, formal lending refers to all commercial institutions which are registered with, regulated by, and taxed by the state.
7 In John S. Mbiti's (1990, 106) *African Religions and Philosophy*, he famously explained the African philosophy of communitarianism. Now referred to as *ubuntu*, this philosophy is often explained using one of Mbiti's most famous lines: "I am because we are; we are because I am."
8 Today, the Swahili term *chama* is much more commonly used as a general term for any kind of self-help group.
9 In the literature and in common development discourse, "unbanked" generally refers to anyone not yet incorporated into the formal financial sector.
10 She made no distinction between microfinance institutions and banks, and when I probed, she said she understood them as being interchangeable.
11 Established at the time of independence in 1963, AFC is a financial institution that is wholly owned by the government. AFC's mandate is to provide short-, medium-, and long-term finance to Kenyan farmers. The local branch in Wote estimates that about 80 percent of its clientele is men due to the fact that the only form of collateral AFC accepts is a title deed (generally signed to the male head of household's name).

References

Akin, David, and Joel Robbins, eds. 1999. *Money and Modernity: State and Local Currencies in Melanesia.* Association for Social Anthropology in Oceania (ASAO) Monograph Series, no. 17. Pittsburgh: University of Pittsburgh Press.

Anderson, Robert T. 1966. "Rotating Credit Associations in India." *Economic Development and Cultural Change* 14 (3): 334–39.

Berry, Sara S. 1993. *No Condition is Permanent: The Social Dynamics of Agrarian Change in Sub-Saharan Africa.* Madison: University of Wisconsin Press.

Binswanger, Hans P., and Donald A. Sillers. 1983. "Risk Aversion and Credit Constraints in Farmers' Decision-Making: A Reinterpretation." *Journal of Development Studies* 20 (1): 5–21.

Bortei-Doku, Ellen, and Ernest Aryeetey. 1995. "Mobilizing Cash for Business: Women in Rotating Susu Clubs in Ghana." In *Money-Go-Rounds: The Importance of Rotating Savings and Credit Associations for Women*, edited by Shirley Ardener and Sandra Burman, 77–93. Oxford, UK: Berg.

Bouman, Frits J. A. 1995. "Rotating and Accumulating Savings and Credit Associations: A Development Perspective." *World Development* 23 (3): 371–84.

de Soto, Hernando. 2003. *Mystery of Capital: Why Capitalism Triumphs in the West and Fails Everywhere Else*. New York: Basic Books.

"Ease Access to Credit for Women." *The Standard*. March 2014. 2b.

Freeman, H. A., Simeon K. Ehui, and Mohammad A Jabbar. 1998. "Credit Constraints and Smallholder Dairy Production in the East African Highlands: Application of a Switching Regression Model." *Agricultural Economics* 19 (1): 33–44.

Geertz, Clifford. 1974. "'From the Native's Point of View': On the Nature of Anthropological Understanding." *Bulletin of the American Academy of Arts and Sciences* 28 (1): 26–45.

Graeber, David. 2001. *Toward an Anthropological Theory of Value: The False Coin of Our Own Dreams*. Basingstoke: Palgrave Macmillan.

Guyer, Jane I. 2004. *Marginal Gains: Monetary Transactions in Atlantic Africa*. Chicago: University of Chicago Press.

Hart, Keith. 2000. *The Memory Bank: Money in an Unequal World*. London: Profile Books.

Johnson, Susan. 2004. "Gender Norms in Financial Markets: Evidence from Kenya." *World Development* 32 (8): 1355–74.

Karim, Lamia. 2011. *Microfinance and its Discontents: Women in Debt in Bangladesh*. Minneapolis: University of Minnesota Press.

Kenya, Ministry of Agriculture. 2006. *Natural Conditions and Farm Management Information*. 2nd ed. Vol. 2 of the *Farm Management Handbook of Kenya* by R. Jaetzold, Helmut Schmidt, Berthold Hornetz, and Chris Shisanya. Nairobi: Ministry of Agriculture.

Kinyanjui, Mary Njeri. 2012. *Vyama, Institutions of Hope: Ordinary People's Market Coordination and Society Organisation*. Nairobi: Nsemia Publishers.

Kurtz, Donald V., and Margaret Showman. 1978. "The Tanda: A Rotating Credit Association in Mexico." *Ethnology* 17 (1): 65–74.

Marx, Karl. [1867] 1976. *A Critique of Political Economy*. Vol. 1 of *Das Kapital*. With translation by Ben Fowkes. [Hamburg, Germany] Harmondsworth: Penguin.

Mbiti, John S. 1990. *African Religions & Philosophy*. 2nd edition. Portsmouth: Heinemann.

Njeru, Enos. 1978. *Land Adjudication and its Implications for the Social Organisation of the Mbeere*. Madison: University of Wisconsin Press.

Osei-Assibey, Eric. 2015. "What Drives Behavioral Intention of Mobile Money Adoption? The Case of Ancient Susu Saving Operations in Ghana." *International Journal of Social Economics* 42 (11): 962–79.

Schreiner, Mark. 2001. "Informal Finance and the Design of Microfinance." *Development in Practice* 11 (5): 637–40.

Scott, James C. 1998. *Seeing Like a State: How Certain Schemes to Improve the Human Condition Have Failed*. New Haven: Yale University Press.

Xaba, Jantjie, Pat Horn, Shirin Motala, and Andrea Singh. 2002. *Informal Sector in Sub-Saharan Africa*. ILO Working Paper 355190, International Labour Organization, Geneva. www.ilo.org/wcmsp5/groups/public/---ed_emp/documents/publication/wcms_122204.pdf.

Yunus, Muhammad. 2007. *Banker to the Poor*. Guragaon: Penguin Books India.

Brazil

12 Participation of women farmers in food procurement programs in Brazil

Andrea Moraes and Cecilia Rocha

Rural poverty and family farms in Brazil

Brazil is a country rich in land and other resources. It has the world's fifth largest land area and a population of over 190 million people, 84.4 percent of whom live in urban areas (IBGE 2011). Once called the "land of contrasts" (Bastide 1957), the country is one of the world's most socio-economically unequal. Poverty is especially prevalent in rural areas. According to the International Fund for Agricultural Development (IFAD), 51 percent of Brazil's rural population lives on less than two dollars a day, while the national average is 35 percent (IFAD 2010). Recent data (IPEA 2014) show that in 2012 extreme poverty was more common among rural households (9.3%) than urban (2.6%).

Small-scale farms in Brazil are called *family farms*, which are defined by law as establishments: (1) that are limited in size to four fiscal modules (a measurement defined regionally); (2) where work is done mostly by the family; (3) that produce income mostly from the farm; and (4) that are managed by members of the family (MDA 2009). In 2006, according to the Brazilian Agricultural Census, 4.3 million establishments were family farms, corresponding to 84 percent of all rural establishments. Although family farms occupy only 24.3 percent of the total agricultural area, they produce 38 percent of the country's agricultural value. Moreover, family farms produce the majority of the staple foods consumed by Brazilians,[1] and employ 74 percent of the rural labor force (MDA 2009; Rocha, Burlandy, and Maluf 2012). Family farms are thus essential for the country's food security and poverty reduction strategies (IFAD 2011).

Although often "invisible" (Melo and Di Sabbato 2006), women's work is central to family farming in Brazil, as in other parts of the world. Strategies to reduce rural poverty and increase food security must consider not only impacts on women as beneficiaries of such strategies, but also recognize women's contributions and value to society as citizens with rights and capabilities. Moreover, "women's rights advocates call for approaches [to reduce rural poverty] that respect the commons and local livelihoods, recognize and value care, restructure production and consumption and pave the way for green transformations" (Agarwal 2010; Wichterich 2012; Women's Major Group 2013 quoted in UN Women 2014, 33). Policies that give visibility, value women's work, and promote equity are essential for real sustainable development (BRIDGE 2015).

This chapter examines public policy initiatives in Brazil, which directly or indirectly promote the visibility and inclusion of women's work in small-scale family agriculture. It looks specifically at two national programs created to support family farming and address food insecurity: the Food Acquisition Program (*Programa de Aquisição de Alimentos – PAA*), and the National School Meals Program (*Programa Nacional para Alimentação Escolar – PNAE*). What are the advances and challenges for women's participation in these programs? The next section of this chapter contextualizes women as family farmers in rural Brazil. Section three examines women's participation in both PAA and PNAE and looks at advances and challenges in these efforts. Finally, the closing section raises ideas that could help explain the Brazilian case and inspire future research on social policies, gender equity in rural areas, and sustainable development.

Brazilian women and family farming

Family farming is characterized by a fusion of family and work, where the organization of production is structured in family relations (Butto 2006b). In Brazil, family relations in rural areas have been historically and predominantly patriarchal (Brumer 2008; Melo 2010; Melo and Di Sabbato 2006; Röhnelt and Salamoni 2010). This means that family relations are basically organized according to a sexual division of labor: men's work is commonly associated with activities that generate income, while women's activities are centered around family consumption and mostly unpaid work.

Brazilian rural women are directly involved in several activities related to agriculture, such as raising birds and small animals, horticulture, floriculture, forestry, and tillage (Butto 2006a). They are also very involved in water management (Moraes and Rocha 2013) and seed saving. The Brazilian Agricultural Census of 2006 reported that one-third of the people involved in family farming (4.1 million) were women (França, Del Grossi, and Marques 2009).

In addition to agriculture, rural women perform a variety of nonagricultural activities that promote the diversification of resources in family farms. These include activities that aggregate value to agricultural products, such as processing foods, craftwork, and participation in local markets (Röhnelt and Salamoni 2010). Along with agricultural and non-agricultural activities, rural women also contribute to family farms though reproductive and self-sufficiency activities, such as food production (including gardens), cooking, washing, fetching and managing water, and caring for children and the elderly. Rural women's work is often perceived (even by themselves) as an extension of their role as mother/spouse/housewife in providing for their families' needs (Melo and Di Sabbato 2006).

Generally speaking, many of these activities are not included in national statistics. According to Melo and Di Sabbato (2006)[2] this is because official statistics' classification of agricultural work excludes activities for self-consumption, which occupies almost 41 percent of rural women's working hours and only 9 percent of men's working hours. This "invisibility" of their work creates a barrier for women's access to social policies and reinforces gender inequalities.

Almost 80 percent of the work performed by rural women is not paid (in contrast to 28% of men's work) and when women are paid, they receive only 56.4 percent of what men receive (Brumer 2008). Rural women are the majority (64%) of Brazilian women workers without payment, which helps to explain the fact that a number of young rural women migrate to the cities for paid work. Despite and because of this scenario of gender inequities in rural Brazil, over the last decades the Brazilian government has been implementing a series of programs that gives visibility to the role of women in family farm agriculture, ranging from documentation campaigns, to new rules for land title, quotas for rural credit and rural insurance. Incentives for women's participation also appear in programs such as PAA and PNAE, to support commercialization of produce from family farmers. This will be examined in the following section.

The participation of women in food procurement programs in Brazil

The objectives of public food procurement programs in Brazil are twofold: they aim to open new channels of commercialization for family farmers and at the same time, promote greater access to fresh and healthy food for people at risk of food insecurity. Currently in Brazil, the main buyers of products from family farmers are the National Food Acquisition Program (PAA) and the National School Meals Program (PNAE) (CAISAN 2014).

The National Food Acquisition Program (PAA)

PAA was created in 2003 by the Brazilian Government under the Zero Hunger Strategy (Rocha 2009). The program involves the purchasing of food crops and milk for governmental institutions and charities, as well as for strategic stock formation (Santos and Costa 2014). Since its creation, the number of family farmers participating in the program has increased substantially: from 42,000 in 2003 to 185,000 in 2012 – when the program had an overall budget of US$450 million (IPC-IG 2013). PAA can be accessed by family unit or by group (cooperative or association) with a maximum per-year selling limit of BR$8,000 (MDS, SESAN, and DECOM 2014).

PAA is coordinated by the Ministry of Social Development (MDS) and the Ministry of Agrarian Development (MDA), and is managed by states, municipalities, or by CONAB (the National Food Supply Company). In order to qualify for the program, farmers must be officially identified as family farmers through a government credential, the DAP: Document of Aptitude to PRONAF.[3]

The Resolution n. 44, from August 16, 2011 by the Managing Group of PAA (GGPAA) stated that women's participation was to be considered a priority criterion for the selection and execution of proposals in the PAA. In concrete terms, this meant that from its annual budget, five percent would have to be allocated to organizations composed of between 75–100 percent women members. This same 2011 resolution introduced a quota system requiring the participation of 30 to 40 percent of women on purchases from the different modalities of PAA.

These policies are having a beneficial effect as the participation of women in PAA has been growing significantly over the last few years. In 2009 PAA had 11,500 contracts with women farmers. In 2012 this number grew to 39,300 – a growth rate of 240 percent (CONAB 2013; MDA 2013). Also in 2012, women corresponded to 29 percent of all PAA contracts (CAISAN 2014).

Table 12.1 provides information on the numbers and values of contracts managed by CONAB between 2011 and 2014. It shows the steady increase of contracts with women farmers, which in 2014 corresponded to just over 50 percent of all projects funded under PAA, both in terms of number of farmers and value of resources (see also Butto et al. 2014, and CONAB 2013, for earlier analysis of this evolution). It should be noted that, while women's participation in the program has increased steadily in the past few years, the number of contracts and the value of government resources dedicated to PAA in general have fluctuated and were lower in 2014 than in 2012.

Previous studies (Siliprandi and Cintrão 2011) had already pointed out the special alignment that some dimensions of PAA had with women's traditional products. The PAA modality of Simultaneous Donation, for instance, buys local fresh produce (fruits, vegetables and herbs) and minimally processed foods (such as cakes, breads, cookies, juices, and jams) to be consumed by government welfare institutions almost immediately. These are traditionally women's food crops and products.

In addition to the introduction of a quota system, the growth in women's participation in the program can also be partially explained by changes in the program's internal processes. As mentioned before, the base document required to create a selling contract with the government under PAA is the DAP. Each household or family can be issued only one DAP, and most DAPs had the name of the man first. Because of pressure exerted by feminists and women's movements inside and outside the government there have been significant changes in the DAP form. Initially, women used to be listed on the last page as dependents; later on, they were included in the first page as second applicants; and most recently the first page contained two spaces for co-applicants, without a set hierarchy. These relatively small changes have helped to give visibility to women's work.

Siliprandi and Cintrão (2011) argue that the name of the person on the DAP is important because, although the selling contract with the government could be made by any member of the DAP, an institutional assumption – not only among people from the staff filling the forms but also among women

Table 12.1 PAA: number of contracts and total resources managed by CONAB (2011–2014)[a]

Year	Farmers				Resources distribution				TOTAL
	Female		Male		Female		Male		
	#	%	#	%	BR$	%	BR$	%	
2011	25,905	28.01	66,576	71.99	105,728,358	27.6	277,382,112	72.4	383,110,470
2012	35,143	31.12	65,758	58.23*	155,432,084	34.6	293,576,511	65.4	449,008,595*
2013	18,352	48.20	19,728	51.80	97,526,671	47.7	106,852,204	52.3	204,378,875
2014	23,495	50.71	22,834	49.29	154,905,800	50.6	151,298,270	49.4	306,204,070

a The PAA data presented here correspond to one category of execution of PAA: CONAB financed by the MDS. This category has the largest number of farmers' participation and resources invested.

(*) The total does not sum 100% because 10.64% did not report sex.

Source: PAA Data from the SAGI – National Secretary for Evaluation and Management of Information at http://aplicacoes.mds.gov.br/sagi/portal/.

and men farmers as well – was that the contract had to be with whomever had the first name on the DAP. The authors suggest that although women's production was being commercialized before, a large number of contracts were signed by the male of the household, constituting what they call a policy bias (Siliprandi and Cintrão 2011).

Another reason why Siliprandi and Cintrão (2011) believed that rural women were underrepresented in the PAA contracts was because of cultural assumptions about gender. The traditional divisions of labor assign women the domestic role of reproduction characterizing it as feminine (and therefore related to production of food to eat); on the other hand, men and masculinities are associated with public participation, and also the commercialization of produce (food for cash). This gender dichotomization of women-domestic and men-public is reinforced when the men sign the contracts in the name of women. It is also connected to other challenges of public recognition faced by rural women such as difficulties accessing documentation, bank accounts, and producing invoices (which can also be complex for low-income men).

An example of the impact of the program on women's organizations was presented by Mota, Schmitz, and da Silva (2013) in a study about *extractivist* women in the state of Sergipe in Brazil. They noted that the women who participated in the program were already beneficiaries from two other national social policies: the *Bolsa Família*[4] and the Program for Eradication of Children's Work (PET). Historically, these women have been extracting fruits such as *mangaba*, mango, and cashew fruit for their consumption and small sales. PAA provided the first opportunity to value their traditional activity and knowledge as well as generate a regular income from it. Thanks to the work of a number of local leaders, the 30 women involved formed a cooperative and in 2007 started to sell regularly to PAA. This produced some interesting results. The authors state, for example, that there were changes in household routines, since the women intensified production (and they were paid a fair price) and they had delivery deadlines. Household chores had to be adapted to those new priorities. The social life of their communities were also enhanced because the women had to go out more often, transporting their fruits using wheelbarrows and meeting and talking with others in the streets about their business. The income they received from their transactions was generally used to pay bills or to purchase household or personal items. There was a greater consumption of meat and chicken and some women also reported putting money into savings. The authors note that the local economy also benefited from the women's participation in the PAA. Small businesses such as small grocery stores and bakeries received a boost in income (Mota, Schmitz, and da Silva 2013).

Other research has reported increased food security of family farmers involved with the PAA (Azevedo, Barreto, and dos Santos 2013) and overall women's empowerment and autonomy (Azevedo 2012). Because the focus of PAA purchases is on food crops, which traditionally have been women's production, the greater value put on these products serves to increase the self-esteem of women farmers. In addition, considering the priority given to cooperatives and associations in some PAA modalities, there is an incentive for the formalization of women's associations. Most rural women's organizations produce crafts, plant and process food, and/or provide services. They are normally small and informal with little access to infrastructure for production or support for commercialization. Most often they are characterized as generating small and irregular incomes (Butto and Leite 2010). The PAA has introduced a challenge and an incentive for their formalization.

The National School Meals Program (PNAE)

The seed for what is now the National School Meals Program (PNAE) started in 1955 as a milk distribution program. More recently, PNAE became one of the largest social programs in South America with a budget of BR$3.5 billion, benefiting more than 45 million basic education students and young adults (IPC-IG 2013). PNAE is funded by the Ministry of Education and coordinated by the National Fund for Educational Development (FNDE). The program is implemented through states, municipalities, schools, and other agencies that buy food for school meals. PNAE has a number of layers of social control: from the local Councils for School Meals, which include representation from civil society members, parents, teachers, and government, to the Federal Union Accounting Tribunal, whose role is to guarantee the accountability and transparency of federal public resources.

Over the last decade, PNAE became part of the National Plan for Food and Nutrition Security. Since 2009, it adopted a new legislation that requires that 30 percent of the program's budget is invested in the direct purchase of food products from family farms. This change supports the dual goal of PNAE of providing healthy food for students on one hand and supporting sustainable rural development on the other.

As with the PAA, in order to sell their produce to PNAE, small family farmers have to be recognized by the state as such through the DAP. However, unlike the PAA, which has modalities for purchases directly from individual farmers, PNAE only buys from cooperatives and farmers associations. Thus, beyond the individual DAP there is another document needed for the participation of cooperatives and farmers associations on PNAE: the National Registry of Legal Entity for cooperatives or associations – also known as Juridical DAP.

The limit of purchase per family farm under the PNAE is BR$20,000 (approximately US$7,000) per year. The program pays a fair price (defined regionally) for family-farming products and offers higher prices to encourage organic food production. Since 2013, priority under the program has been given to the purchase of products from family farmers in agrarian reform settlements and in indigenous and *quilombola*[5] communities. A proposal to include women in the program's priorities is under debate (in 2015) in the Brazilian Senate (Chagas 2012; Câmara dos Deputados 2014).

In a study of women farmers in Seabra, in the state of Bahia, Santos and Costa (2014) noted a cultural affinity between the food needed for schools and the products traditionally produced and processed by women. Among the products sold to PNAE in the region are manioc, manioc cakes and cookies, fruits and juices, and vegetables such as carrots, beets, lettuce, pepper, tomatoes, and cucumbers – all of which are usually produced by women.

The women interviewed in the Seabra study reported a number of challenges accessing the program, ranging from difficulties in getting information about how the program works to how to be included in it (Santos and Costa 2014). They reported having difficulties in obtaining all the documentation necessary for requesting the Juridical DAP and formalizing their associations (Santos and Costa 2014). Moreover, the effort required for effective mobilization and organization created an extra burden for women, given their responsibilities with household and family care.

When the women were able to organize themselves and create a contract with an executing agency to sell to PNAE they faced production challenges common to all small family farmers (men and women). Changes in weather patterns, as elsewhere, could interfere with the production, creating extra risks for small farmers. Women also reported difficulties in planning their production capacity, guaranteeing the quality of their products and the volume of production needed for the schools. Butto et al. 2014 also state that official food safety requirements commonly based on agribusiness models, offer extra challenges for small family farms. Another issue that interferes with the regularity of PNAE as a new market for family farmers is the income disruptions due to school summer and winter vacations (Santos and Costa 2014).

Despite those challenges, all women interviewed in the study evaluated their engagement with PNAE positively. First, there were financial gains. Santos and Costa argued that gains from selling food products to PNAE corresponded to approximately 15 percent of their overall incomes.[6] But equally important were gains related to improved quality of life and a greater sense of value. Before selling to PNAE most women were working at home and in gardens, helping men in the fields and doing small informal services. Selling to PNAE involved being connected to farmer's organizations, working together, and participating in meetings and small trips. The quote below from one of the women illustrates the effects PNAE has had on women's lives.

> Today my routine changed a lot. I still have my things to do at home, but now I have the production, together with my colleagues. We have a lot of fun together, we talk a lot. After we started selling to PNAE our lives changed, in all aspects. Not only our income improved, but also our self-esteem.
>
> (Sirleide Rosa de Sousa, quoted in Santos and Costa 2014, 360)

The participation of women in the program not only enabled them to leave the environment of the house, to start having a public life, and to be recognized as producers, but also allowed them to access other programs and education opportunities and "reach new heights" (Santos and Costa 2014, 360). Still, the authors of the study also noted that despite many advances, only 20 percent of men farmers from the region reported that they help in the house with domestic work and none shared household duties. This poses an extra burden to women's empowerment and gender equity.

Recognizing the challenges that the rural poor still face in accessing public policies in support of family farming, the Brazilian Government in 2008 created a pilot program called Territories of Citizenship. This program selected 86 territories in Brazil as pilots for the implementation of a diversity of actions, including research, knowledge sharing, outreach, and training for poor rural communities. A strong focus on gender equality had also been developed. From the 86 territories selected, 80 have already formed groups of women producers organized as committees (Butto et al. 2014). Since one of the components of this program is to support family farmers in accessing social policies, an increase in women's participation in PAA and PNAE in those territories is expected.

Conclusion

The advances and gains in the participation of small rural women farmers in food procurement programs such as PNAE and PAA are undeniable, despite innumerous challenges. Real changes seem to be taking place in the greater recognition and visibility of rural women's work. These results are connected to a history of democratization of the country, based on an unusual proximity and collaboration between government and civil society. Over the last decade, the Brazilian government has engaged in pragmatic public policies that are effectively tackling one of its worst problems: social inequalities. In addition, there is a history of feminist mobilization, and women's and rural workers movements that are participating and helping in framing policies. Furthermore, because new programs and policies emerge from different areas at the same time, a synergy is created that has a true effect on the lives of poor rural women and men farmers. There are not only PAA and PNAE, but also PRONAF, Territories of Citizenship, *Bolsa Familia*, Cisterns Programs, Rural Universities, and others. We conclude by arguing that it *takes a village* to create policies that empower women, promote sustainable development, and food security. The Brazilian case, although not perfect or finished, reminds us of what is possible.

Notes

1 For instance, family farms are responsible for the production of cassava (87%), beans (70%), corn (46%), coffee (38%), rice (34%), milk (58%), pork (59%), birds (50%), beef (30%), and wheat (21%) consumed in Brazil (MDA, 2009).
2 Using data from the National Survey of Households (Pesquisa Nacional por Amostra de Domicilio/ PNAD) by the Brazilian Institute of Geography and Statistics (IBGE). See Melo and Di Sabbato 2006.

3 PRONAF is the National Program for the Strengthening of Family Farming (PRONAF) that offers small loans to family farmers (microfinance) to support their production with less bureaucracy and lower interest rates. It supports individual and collective projects that generate income to family farmers and settlements from the agrarian reform.
4 *Bolsa Familia* is currently the largest conditional cash transfer program in the world. For more, please see Rocha 2009.
5 *Quilombolas* are traditional communities formed originally mostly from escaped black slaves in Brazil. The Brazilian constitution of 1988 recognized their land rights.
6 Santos and Costa (2014) also reported that on average 60% of their income originated from the *Bolsa Familia* program.

References

Agarwal, Bina. 2010. *Gender and Green Governance: The Political Economy of Women's Presence Within and Beyond Community Forestry*. Oxford: Oxford University Press.
Azevedo, Heloisa, Francisca Barreto, and Maria Leila dos Santos. 2013. "A Participação de Mulheres como Critério de Avaliação dos Projetos do Programa de Aquisição de Alimentos." Paper presented at the Seminário Internacional Fazendo Gênero 10: Desafios Atuais dos Feminismos, Florianópolis, September 16–20.
Azevedo, Vilma M. 2012. "Os desafios para o Empoderamento da Mulher Agricultora a Partir do Programa de Aquisição de Alimentos: o Caso de Barbacena." Master's Thesis, Universidade Federal de Viçosa.
Bastide, Roger. 1957. *Brésil, terre des contrastes*. Paris, Éditions L'Harmattan.
BRIDGE. 2015. "Gender and Sustainable Development." *Gender Update 108*. www.bridge.ids.ac.uk/updates/gender-and-sustainable-development.
Brumer, Anita. 2008. "Gender Relations in Family-Farm Agriculture and Rural-Urban Migration in Brazil." *Latin American Perspectives* 35: 11–28.
Butto, Andrea. 2006a. "Políticas para as Mulheres Trabalhadoras Rurais: um Compromisso de Aodos os Dias." In *Gênero, Agricultura Familiar e Reforma Agrária no Mercosul*, 87–116. Brasília: Ministério do Desenvolvimento Agrário.
———. 2006b. "Prefácio." In *Agricultura Familiar e Gênero: Práticas, Movimentos e Políticas Públicas*, edited by Parry Scott and Rosineide Cordeiro, 9–15. Recife: Editora Universitária UFPE.
Butto, Andrea, Conceição Dantas, Karla Hora, Miriam Nobre, and Nalu Faria. 2014. *Mulheres Rurais e Autonomia: Formação e Articulação para efetivar Políticas Públicas nos Territórios da Cidadania*. Brasília, Ministério do Desencolvimento Agrário.
Butto, Andrea, and Renata Leite. 2010. "Políticas para as Mulheres Rurais no Brasil: Avanços Recentes e Desafios." Paper presented at the VIII Congreso Latinoamericano de Sociología Rural, Porto de Galinhas. Brazil.
CAISAN (Câmara Interministerial de Segurança Alimentar e Nutricional). 2014. *Balanço das Ações do Plano Nacional de Segurança Alimentar e Nutricional PLANSAN 2012/2015*. Brasilia: CONSEA. www4.planalto.gov.br/consea/publicacoes/balanco-plansan.
Câmara dos Deputados. 2014. "Agricultura Aprova Prioridade para Mulher na Venda de Alimento para Merenda Escolar." *Câmara Notícias*. www2.camara.leg.br/camaranoticias/noticias/AGROPECUARIA/465819-AGRICULTURA-APROVA-PRIORIDADE-PARA-MULHER-NA-VENDA-DE-ALIMENTO-PARA-MERENDA-ESCOLAR.html.

Chagas, Marcos. 2012. "Projeto Define Cota Mínima de Participação de Mulheres na Venda de Alimentos para a Merenda Escolar." *Notícia.* http://ultima-instancia. jusbrasil.com.br/noticias/3054634/projeto-define-cota-minima-a-mulheres-na-venda-de-alimentos-para-merenda-escolar.

CONAB (Companhia Nacional de Abastecimento). 2013. "Dispara a Participação das Mulheres no PAA." *Notícias.* March 15. www.conab.gov.br/imprensa-noticia. php?id=29303.

França, Caio Galvão, Mauro Eduardo Del Grossi, and Vicente Azevedo Marques. 2009. "O Censo Agropecuário 2006 e a Agricultura Familiar no Brasil." Brasília: Ministério do Desenvolvimento Agrário.

IBGE (Instituto Brasileiro de Geografia e Estatística). 2011. *Sinopse do Censo Demográfico 2010.* Rio de Janeiro: Ministério do Planejamento, Orçamento e Gestão and IBGE. www.ibge.gov.br/home/estatistica/populacao/censo2010/default_sinopse. shtm.

IFAD (International Fund for Agricultural Development). 2010. "Rural Poverty in Brazil." *Rural Poverty Portal.* www.ruralpovertyportal.org/country/home/tags/brazil.

———. 2011. "Habilitando os Pobres Rurais a Superar a Pobreza no Brasil." www. ifad.org/operations/projects/regions/PL/factsheet/brazil_p.pdf.

IPC-IG International Policy Centre for Inclusive Growth. 2013. *Structured Demand and Smallholder Farmers in Brazil: The Case of PAA and PNAE.* Brasília: International Policy Centre for Inclusive Growth.

IPEA (Instituto de Pesquisa Econômica Aplicada). 2014. *Objetivos de Desenvolvimento do Milênio – Relatório Nacional de Acompanhamento.* Brasília: Instituto de Pesquisa Econômica Aplicada.

MDA (Ministério do Desenvolvimento Agrário). 2009. "Censo Agropecuário 2006: Agricultura Familiar Produz Mais em Menor Área." *Portal MDA.* www. ecodebate.com.br/2009/10/01/censo-agropecuario-2006-agricultura-familiar-produz-mais-em-menor-area/.

———. 2013. "Oficinas visam ampliar acesso das mulheres rurais ao Programa de Aquisição de Alimentos." *Portal MDA.* http://portal.mda.gov.br/portal/noticias/ item?item_id=13835462.

MDS (Ministério do Desenvolvimento Social e Combate a Fome), Secretaria de Segurança Alimentar e Nutricional (SESAN), and Departamento de Apoio a Aquisição e a Comercialização de Produção Familiar (DECOM). 2014. *PAA – Programa de Aquisição de Alimentos: Manual Operativo: Modalidade de Compra com Doação Simultânea Operação por Meio de Termo de Adesão.* Brasília: MDS, SESAN and DECOM.

Melo, Hildete Pereira, and Alberto Di Sabbato. 2006. "Mulheres Rurais – Invisíveis e Mal Remuneradas." *Gênero, Agricultura Familiar e Reforma Agrária no Mercosul,* 47–86. Brasília: Ministério do Desenvolvimento Agrário.

Melo, Ligia Albuquerque. 2010. "A Mulher Agricultora: Relação Íntima com a Água." Paper presented at the Seminário Internacional Fazendo Gênero: Diásporas 9: Diversidades, Deslocamentos. Florianópolis, August 23–26.

Moraes, Andrea, and Cecilia Rocha. 2013. "Gendered waters: the Participation of Women in the 'One Million Cisterns': Rainwater Harvesting Program in the Brazilian Semi-Arid Region." *Journal of Cleaner Production* 60: 163–69.

Mota, Dalva Maria, Heribert Schmitz, and Josué Francisco da Silva Jr. 2013. "Políticas Públicas para as Mulheres Extrativistas: Reforço no Desenvolvimento Local?" Paper presented at 29th Congreso de la Asociacion de Sociologia. Santiago, Chile. Acta Cientifica FACSO. 2013. www.alice.cnptia.embrapa.br/handle/doc/976704

Rocha, Cecilia. 2009. "Developments in National Policies for Food and Nutrition Security in Brazil." *Development Policy Review* 27 (1): 51–66.

Rocha, Cecilia, Luciene Burlandy, and Ronaldo Maluf. 2012. "Small Farms and Sustainable Rural Development for Food Security: The Brazilian experience." *Development Southern Africa* 29 (4): 519–29.

Röhnelt, Priscila, and Giancarla Salamoni. 2010. "O Papel da Mulher nas Transformações da Agricultura Familiar: a Pluriatividade como Estratégia de Reprodução Social." Anais XVI Encontro Nacional de Geógrafos. Porto Alegre, July 25–31.

Santos, Cristiane Nascimento, and Edimare Ribeiro Costa. 2014. "A Inserção das Mulheres Agricultoras Familiares do Município de Seabra no PNAE: Uma Analise de Gênero." *Bahia: Análise e Dados* 24 (2): 349–63.

Siliprandi, Emma, and Rosangela Cintrão. 2011. "As Mulheres Agricultoras e Sua Participação no Programa de Aquisição de Alimentos (PAA)." *Segurança Alimentar e Nutricional* 18 (2): 12–32.

UN Women. (United Nations Entity for Gender Equality and the Empowerment of Women). 2014. *The World Survey on the Role of Women in Development 2014: Gender Equality and Sustainable Development.* www.unwomen.org/en/digital-library/publications/2014/10/world-survey-2014

Wichterich, Christa. 2012. *The Future We Want: A Feminist Perspective.* Publication Series on Ecology, No. 21. Berlin: Heinrich Böll Stiftung.

13 The rise of institutional food procurement

A tool for empowering women or furthering the status quo?

Bryan Crawford-Garrett, Clare Mbizule, Karin Wachter, and Brian Sage

Introduction

The growth over the last several years of food procurement through institutional demand markets in the developing world represents a significant opportunity for women in agriculture. Institutional demand (ID) refers to public, demand-side market interventions in which markets are established and facilitated by a public or not-for-profit institution – a host-country government, multilateral agency, or non-governmental organization (NGO). Programs that include ID purchasing often promote social welfare objectives that provide preferential procurement terms for the smallholder farmer,[1] such as a guaranteed price at harvest, seeking to address the problem that even with support on inputs and improved techniques, small-scale farmers might not invest the additional resources if they are not certain to sell the surplus. In this way, institutional purchases of food commodities from local farmers by public or not-for-profit sector entities present opportunities to improve access to market outlets for smallholder farmers and even more particularly for female smallholders. An increase in targeted demand from an institutional buyer, however, may not stimulate a supply-side response if resource-constrained smallholders do not have access to improved inputs or the know-how to increase production to meet the demand. As a result, for ID procurement to succeed in sourcing from smallholders, supply-side interventions in agricultural production and marketing are often typically also required.

This chapter presents a theory of change (ToC) and theoretical framework for increasing women's engagement in ID programming, along with concrete examples of certain components of the framework from the UN World Food Programme (WFP) Purchase for Progress (P4P) pilot program. In this way, the chapter considers how theory and practice might be leveraged to improve opportunities for women smallholder farmers and offers lessons that can help to inform other ID and broader agricultural development programs that still struggle to improve outcomes for female farmers. While the examples provided

Figure 13.1 Female farmers in a paddy rice field in Bangladesh. ©WFP/Shebab Uddin.

and much of the literature cited in the chapter are from Sub-Saharan Africa, the framework was developed for general use in ID programming in places where significant inequalities between male and female farmers exist.

The chapter proceeds as follows: after this introduction we provide an overview of the current status quo for women smallholder farmers in agriculture in the developing world. We then discuss the WFP-P4P experience, including concrete successes and challenges related to women's engagement programming during the P4P pilot, in which activities were implemented from 2009–2013. This is followed by our presentation of the theoretical framework, which was originally developed based on learning from the P4P experience along with the experiences of other agencies implementing ID projects – most notably the Alliance for a Green Revolution in Africa (AGRA), the Partnership for Child Development (PCD) at Imperial College, and SNV (Netherlands Development Organisation), as well as a review of the literature and consultations conducted in June 2013 with practitioners with expertise in gender and agricultural development. In this manner, the framework theory benefits from and is grounded in practice and learning across a number of contexts. After the theoretical framework we offer a discussion of a number of relevant themes that are important for future consideration and then concludes the chapter.

The status quo: challenges and risks for female farmers

Many of the challenges that women smallholder farmers face in the developing world, especially as compared to their male counterparts, are well documented in the literature (see for example Quisumbing and Pandolfelli 2010 and O'Sullivan et al. 2014, among others). These same constraints are present within programming that introduces the purchasing of food crops through an ID buyer. Indeed, in many geographic areas where smallholders have access to some level of market opportunities, in addition to the injection of demand through the institutional buyer there must be accompanying supply-side support for improving production and marketing in order for smallholders to benefit (Sumberg and Sabates-Wheeler 2010). This is even more the case for women smallholders, given the immense obstacles they face.

First and foremost, women farmers have less access than men to productive resources and assets, including land, water, labor, agricultural inputs (seeds, tools, fertilizers, etc.), technologies, and financial, human (specifically the gender gap in levels of education), and social capital (O'Sullivan et al. 2014). As a result, women's productivity suffers, and opportunities for increasing production and capacity are limited. Land in particular may be the most critical asset for the rural poor, and there is evidence linking secure land rights for women with household wellbeing (Landesa 2012). Moreover, secure land rights are often seen as fundamental for investment and improving productivity (Deininger 2003). Second, women often have significantly greater household-level workloads and responsibilities than their male partners, have less access to technologies that would reduce their farming-related labor (O'Sullivan et al. 2014), and have less access to hired farming labor (Udry 1996; O'Sullivan et al. 2014). Each of these disadvantages has a negative impact on production and marketing potential and can also result in women taking their younger daughters (but not sons) out of school to work on the farm or help with household tasks (Quisumbing and Pandolfelli 2010). Third, women have less control over resources and decisions in the household and community (Mehra and Rojas 2008). Finally, agricultural polices often do not take women's needs into consideration (Quisumbing 2003). Policies that make no distinction around gender can further institutionalize and exacerbate the gap between male and female farmers.

In addition to the general challenges female farmers often face, there are also risks involved in the introduction of programming that targets women's empowerment, especially given the deep structural roots of gender inequality throughout much of the world. Although women's income earning can provoke positive change and begin to improve the status quo – if seen as adding to the household's overall income – women may face backlash or pushback for their participation in economic empowerment activities, including the potential for an increased risk of violence (Some and Hildyard 2013; Vyas and Watts 2009). Women farmers also often face gender-specific barriers to market participation, and intentionally engaging women in new or expanded market opportunities opens up a second risk: once there is a formal market opportunity at a profitable scale for traditional women's crops, men may take over production and/or marketing of the crop (The World Bank, Food and Agriculture Organization, and International Fund for Agricultural

Development 2009). A third risk relates to women's resources. Women have heavy workloads and any activities that engage women must consider the time requirements and impacts on the women and their households. Without such consideration, there is a risk that female-friendly agricultural development programming can inadvertently over-burden women's time and physical and emotional energy by placing additional responsibility on them versus other members of the household to increase household income.

The current state of program capacities of implementing agencies involved in gender-specific agricultural development and ID programming is also a significant barrier to increasing impacts on women smallholders. Consultations with practitioners revealed that while organizations struggle to introduce change at the strategy level, it is even more difficult for program staff at the implementation or field level to challenge systemic and cultural barriers female smallholders face. Moreover, staff in the field often do not have the skills, knowledge, or impetus to do this sensitive work – or to do it well – because it is already challenging enough to work with those better positioned to participate in agricultural development initiatives (typically men, typically not the poorest) or within existing structures. Male farmers, for instance, are far easier to access, as men in the developing world are by and large more educated than women (Mehra and Rojas 2008), more likely to have been reached by extension services than women (The World Bank and International Food Policy Research Institute 2010), more likely to be in farmer producer groups or cooperatives (Mehra and Rojas 2008), and anecdotally more likely to hold positions of leadership in such groups (Aris 2013). As farmer groups and extension services are two of the main avenues for working with poor farmers, and current systems are effectively more accessible to men, it takes a concerted and deliberate effort to work closely with women farmers.

Intentional interventions for women within ID programs are critical to ensure that benefits accrue for women smallholders and their households; not doing so risks further institutionalizing and potentially widening the gap between men and women farmers. Transforming the status quo therefore requires improving women's access to and use of productive resources and assets, coupled with shifts in power dynamics and structures at the household, community, and institutional levels.

Introducing the WFP Purchase for Progress experience

The United Nations World Food Programme's (WFP) Purchase for Progress (P4P) initiative is one program whose experience helps provide a solid linkage between the challenges and risks articulated in the preceding section and the theoretical framework introduced in the next section. The P4P initiative – launched as a five-year pilot in 2008 covering 20 countries[2] – combined the leverage offered by WFP's institutional purchasing power with capacity-building efforts of supply-side partners, as P4P used pro-smallholder procurement mechanisms coupled with production and marketing support to link smallholder production of staple crops to WFP purchases and to support and incentivize smallholders to access other formal markets. Over the five years since the inception of P4P, smallholders have delivered staple crops valued at nearly US$150 million for use in WFP's food assistance programs.

From the beginning, P4P was conscious of the project's potential to positively impact female smallholders' economic opportunities and set a goal of having 50 percent women participants. However, the challenges of reaching this numerical target along with the need to consider programming impact beyond mere participation numbers became quickly apparent. In particular, women were required to be members of a farmer organization to access the procurement opportunity offered by WFP, but the predominantly mixed-gender farmer organizations participating in the P4P program had low proportions of women members and leaders. In addition, fewer women than men were actually involved in the sales to WFP and the average volumes they contributed were lower than for men. In the third year of the initiative WFP commissioned the Agriculture Learning Impacts Network (ALINe) to work with P4P staff to define strategies and boundaries for how P4P could most meaningfully promote the economic empowerment of women smallholders beyond the set numerical targets.

Based on the P4P experience, a number of important lessons emerge related to addressing many of the issues women smallholders face:

1. Consider ways of engaging with and shifting household and community power dynamics

The P4P Global Gender Strategy noted that the overwhelming majority of rural communities where P4P works "are characterised by male-dominated cultures, which are used to justify and even legitimise inequalities in gender relations ... To bring about change it is necessary to work towards changing mindsets, and to support women in their constant process of negotiation to achieve change in their unequal position" (UN World Food Programme 2011, 13). Yet, access to and control of money influences the power dynamics at household and community levels. One P4P-supported female farmer in Zambia, speaking to WFP staff during a routine project monitoring visit, noted, for instance, that "a person with money and assets is given respect whether or not they are a woman." P4P has used its ability to place money directly in the hands of women selling staple commodities to WFP as a powerful entry point into the dialogue about the role and rights of women. No proxies are allowed to receive payment on behalf of any woman who registers a contribution to a collective sale made to WFP. Local financial institutions have played their part by easing account opening procedures and ensuring that banking services better meet the needs of both literate and non-literate smallholders. Women have been encouraged to opt for payment into their bank accounts to enhance security of their financial transactions and also increase their control over the resources earned from their labor.

On a sobering note, as mentioned in the preceding section more income in the hands of women can potentially result in forceful male resistance to their partners' growing economic empowerment and every effort must be made to avoid increasing women's vulnerability both inside and outside the home. P4P has worked to address this issue by situating gender equality as an economic issue, stressing to both men and women the gains to be realized through fully including women in agricultural value chains and providing them with productive resources, including land. P4P developed and used a household negotiation tool for this purpose. The essence of the negotiation approach was to emphasize the economic benefits of the inclusive management of household resources, through looking at household budgets, decision-making between men and women, and who holds power and control of productive resources in the household. This simple yet deliberate move to improve communication between men and women within their households gained the support of men and customary leaders – the power holders and gatekeepers often with the most influence in these settings. This is evident in some of the actions that have resulted from P4P's work with women, such as communities granting women joint access to land in a very conservative society in Mali, and allowing the women as a collective to grow and sell sorghum which is generally regarded as a crop for men (and not for women) to plant and sell. In the case of Mali, a local village chief sanctioned the allocation of land to the women based on the positive results he had seen from their participation in P4P.

Women are therefore increasingly leveraging their affiliation to P4P as a negotiation tool to help win support at both intra-household and community levels. Because of the tangible economic benefits that women can show from their participation in the program, men seem more inclined to see their wives as key partners in advancing the welfare of the household and community rather than as a threat with potential to destroy the social order.

2. *Promote women's participation in beneficial aggregation structures or institutional purchasing mechanisms*

By acting collectively, smallholder farmers are able to increase the volume and quality of commodities sold within a single transaction, making them a more attractive supplier to the better paying institutional buyers. A number of options exist for collective action. P4P worked primarily through farmer organizations, but also facilitated the linkage of smallholder farmers to commodity exchanges and warehouse receipt systems. Each has challenges. In the case of farmer organizations, men tend to dominate both membership and leadership of farmer organizations, particularly when membership is tied to land ownership. As the prevailing sociocultural framework in many P4P countries privileges land ownership towards men, very few women meet the essential criteria of land ownership which would allow them to register as members of the farmer organizations with which WFP contracted for the supply of staple commodities. To address this issue, the P4P program incorporated more women-only organizations and set targets for mixed-gender farmer organizations wishing to remain part of the P4P program. Over the lifetime of the pilot, the proportion of women in P4P-supported farmer organizations rose from 19 percent in 2009 to 29 percent at the end of 2013. Moreover, WFP found that "this result is significantly skewed by the data from Ethiopia which accounts for half a million of the global P4P farmers' membership and yet just 13 percent of members in P4P-affiliated FOs in Ethiopia are women. When the participation of women in FOs is considered in the absence of Ethiopia, the current global female membership rises to 48%" (UN World Food Programme, 2014, 26). In addition, the proportion of female leaders reached 36 percent by the end of the pilot; this increase may be attributable to gender awareness training on the benefits of having women participate in the leadership and providing leadership and literacy training to women to help them gain confidence in their abilities.

P4P supported smallholder participation in commodity exchanges and warehouse receipt systems in Uganda, Ethiopia, Zambia, and Malawi. In Malawi, the Agricultural Commodity Exchange (ACE) established local certi-fied warehouses close to targeted farming communities. Individuals or groups deposited any volume of produce in exchange for a receipt of acknowledg-ment against which they could borrow funds from a participating bank. The loans were repaid on sale of the crops and the farmer received the balance of funds remaining after deduction of interest as well as storage and cleaning fees. P4P Malawi encouraged women farmers to use this solution as it allowed women to access a remunerative quality market in close proximity that was willing to accept small volumes and provided access to an immediate cash advance on delivery of their produce into the warehouse.

3. Women's participation is a necessary but insufficient condition to change the status quo

While the P4P initiative was ultimately able to achieve a 300 percent increase in the actual numerical representation of women in P4P-supported farmer organizations, this alone was not sufficient to achieve gender equity in two important respects: the number of women contributors and the volumes they contributed towards WFP contracts was invariably lower than for their male counterparts. For example, between 2010 and 2012 in Kenya, women accounted for 44 percent of the contributors but just 32 percent of the aggregated quantity. As well, annual earnings from participation in collective sales were on average $48 per woman as compared to $68 per man. Globally, women have earned about 38 percent of the total amount paid out to smallholder farmers under the P4P program (UN World Food Programme 2014).

To address these differences, farmer organizations were encouraged to pri-oritize the purchase of crops from women farmers when fulfilling WFP con-tracts. Women's participation was monitored through contribution records submitted to WFP either directly with the payment invoice or through regular reporting at quarterly intervals. Over time, WFP also increased the procurement of pulses, which are more traditionally farmed and controlled by women. P4P partners also stepped up efforts to improve women's access to farming inputs and public extension services where opportunity allowed. Across the implementing countries, the contributions of women have increased over time, especially for certain crops. By 2012, in Burkina Faso, for example, 100 percent of the 102 metric tons of cowpeas procured by WFP from P4P-supported farmer organizations were supplied by women, compared with less than 20 percent in 2009 (see Figure 13.2 below).

4.   *Address individual women smallholder labor and time constraints as a priority*

In the absence of support to reduce women's labor burdens and ease time constraints, women's ability to participate in farmer organizations and occupy leadership positions will continue to be severely limited. With this reality in mind, P4P prioritized the provision of time and labor saving technologies that benefit women, supporting the provision of equipment ranging from simple manual tools to more sophisticated mechanical devices. Equipment such as manual and motorized maize-shellers, tractors, rippers, and milling machines were provided to facilitate production and post-harvest activities. These were complemented by appropriate technologies to facilitate quality enhancement such as tarpaulins, rice parboiling equipment, and bag stitching machines. The choice of a technology in each case was based on its relevance to the local

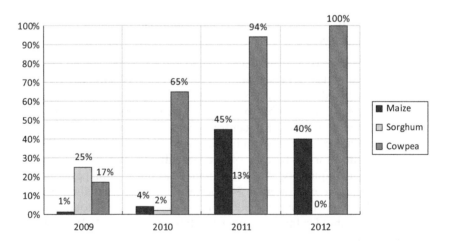

Figure 13.2 Percentage of P4P-participating farmer organization stocks in Burkina Faso contributed by women, by crop.

Source: WFP monitoring data – Burkina Faso.

context, as well as to women's needs, and was provided on a full or partial cost recovery basis. Some tools were targeted for individual household use while others were to be used and managed collectively by the farmer organization or by entrepreneurial members of the community who could run the equipment as a business, providing services to members of the community at large. The introduction of semi- and fully-mechanized post-harvest equipment prompted a transformation of the dynamics of the traditional gender division of labor, as the project saw that men more readily took over the performance of chores such as shelling that would normally be considered women's work thus freeing up women's time. However, caution had to be exercised to ensure that men would not impede women's power to control and benefit fully from the technologies provided (UN World Food Programme 2014).

From practice to theory: a theoretical framework for transforming the status quo

The theoretical framework detailed in this section lays out how women smallholders can begin to overcome the challenges they face at individual, household, community, and structural levels in terms of gender inequality in agricultural production and marketing. Development of the framework benefited from many of the lessons learned from the P4P experience as well as experiences of other agencies implementing or supporting ID programming – most notably AGRA, PCD, and SNV – across a variety of countries and contexts, coupled with a review of the literature and practitioner consultations. The P4P experience in particular helped lead to the focus on dynamics within the household, based on the recognition that household power structures must change so that more money in women's hands can be an asset rather than a liability. The theory found in the framework is therefore deeply informed by practice and existing empirical evidence.

The framework suggests an emphasis on the smallholder farmer *household* as a locus of gender transformative change. Specifically, this locus of change involves shifting intra-familial dynamics so that profits and sales are invested back into businesses and the household, with women engaged in decision-making processes. This type of change requires moving beyond traditional frameworks focused on individual productivity gains or on women's individual sales or incomes to reflect the reality that smallholder agriculture is frequently a household activity, and one that involves significant female labor (O'Sullivan et al. 2014). The framework further posits that while the highest-level result is focused on the household, to achieve that result change must occur at multiple levels: individual, household, community, and structural.

Three hypotheses underpin the framework: (i) households are more productive when women famers are meaningfully engaged in agricultural opportunities, enabling them to directly benefit from those opportunities and have influence over the benefits produced from them; (ii) women are more likely than men to reinvest their income in the health and well-being of the family when they have the opportunity to do so (Quisumbing 2003; Thomas 1997); (iii) and to bring about meaningful change benefiting women, men, and their families, a range of interventions are required targeting the individual, household, community, and structural levels. These hypotheses highlight the extent to which ID interventions can maximize impact only through the inclusion of women.

Theory of change

The detailed theory of change (ToC), illustrated in Figure 13.3, shows three main channels of causal logic focused at the individual, household, and structural (enabling environment) levels, with community also being incorporated as part of each of the three main levels. While these can be considered stand-alone pathways with their own set of specialized interventions that would spark the intended chain of events, they are also interrelated, as indicated by the arrows showing the horizontal and vertical relationships amongst the various components of the ToC. In addition, change is necessary in each of the three main pathways to lead to the framework's ultimate goal of smallholder households managing and investing profits and sales back into the household with the explicit involvement of women in the decision-making process.

Long-term and highest-level outcomes/goals. The three main pathways contribute to the framework's ultimate goal of smallholder households strategically managing and investing profits and revenues back into the business and household with the explicit involvement of women in the decision-making process. This higher-level outcome is also linked to other long-term broad agricultural development goals, including increasing income from agricultural sales and improving overall household welfare of smallholder farmer families.

Individual and community level: Women smallholder production and marketing capacities increase. In order for women's production and marketing capacities to increase, four shorter-term outcomes should be achieved. The first is that women smallholders have access to key productive resources and assets, including but not limited to: inputs, land, labor, saving/credit and other financial services, water, and gender-appropriate agricultural technology. The second is that women smallholders have increased knowledge and skills related to production and marketing. The third is that women smallholders have the opportunity to participate in farmer organizations and hold formal membership in the group. This would include formal registration, regular participation, receipt of benefits and contribution to decision-making as an equal member. Additionally, they would have the opportunity to take on leadership positions within the farmer organizations, and receive training and mentorship to be effective in those roles. The fourth, shorter-term, outcome is that women, through the farmer organizations, would have the opportunity to expand their social networks and access social support from other women, which reduces isolation and can support in the uptake of new practices and technologies.

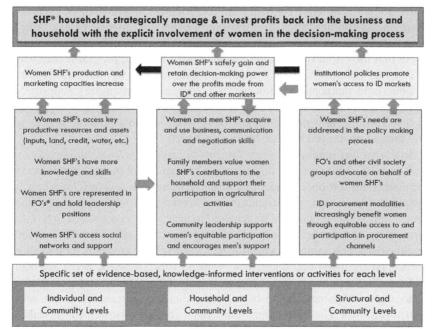

Figure 13.3 Theory of change for women's engagement in institutional demand programming.[3]

Household and community level: Women smallholders safely gain and retain decision-making power over profits from ID and other market sales. While women may significantly contribute to their household's agricultural production and increase their abilities to market their own and/or their household's production, they may not have control over decisions regarding production or the sale of the produce. No matter the additional production and/or marketing capacities women may attain, they will not fully reap the benefits if they lack control over planning, sales, and how to spend/ invest profits within the household.

There are three shorter-term outcomes required to bring about this change. The first is that men and women acquire and use business, communication, and negotiation skills. This might involve inviting household members (i.e., couples) to reflect upon their household's financial well-being and the value of women's contributions to the household, as well as to learn concrete financial planning skills. The second is that family members value women's contributions to the household and support their participation in agricultural activities by pooling their resources to contribute to the myriad of responsibilities women typically carry so as not to unduly tax women's time and energy or sacrifice daughters' educations by pulling them from school to help cover household activities. The third is that the community leadership supports women's equitable participation in agricultural development programming and encourages men to contribute in the best interest of the family/household. Given the sensitivity around household finances and a common norm that men hold the cash and decide how it is spent, programs may want to consider behavior change components that support women's involvement in household financial decision-making. Increasing community support for changes in how households approach financial decision-making along gender lines is an important programmatic consideration and a possible way to try and mitigate potential risks of harm to women.

Structural and community level: Institutional policies promote women's access to ID markets. Given gender disparities and pragmatic obstacles women face in the market, institutional policies that promote women's access to ID markets are instrumental to making the agricultural market more accessible to women. Three shorter-term outcomes should be achieved to increase this access. The first is that farmer organizations and other civil society groups advocate on behalf of women smallholders. This joint advocacy at the local level will ensure achievement of the second short-term outcome: that women's context-specific needs are being addressed in the policy-making process around land ownership and access, inheritance rights, infrastructure, access to legal rights and representation, and other related priorities. The third related outcome is that ID procurement modalities increasingly benefit women through equitable access to and participation in procurement channels. This could include, for example, promoting and increasing demand for women-led crops (such as, depending on the context, certain vegetables, cowpeas, groundnuts, etc.), more decentralized procurement models and/or procurement of smaller quantities than are often purchased for many of the male-dominated staple crops, using mechanisms such as the warehouse receipt system that provides cash on delivery, and using contracting mechanisms that best meet the needs of female farmers. This would also potentially include having local social accountability measures in place to track implementation of policies promoting women's participation in ID markets at the local level.

Discussion

A number of the challenges and opportunities for women's participation in ID programming are not unique, but also apply to other agriculture development programs that might specifically target women. For example, understanding the starting point for change for women requires deep contextual knowledge combined with an understanding of the potential impact and limitations for specific programming approaches, as no single intervention can alone address the breadth of challenges women face in agriculture. To ensure the greatest effect, it is important to implement a coherent and precise approach focused on those changes that a given program can most effectively or efficiently influence, and the specific actions that will help bring about those changes. P4P's global gender strategy for instance identified persistent constraints for women

Figure 13.4 A female farmer in San Pablo Village in Colombia at work. ©WFP/
Paul Smith.

smallholders and articulated corresponding general objectives with menus of
activities that set the vision and boundaries of what P4P aimed to achieve
through its gender-related activities (UN World Food Programme 2011).

Rather than a one-size fits-all approach, the P4P strategy provided a concrete framework from which to tailor contextually appropriate activities that
best fit the sociocultural, political, and bureaucratic environment in their specific settings, based on the recognition that women from smallholder farmer
families in the developing world are not a homogenous group: they are not all
legally married, not all cohabitating with a male partner and many live within
a polygamous family structure. Furthermore, women may or may not be producers of agricultural products typically sought by ID or other markets; they
may be unpaid laborers in their households; they may contribute to some or
all aspects of agricultural production; and they may even be landless laborers
contributing to other households' production.

The policies that will be necessary for promotion of women's production,
sales, and control over profits will additionally be context-specific. Such
context-specific policies may focus on women's access to and legal rights
(in practice) to land; women's legal and customary rights to inherit land;
ID procurement mechanisms that will ensure the most equitable access for
women smallholders; investments in local infrastructure that reflect the priorities of women vis-à-vis their agricultural ambitions (e.g., water systems,

transportation, schools, etc.); women's legal rights to sign contracts; and access to legal representation.

The systematic focus on the household level proposed in the ToC presented above reflects the reality that, for smallholder farmers, agricultural production is almost always a family endeavor. Moreover, it is an opportunity to conceptualize that endeavor as a family business, in which women's explicit involvement is essential to bolster and maximize productivity, as well as to encourage the reinvestment of profits back into the household. The family risks not truly realizing the benefits of increased sales if additional revenues (or the financial rewards) are not then reinvested into the family priorities related to education, health and nutrition, priorities often emphasized more by women. Therefore, programming should not stop at investing in interventions that seek to increase female farmer agricultural production and sales, as programming needs to go further to address power dynamics in the household as well as in the community to increase women's ability to influence decision-making about how sales and profits from agricultural production are used and re-invested back into the household and household business. Women need to be safe and supported in contributing to decision-making often not considered within the purview of a woman's role, and men need the opportunity to consider new approaches to collaborating with their partners and other female family members in the best interest of the household.

While it is necessary to build the individual capacities of women to increase production and engage in market activities, this individual focus is not sufficient, because women live and operate within larger structures. Women will only be able to operate as productive market agents if household, community, and larger social forces support their economic empowerment. In households, farmer organizations, and communities, women need to have influence over investment decisions, especially from income that results from their economic activity. In addition, local leaders must support the participation of women in the marketplace, and policy frameworks must be established that protect the economic rights and interests of women.

At the level of implementation, gender-transformative ID programming requires atypical skillsets for program delivery. Many of the programmatic approaches and interventions which may have the greatest impact on women gaining and retaining decision-making power are not as typically related to agriculture techniques. Changes related to issues like land tenure and household decision-making are more associated with behavior change and the enabling environment, rather than purely technical agricultural production interventions. These kinds of programs require specialized skillsets, different staff profiles, and integrated program models in order to achieve meaningful change for women. Providing skill-based training, not limited to "gender" but specific to carrying out particular components of a gender transformative program, must be part and parcel of engaging women and men, so as to facilitate new opportunities, avoid reinforcing unequal social norms and ensure change promotes women's safety and well-being. Integrated programming and gender mainstreaming is often times difficult for specialized, international organizations to achieve; however with the proper toolkits, mindsets, and staff there can be opportunity for change.

Conclusion: looking forward

The theory of change presented in this chapter can be adapted and improved upon as different programs and activities identify how to support greater engagement and participation of women in ID programs. This would entail a dialogue which continues beyond this chapter and this book, and should involve communities themselves, implementing organizations, local and international institutions, donors, governments, researchers, and other relevant stakeholders. While understanding and documentation of gender gaps have increased, there are far fewer consistent program models which have documented what works for improving engagement of women in agriculture, to which ID brings an additional perspective.

There is still a limited body of evidence about what works and does not work to overcome the myriad challenges and risks women encounter in agriculture. Research initiatives to better understand the various components of the ToC above are important to refine approaches for field-based programming. Rigorous impact and process evaluations, as well as strong quantitative and qualitative monitoring, can be synthesized and shared to help further develop collective learning around impacts of ID programming on female smallholders. It will be of particular importance for institutions that implement ID activities to develop and use mechanisms to track and disaggregate information at the smallholder level for different procurement modalities across various types of crops. Specific strands of further ID program research could include: determining the procurement policies and modalities (in terms of sizes of purchases, types of crops, contract types, etc.) that benefit women under certain contexts and conditions; considering differing impacts of focusing on female smallholder farmers as opposed to all female farmers in targeted areas and the implications of each approach (recognizing that the majority will be smallholders but those that have greater resource and asset bases are less likely to be smallholders and more likely to be early adopters); the usefulness of considering a focus on women's engagement at the household level; and best practices for risk mitigation to address the greatest risks inherent in ID programming focused on women.

Finally, the success of future efforts to empower women through ID depends upon four interrelated factors: (i) deep understanding and analysis of the specific contexts of ID programming; (ii) ambitious program design that intentionally promotes greater women's participation in institutional markets and recognizes the household as the locus of change; (iii) implementation of activities by staff that have adequate skills, attitudes, and knowledge to carry out their work; (iv) and robust measurement systems that not only disaggregate data by gender, but also assess how and why changes are or are

not happening for women. While women stand to benefit greatly from institutional food procurement, focused effort is required to achieve such change;
otherwise, the status quo will continue unabated.

Acknowledgment

Please note that some of the information in this chapter – especially around
the detailed theory of change that we present – was developed through work
that Oxu Solutions did for the Bill & Melinda Gates Foundation in 2013, when
Oxu worked with the foundation and grantees within the Structured Demand
portfolio to develop a theory of change explicitly for women's engagement in
Structured Demand (SD) programming. The World Food Programme (WFP)
Purchase for Progress initiative was one of the four SD grantees (along with
the Alliance for a Green Revolution in Africa (AGRA), the Partnership
for Child Development (PCD) at Imperial College, and SNV (Netherlands
Development Organisation). The findings and conclusions contained within
the chapter are those of the authors and do not necessarily reflect positions
or policies of the Bill & Melinda Gates Foundation.

Finally, the current version of this chapter benefited from the review of
Musa Kpaka and Vicki Wilde at the Bill & Melinda Gates Foundation.
Previous versions of the theoretical framework were reviewed by staff from
the foundation as well as AGRA, PCD, SNV, and WFP.

Notes

1 The term "smallholder farmer" has no universally accepted definition, and the definition can vary by country based on the local context (including level of agricultural development, land availability, etc.). For example, in more densely populated
  and fertile areas smallholders often cultivate less than one hectare, whereas in more
  sparsely, semi-arid geographies a "smallholder" could cultivate ten or more hectares.
  In spite of this, smallholders throughout the world do share a number of characteristics. Generally speaking, they are poor, have limited and low productivity assets, rely
  heavily on family labor, and have limited access to other productive resources.
2 The P4P pilot countries included: Afghanistan, Burkina Faso, Democratic Republic
  of Congo, El Salvador, Ethiopia, Ghana, Guatemala, Honduras, Kenya, Liberia,
  Malawi, Mali, Mozambique, Nicaragua, Rwanda, Sierra Leone, South Sudan,
  Tanzania, Uganda, and Zambia.
3 Figure 13.3 is adapted from the work done by Oxu Solutions with input from
  Structured Demand grantees for the Bill & Melinda Gates Foundation, as mentioned in the Acknowledgment.

References

Aris, Giselle. 2013. "Challenging Barriers to Women's Leadership in Cooperatives."
    Shoreview, MN: Land O'Lakes International Development. http://agrilinks.org/
    sites/default/files/resource/files/Challenging%20Barriers%20to%20Women's%20
    Leadership%20in%20Cooperatives%20-%20FINAL.pdf.

Deininger, Klaus. 2003. *Land Policies for Growth and Poverty Reduction.* Washington, DC: The World Bank and Oxford University Press.

Landesa. 2012. "Issue Brief: Women's Secure Rights to Land: Benefits, Barriers, and Best Practices." Seattle, WA: Landesa. www.landesa.org/wp-content/uploads/Landesa-Women-and-Land-Issue-Brief.pdf.

Mehra, Rekha, and Mary Hill Rojas. 2008. "A Significant Shift: Women, Food Security and Agriculture in a Global Marketplace." Washington, DC: International Center for Research on Women (ICRW). www.icrw.org/files/publications/A-Significant-Shift-Women-Food%20Security-and-Agriculture-in-a-Global-Marketplace.pdf.

O'Sullivan, Michael, Arathi Rao, Raka Banerjee, Kajal Gulati, and Margaux Vinez. 2014. "Levelling the Field: Improving Opportunities for Women Farmers in Africa." Washington, DC: The World Bank and One Campaign. http://documents.worldbank.org/curated/en/2014/01/19243625/levelling-field-improving-opportunities-women-farmers-africa.

Quisumbing, Agnes. 2003. "What Have We Learned from Research on Intra-household Allocation?" In *Household Decisions, Gender, and Development: A Synthesis of Recent Research*, edited by Agnes Quisumbing,. Washington, DC: International Food Policy Research Institute. http://ebrary.ifpri.org/cdm/ref/collection/p15738coll2/id/126037

Quisumbing, Agnes, and Lauren Pandolfelli. 2010. "Promising Approaches to Address the Needs of Poor Female Farmers: Resources, Constraints, and Interventions." *World Development* 38 (4): 581–92. doi:10.1016/j.worlddev.2009.10.006

Some, Batamaka, and Leigh Hildyard. 2013. *Female Smallholder Farmers Empowerment: Understanding Gender Subtleties and Preserving Household Harmony; Learnings from WFP.* Rome: World Food Programme.

Sumberg, James, and Rachel Sabates-Wheeler. 2010. "Linking Agriculture Development to School Feeding." *PCD Working Paper no. 213*, London: Institute of Development Studies and Partnership for Childhood Development.

Thomas, Duncan. 1997. "Incomes, Expenditures, and Health Outcomes: Evidence on Intrahousehold Resource Allocation." In *Intrahousehold Resource Allocation in Developing Countries*, edited by Lawrence Haddad, John Hoddinott, and Harold Alderman, 142–64. Baltimore: Johns Hopkins University Press.

Udry, Chris. 1996. "Gender, Agricultural Production, and the Theory of the Household." *Journal of Political Economy* 104 (5): 1010–46.

UN World Food Programme. 2014. *P4P Women's Empowerment Pathways: Roadblocks and Successes.* Rome: WFP. http://documents.wfp.org/stellent/groups/public/documents/special_initiatives/wfp265434.pdf.

———. 2011. *P4P Global Gender Strategy.* Rome: WFP.

Vyas, Seema, and Charlotte Watts. 2009. "How Does Economic Empowerment Affect Women's Risk of Intimate Partner Violence in Low and Middle Income Countries? A Systematic Review of Published Evidence." *Journal of International Development* 21 (5): 577–602. doi: 10.1002/jid.1500

World Bank, Food and Agriculture Organization, and International Fund for Agricultural Development. 2009. *Gender in Agriculture: Sourcebook.* Washington, DC: The World Bank.

World Bank, and International Food Policy Research Institute. 2010. *Gender and Governance in Rural Services: Insights from India, Ghana, and Ethiopia.* Washington, DC: The World Bank.

Part IV
Working for social change

Morocco

14 From empowerment to transformative leadership

Intersectional analysis of women workers in the strawberry sector of Morocco

Julie Théroux-Séguin

Introduction

"Be careful with the strawberries because they're worth more than you."[1] This statement was shared by a woman worker explaining the type of verbal violence many women workers are facing in the strawberry sector. She said it with a smile. Amused. As if mocking the insults of the supervisors gave her the strength to face these indignant situations. How do you go from accepting this verbal and physical violence every day, not receiving the salary and getting the working conditions you should according to the labor code, to being a "women promoter", an "activist," engaging with other women and other influencing actors, to claim your rights, but more so, to claim your dignity as workers, as women?

This chapter looks at the stories of female workers in the agricultural sector of Morocco, focusing especially on two structural issues identified here as the normalization of women's hardship and the challenges caused by gender stereotypes. Acknowledging the possible bias this could introduce, their stories will be told and analyzed from the point of view of a development worker specialized in gender and involved in this field for more than ten years, born and raised in a western country with no personal religious inclination.

To set the scene, the overall context of agriculture in Morocco will be presented with a specific focus on the strawberry sector. Then, details of some of the difficulties women workers are facing in terms of having their rights and dignity respected will be outlined. Through the testimonies of women workers, the two structural issues will be explored using intersectionality to demonstrate how the different oppressive systems at play (e.g., colonialism, sexism, and classism) are structuring women workers' discrimination. Intersectionality allows us to illustrate the enabling factors supporting women's empowerment, not only to enrich the construction of a sensitive development program but also to understand how women themselves can challenge the inequality patterns in their environment and enhance their ability to use the tools provided by external initiatives (national or international) to become actors of change. Finally, the chapter will present how a Transformative Leadership for Women's Rights strategy can contribute to sustainable changes in practice, but also in attitudes and beliefs.

Context and issues[2]

In April 2008, the Moroccan government presented its new agricultural development strategy up to 2015, the Green Morocco Plan (GMP), which included poverty reduction among its objectives. The Green Morocco Plan intended to make agriculture one of the main drivers of the Moroccan economy, particularly through mobilizing investment, creating jobs, increasing exports and their value, and land use planning. However, according to public documentation, the GMP does not strive to address gender inequality in this sector.

In the Loukkos and Gharb Chrarda Beni Hssen (GCBH) region, the GMP aimed to increase the scope of production of berries and the potential export market. Over the past 15 years, Morocco has increased its production of berries from 10,000 tons in 1995 (FAO 2014) to 150,000 tons in the 2013–2014 season according to the Regional Office of Agricultural Development of Loukkos (ORMVAL 2014), for a total cultivated area of 4,400 hectares. The sector is characterized by the presence of large farms, 12 percent of farms with more than 20 hectares, and a strong presence of industrial foreign investors (Oxfam 2010, 5). Due to the added value of berries, 75 percent of berry production is exported (ORMVAL 2013). In 2013, Morocco was the fourth largest exporter of processed strawberries (frozen, chopped, or in purée) and the eleventh largest exporter of fresh strawberries (Trade Map 2013). The sector has an ambitious plan for the period 2014–2020 with the aim to increase land use for strawberry growing to 5,000 hectares (generating 200,000 tons for export).

In 2009, Oxfam commissioned a study to document working conditions of workers in the berry sector, specifically for strawberry production. The study found that the rapid growth of the sector, although creating an economic boom, had not led to a substantial improvement in the living conditions of workers, especially of women workers. The number of workers is estimated to be 20,000 in the Loukkos and GCBH regions for both farms and industries (processing factories and pack houses) with the overwhelming majority women (75–90%).

The conclusions of the 2009 Oxfam study stated that the conditions of employment evolved in a predominantly informal and precarious environment. For example, women had to travel distances of up to 100 km to reach their workplace, often in overloaded vehicles not designed for transporting people. The employment relationship between the employee and the employer was blurred by the presence of labor providers who served as intermediaries and allowed some employers to disengage from any responsibility with regard to the workers, especially since in the majority of cases no written contract existed between the two parties.

Working hours were exhausting, often exceeding that determined by the labor code. Most of the time, women were working up to 10 or 11 hours per day or more during the high season. Weekly rest was rarely respected, and overtime did not give rise to increased payment as the law prescribes it. Opportunities for promotion were very rare, often involving blackmail by the supervisors to the workers; some workers also experienced harassment from supervisors. This abuse of power was alarming and in some cases was also used by supervisors and transporters when making decisions to grant jobs.

Wages paid remained low and did not exceed, in the best case, the minimum wage guaranteed by law. The wage level was particularly low on farms, where the Guaranteed Minimum Agricultural Wage was rarely respected. The situation was more favorable in the processing factories where employers seemed to comply, at least formally, to the Guaranteed Minimum Wage.

Registration with the National Social Security Fund (CNSS) was not applied to all workers and did not benefit seasonal workers. The situation was slightly better in pack houses and factories, but only a few employees actually benefited from the family allowance and medical insurance. Access to benefits from CNSS could lead to significant improvements in women workers' living conditions. For example, a woman with two children could access a 40 percent increase in her income by accessing the family allowance. In addition, CNSS registration also provides access to free health care services and paid maternity leave, and can contribute to a retirement allowance.

Several factors contributed to this non-compliance with labor rights and hence the poverty of women working in the strawberry sector; these reflect issues that are widespread throughout the agricultural sector. The current Moroccan labor code is fairly advanced, despite the fact that it is not quite suitable for agriculture (for example regarding seasonal contracts). Morocco has ratified 23 international conventions on labor. The Labor Code published in 2004 includes regulations on issues such as employment contracts, working hours, working conditions, relationships at work, rights and duties, conflict and arbitration, and the principles of equity.

One of the challenges for women to enjoy their labor rights remains the implementation of the law. Violation of labor law is possible because of lack of and/or limited resources of public authorities, especially for labor inspection and the National Social Security Fund (CNSS). As for audits commissioned by international customers, these are often oriented toward monitoring quality standards, hygiene, and safety, rather than looking at compliance with norms for decent working conditions.

The possibilities for improving socio-economic conditions for women workers in the agricultural sector are to some extent linked to government actions to promote fair economic and social development of the region. However, while the GMP promises to attract private investment into agriculture and create thousands of jobs, it does not take into account the interests of workers and the importance of decent working conditions. In addition, the local population, and in particular women, through their representation in civil society organizations, have limited access to spaces to defend their rights and influence local and national political decision-making. As a result, agricultural policies very often do not align with their priorities and needs.

Unions are not very present in the berry sector of Morocco, and women workers have not felt represented by the predominantly male-dominated unions of the area. In addition, there is a lack of knowledge and understanding among workers of their rights; they are afraid of being fired and have no or access time to organize in order to defend their rights and strive for change.

Oxfam's program

This analysis has led Oxfam to believe that improving the situation for women workers in the berry sector in the GCBH and Loukkos region can be achieved by strengthening the autonomy and leadership of these women workers and their capacity to organize. First, this would allow them to defend their rights and to influence decisions among the various stakeholders involved in the sector. Second, Oxfam believes it is crucial to increase accountability of all actors involved in berry production, including both the private sector and government bodies, to achieve long lasting changes.

The intervention proposed by Oxfam and its local partners[3] covers the regions of GCBH and part of Loukkos. Oxfam implemented this program with financial support of the Spanish International Cooperation Agency for Development (AECID), the Autonomous Government of Valencia, the European Union, the Norwegian Embassy of Morocco, and Oxfam's own funds. Oxfam's program has adopted a positive approach, collaborating with key stakeholders on a series of joint initiatives. At the national level, synergies have been developed between Moroccan civil society associations, state institutions, academics, and berry producers in Morocco as well as the women workers themselves. Concrete actions and joint advocacy was done with local associations, creating the ability to act with the population and the government to regularize the situation of marginalized people. Whether by increasing access to information and building trust between local stakeholders, authorities, and government bodies or through building a better understanding of the constraints that each actor faces, the program has worked to improve these dynamics, thereby promoting greater collaboration in the area.

At the international level, the aim was to highlight the realities of the women workers to European berry importers while taking into account the constraints and complexities of global supply chains. The international strategy was based on dialogue with the importing companies, the retailers, and major brands using strawberries in their product and was aimed at harmonizing their expectations with regard to the Moroccan producers. The link between the national and international levels was also a mechanism to encourage transparency and joint problem solving. The approach allowed stakeholders to come together to address the challenges faced by all involved, and to work to address the systemic causes of the problems.

Methodology and results of the program

After almost six years of implementation, the Oxfam program has undergone a progress evaluation to analyze its impact both at local and international levels. The quantitative data were collected by local associations collaborating with the program and compiled over the last four years working in the field with women workers. It includes a representative sample of 2,857 people out of approximately 20,000 women working in the sector. However, data from the last two years have been predominantly used to analyze the program's achievements, as the majority of the changes have occurred during this period. These quantitative data were collected during meetings and interviews conducted with nearly 1,500 women. Qualitative data were also gathered during the outreach work in the villages, during focus group discussions on specific issues, and through discussions and interviews held with people using services of the different proximity organizations. The data were then crosschecked with different entities to verify the main conclusions. The data verification was done in consultation with key program partners, local authorities, government officials at local levels (e.g., social security officers, labor inspectors), European importers, and producers of berries in Morocco. Most of the stakeholders agreed on the conclusions of Oxfam's analysis, but few of them were able to provide official data or be proactive about providing it.

Up to now, the results of the program have been positive in many aspects but less so in others. Regarding the positive impacts, we have seen tangible progress in terms of paying minimum wage (more frequent in industrial facilities than on farms) and in registration to social security. We estimate that, following implementation of the program, 70 percent of the pack houses or processing factories for which we have information are ensuring payment of minimum wage and, more importantly, women who know their rights are increasingly refusing jobs that do not pay the minimum wage.

As for social security, the number of people registered in the GCBH region increased by 40 percent in 2012 and 70 percent in 2013. In 2014, according to Oxfam's estimates, the total registration of workers was around 65 percent for both Loukkos and GCBH in the berry sector. The program has supported more than 3,025 people, including nearly 2,700 women, to get their CNSS card or check its functionality. If we compare this rate to the national rate, in 2008, only 3.6 percent of the working population engaged in agriculture were declared to the CNSS while in 2013, this rate increased up to 5 percent (Morocco, Ministry of Labor and Social Affairs 2013; Morocco, High Commissioner for Planning 2014). As such, the impact of the outreach work by Oxfam's local partner associations and by women workers themselves, combined with the international pressure by importers on producers to comply with this legal requirement, is obvious.

Another area where improvement occurred was that of working hours, again more so in the factories and pack houses where the eight-hour daily limit is increasingly respected. On farms, this remains a challenge, especially in the high season. Overtime payment is rarely honored either on farms or in industrial facilities.

However, progress on transport conditions and the informality of work in the whole sector (which increases the risk for rights violations) is less than expected. Many factors can explain this slower improvement: multiplicity of the actors involved; complexity of the issue; lack of political willingness from producers to improve the situation; and time constraints, as the strawberry season is quite short, lasting from three to six months.

Beyond these factors preventing a rapid change in women workers' situation, it is important to explore the structural constraints for women. The first such constraint is *normalization of hardship for women*, which contributes to the acceptance of the violation of women workers' rights, and the second is *the magnitude of gender stereotypes*, which reinforces the violation of women's dignity.

Normalisation of hardship and gender stereotypes

One of the dilemmas of women workers in Morocco can be understood within the theoretical framework provided by Asma Lamrabet who seeks to reconcile the "universalist feminist theories" as she called them, which are based on a human rights approach, together with a modern and reformed Islam that would value gender equality.

> Caught in between these two extreme views [religious and western], it is not easy today, for many Muslim women, to go out of the box and to overcome these stereotypical frameworks. Muslim women, in most cases, are disconcerted and even torn between their desire for emancipation and freedom, and their need for identity ties and spiritual roots.
>
> (Lamrabet 2015, 10)

These tensions between the desire for empowerment and the need for identity rooted in cultural values (and all the grey areas in between) cast light on the contradiction women workers have to deal with when they engage in paid employment, particularly in the strawberry sector.

Normalization of hardship for women: it's natural, it's easy!

On one side, women enter into paid employment with the desire to contribute to the household income and have their autonomy ("desire for emancipation") but they also wish to respect the cultural values and the gender role expectations that are part of the still quite vivid patriarchal system,[4] referring regularly to Islam to justify it. "Patriarchal ideology has, in its interaction with social structure, a relative autonomy, that makes it survive to the structural social transformation that evolves in parallel with it" (Mouaqit 2003, 288–89).

Keeping this tension in mind and looking at women workers' situation, the fact that paid employment is not seen as a continuation of the traditional caring roles of women, but rather as male role, could restrict women from accessing paid work.[5] However, work in the strawberry sector is considered a women's job. The most common stereotypes are that only women's hands have the carefulness needed for the delicate fruits, and that bending for harvesting the fruits is said to be more suitable for women's bodies. The roles within the strawberry sector are clearly divided: among other tasks, women harvest strawberries or work inside the pack house packing fruit into boxes or cutting stems off fruit to be frozen, while men are mainly truck drivers, supervisors, or owners. Many women also mentioned during group discussions that men would not accept supervision by other men as women do, implicitly reaffirming the male domination over women. As such, the primary discourse surrounding the strawberry sector is that it is "naturally" more suitable for women and therefore not so difficult for them. This normalizes the hardship of the work for women since they are seen as "suited" for this job and what would be considered difficult for men, is "natural" (so necessarily easier) for women.

For that reason, if women are not working fast enough according to the supervisor and to the productivity rate expected by the producers, it is legitimate for supervisors to yell at the women workers, since the work is supposedly easy for them. If they do not work fast enough it is because "they are being lazy and because women like to chat all the time" as a supervisor explained to Amira.[6] Amira explained that on the strawberry farms (in comparison to the factories), supervisors yell all the time for women to go faster and even insult them. Amira shared also the belief amongst workers that, "If one day the supervisor does not yell so much, we believe he is sick." Amira started working when she was 15 years old, which is the legal age according to the Moroccan labor code. She is now 19 years old. For her, this verbal violence is part of the work and she has seen it on each of the farms where she has worked. The majority of women consulted for the progress report agreed that this attitude from supervisors is not exceptional.

To partly explain this, Djemila Zeneidi, who has closely studied the journey of Moroccan women seasonally picking strawberries in Spain, illustrates that economically marginalized women, especially those coming from rural areas, are accustomed to working hard, that hard work is part of their day-to-day experience and the way they envision their life: "In reality, they submit because they are used to being dominated, their professional trajectory in the rural areas of Morocco is marked by employers' abusive behaviors" (Zeneidi 2013, 88). However, and agreeing with Zeneidi, to submit is not to accept (Zeneidi 2013, 89). And that is the starting point for empowerment.

Twenty-year-old Jahida, who has worked in the sector for three years, explains that what she finds most difficult is the transport conditions. She wakes up at 5:00 a.m. and waits for the transporter to pick her up. The most common vehicle is a Mercedes 207 van, legally suited for nine people.

Generally, there are 30–35 people fitted inside and sometimes the number can go up to 55. Jahida reported that, "Sometimes there is no more space in the van; we are 30 people and the driver says that there is not many people inside and puts more women in. Some girls faint when there are too many people." This situation happens daily and for some women, they have endured it two to three hours, morning and evening. The need for a high number of workers during the peak of the season and the fact that most of the transporters are paid by number of workers (between $1.00–1.50USD per person brought to the farm) can partly explain why the truck continues to be overloaded.

Women do not have other affordable options to reach the farm. Knowing that in 75 percent of the cases, transporters are also labor providers (Oxfam 2012, 2), the transport conditions are "part of the deal." What kind of negotiation power can women workers realistically have to claim for respectful transport conditions when the transporter is also the one to grant or not grant the job? For women traveling regularly with an overloaded truck with 55 persons in which men and women are mixed together, increasing occurrence of sexual harassment and assault, 30 people seems, again, normal. This terrible situation makes awful conditions seem acceptable.

Testimonies regularly draw attention to the high prevalence of sexual harassment and aggression both in transport and in the farm site. Transporters or supervisors will offer better conditions to some women expecting sexual favors in return. Malika, who has worked in the sector for five years, explained: "Pretty girls are always favored by the supervisor. They can sit in front of the truck, they get easier tasks, have more time to rest ... however, if they refuse their advances, supervisors can change their attitude and become very cruel." Unequal power relations are coupled with the normalization of such attitudes. Most of the time owners deny that harassment is happening on the farm. This makes the situation invisible, but adds to the existing taboo and the guilt of women who are accused of causing such situations or from benefiting from it. Harassment contributes to the hardship of the work on the strawberry farms, but a lot of women do not dare to denounce it for fear of losing their job or losing their family's respect. Denouncing it would also mean confronting the engrained idea of the superiority of men over women:

> This kind of patriarchy imposes unequal principles between men and women by manipulating religious concepts in favor of male supremacy and tries to root in the minds and mentalities a notion of worthlessness and disregard for women as subordinated human beings because they are women.
>
> (Lamrabet 2010)

These three issues presented (transport problems, excessive power of labor providers, and harassment) are the ones women express the most frustration about. On one hand, they are gaining more autonomy due to more economic power and the increase of mobility and knowledge, but on the other hand they remain structurally constrained and are prevented from enjoying fully their rights and dignity.

Gender stereotypes: social pressure, social control

There are tangible tensions between having paid employment and the necessity to still honor gender roles despite the stereotypes that prevail in the strawberry sector. The sexism inherent in this tension is linked to the dominant patriarchal order: "Opposition to the shift towards gender equality is, in fact, more motivated by attachment to the patriarchal society and male privilege than by faithfulness to religion" (Benradi 2003, 86).

As mentioned, sexual harassment is common in transport and on the strawberry farms. Families fear that their daughter, sister, or wife could be raped or would "accept" sexual favors in exchange for better conditions (Bouzidi, El Nour, and Moumen 2011, 13). This fear has become widespread. It is also expressed in the social environment as insults or threats. "My family does not like the fact that I work in the strawberries and they never ask questions when I come home after work. There is discomfort when I come back home. They hear what the people in the village say about it, that the girls have to sleep with the supervisors and so on," explains Houriya. "I'm 27 years old and not yet married and I know no man in the village would like to marry me because of this."

Hana, a married woman, expressed the same sentiment and noted the increased tension in the household because of these beliefs: "My husband believes me, but people talk a lot. Women working in the strawberry sector have a bad reputation because they work with men," implying that workers' relationships can lead to other types of relationships, especially in a hierarchical setting. Multiple testimonies have expressed different stereotypes surrounding the idea that women working in the strawberry sector are having sex with their supervisor or transporter. In all cases, women are blamed. If a woman is married, people will believe she will be unfaithful; if she is not married, people will believe she will engage in sexual activity for better conditions; if she is divorced, people will believe it is because she had relations with someone else at work.

To continue working, women workers have used different coping mechanisms, such as going to work on the farms with other members of the family and neighbors, thus reassuring others that their "honor is safe"; not paying attention to the gossip; or inventing poems and songs they sing while working in order to externalise the tension that comes from the social pressure. "Indeed, women workers travel in groups to work on the same farms, they share meals together during the break, jointly discuss their problems, sing and return together in the village at the end of the day. These groups give the opportunity to create some solidarity during work time but also a kind of social control and assurance for the families of women workers" (Bouzidi, El Nour, and Moumen 2011, 17).

If we look at the different issues from an intersectionality perspective we can see what they have in common from a conceptual point of view. Sirma Bilge describes intersectionality as follows: "The intersectional approach goes beyond a simple recognition of the multiplicity of systems of oppression operating from these categories [sex / gender, class, race, ethnicity, age, disability and sexual orientation] and postulates their interaction in the production and reproduction of social inequalities" (2009, 70). As such, we can analyze that on one hand, women face the imperative of safeguarding the "Moroccan values" (colonialism), and on the other trying to overcome poverty (classism), but that they also face issues associated with gender roles and male supremacy in hierarchical work relations and in interaction with their social environment (sexism).

As Lamrabet argued regarding the influence of colonialism over culture, modernity and women's autonomy are often not seen as a social evolution, but rather as a denial of the complexity of the Moroccan identity: "The colonised Muslim countries have had a chaotic relationship with modernity as it was imposed by a coloniser supposed to bring civilisation to the culturally and economically decadent Muslim populations. Modernity was experienced as a power struggle and not as an attempt to liberate oppressed peoples" (Lamrabet 2010, 1). As a result of this, it appears that it is necessary to reaffirm traditional values against the colonial values. In that regard, women becoming more autonomous economically, freer to move, and working outside of the private sphere is not always perceived socially as a progression, but rather as a submission to the external order. However, the idea is not to undermine the social movement existing in Moroccan society or give a dichotomous portrait of it that would be "static, bounded and internally monolithic," thus essentializing the culture (Puar and Barker 2002, 613). Rather, the idea is to examine and interrogate how women challenging conventional gender roles are often understood within their social environment as disloyally internalizing colonialist ideology.

Economic necessity is the first incentive for women to work in the strawberry sector. The centrality of economic necessity in women's motivation to access employment will remain a priority and guides the attitude women workers adopt and mechanisms they will use. In other words, their negotiation power is already reduced by the unequal relations between men and women; the need to preserve a livelihood might prevail when facing tensions and rights abuse (classism).

Having said this, it does not mean that women workers are passive victims of a situation they are unable to control. Women workers do not present themselves as victims; furthermore, such a discourse is too disempowering (hooks 1997, 396). On the contrary, women are discriminated against in a specific way that intersects with all of these systems, but they are also proud of earning a salary and supporting their family. They explained to us how they live within this tension between pride, empowerment, and loss of dignity. Zeneidi (2013, 158) explains this mixed feeling as a quest for recognition that is never really achieved: "False recognition allows us to understand the ambivalence of domination and its way to live with a sense of empowerment."

Figure 14.1 Two women workers in the strawberry sector wearing traditional hats, village close to Larache, Morocco, 2014.

Source: Luigi Forese/Oxfam.

Transformative leadership for women's rights

Oxfam is committed to promoting gender justice while recognizing its role as a foreign organization and the associated possibility of being perceived as part of an oppressive system. To address this challenge, links with local communities and women workers are made in collaboration with local associations who share Oxfam's values and are part of the design of the program and main actors in it. The shared values and vision with local associations help to design sensitive actions, but also enrich the evolving analysis.

Oxfam tries regularly to question its approach to achieve gender justice. Like many other organizations, its approach has gone through transformation from the women and development approach, to gender and development approach, then aiming at achieving gender equality through gender mainstreaming and gender as standalone programs promoting women's empowerment. Now, at the crossroads of new concepts and moved by internal and external contexts, Oxfam is looking at "going beyond gender mainstreaming" (Sweetman 2012, 390) toward Transformative Leadership for Women's Rights (TLWR) as a strategy to inform their work. The intersectionality analysis supports the design of programs using this strategy to adapt to the context of program implementation. "Transformative leadership which is leadership for sustainable change addresses the root causes of inequality. On the one hand, TLWR is about the improvement of leadership, or how people exercise their leadership. At the same time, leadership capacity is being built in order to achieve or change something" (Oxfam2014b 6). In other words, Oxfam is interested in how to support women's empowerment not only to provide individuals with capacities to increase their decision-making power as achieved with a gender mainstreaming approach, but to support women to become leaders for change that will promote and embody gender justice.

As an example illustrating the TLWR approach, around 100 women workers during this Oxfam program in Morocco became "women promoters." They were first trained on labor rights and communication (among others) and then started doing awareness-raising activities on labor rights in the villages. As such, they were fulfilling the strategic interests of other women workers and supporting their own empowerment process. These women were playing a key role in providing and gathering information on rights violation. Moreover, they were doing it from the perspective of a worker, giving them even more legitimacy in communities and helping to reduce the "bad reputation" and stereotypes of women workers. They gained confidence from the awareness-raising sessions: their knowledge and experience benefited others. They formed a Women's Association that would continue to raise awareness on labor rights. Going from accepting insults inside a strawberry farm to questioning the root cause of inequality was an encouraging step they were also proud of making.

In order to understand the causes of the abuse in the strawberry sector, the Women's Association, with the support of local associations and Oxfam, conducted an exercise called the "problem tree analysis" which consists of finding the "roots" of the problem (tree trunk) by looking as well at the leaves being the consequences of it. This visual and interactive tool gives a quick overview of how the difficulties are interlinked and shows that short-term solutions will never address the right issue. After doing the exercise, the Women's Association determined where to focus their energy to improve women workers' life conditions and the overall wellbeing of the community. They identified two elements. First, to continue the sensitization of European importers with the updated information they gathered during the sessions in villages. They reaffirmed that importers should not allow producers to have exploitative practices, understanding the strong inter-linkages between the exporting countries and the productivity pressure they were suffering from (in other words, the influence of the global supply chain). They wanted to influence producers to implement respectful practices for their workers.

The second solution they identified was to keep young girls in school, in order to enable them to claim their rights. Currently, two-thirds of the women workers are illiterate and the rest have very low levels of education. In the summer of 2014, the Women's Association, in coordination with the Department of Education of their localities, started organizing activities with school students aged 10–12 years old. Dropping out of school usually happens around this age. The women shared how they did not have the opportunity to continue school beyond primary school and described the consequences this had on their lack of knowledge about their rights as workers.

Salma explained, with emotion: "Last time I was in a school was ten years ago, when I was 12. I somehow regret to have left school because now I understand it could have given me other opportunities. But it was not possible at that time. The school was too far and my parents could not let me go alone to school. Today, by coming back here I feel I have a mission for the girls who have more opportunities to go to school." The women's suggestions were not to prevent people from working in the strawberry sector or stop European importers from buying in Morocco. On the contrary, what they wanted was to have their rights respected, the end of violence and harassment, and the reduction of stereotypes to ensure their dignity is respected.

The aim of the Transformative Leadership strategy was not only to provide women workers with tools, such as information on labor rights. The objective was to create empowerment spaces where their experience and knowledge could be valued and transferred to influence others and advance the goal of gender justice. The strategy was to find ways to discuss and address the issues that are at the center of their life and their communities. By doing this, women workers want not only to improve their own situation, which was shaped by choices based on the limited opportunities they had, but they now would like to open up more possibilities for others. If organizations have the capacities and resources to broaden these opportunities, they should continue to do it.

Conclusion

Women workers are challenging complex and sensitive issues by claiming their rights to dignity. They are directly or indirectly questioning social order (gender roles, stereotypes, sexism) and cultural identity (religious discourse, colonialism), as well as economic systems based on global supply chains and the expansion of export agriculture dependent on unskilled, low-paid workforce (classism). They are able to pursue this by keeping the right balance between confrontation and positioned dialogue.

Intersectionality in this context is relevant not only to analyze the diversity of oppressive systems faced by women workers, but also to identify the most suitable approaches to support them in addressing these issues. A tool such as Transformative Leadership for Women's Rights would build on this analysis to tackle different levels of change and create spaces for opportunities.

"Every story needs a public" (Huston 2010, 125). The women cited in this chapter are raising their voices and claiming their rights. Through their stories, they are denouncing and challenging unacceptable conditions. As a public, you are now part of their story.

Acknowledgments

This chapter is based on a program implemented by Oxfam and its local partners in Morocco. The analysis and views set out in this text are those of the author and do not necessarily reflect the official opinion of Oxfam. I would like to thank the editors, A. Baril, C. Maillé, T. Janny, and my Oxfam colleagues, S. Sotelo Reyes and N. Gravier for their useful comments.

Notes

1 Translation of interview quotations, as well as some secondary literature cited in this chapter, has been provided by the author.
2 Some of this information can also be found in the published Oxfam report, *Social Protection, Building Dignity!*, 2014.
3 Local association partners of this program are Democratic League for Women's Rights of Larache (LDDF), Development Associations Network (RADEV), Hands of Solidarity Association, the Moroccan Association of Support for the Promotion of Small Enterprise (AMAPPE), Chaml Association, and Youth for Youth Association (AJJ).
4 The concept of patriarchal system is utilized here to respect the Moroccan literature consulted for this text using this concept and do not reflect an ideological choice of the author.
5 A recent example was provided by the Prime Minister of Morocco, Abdel-Ilah Benkiran, who publically affirmed that the place of women was in the household to preserve "light" among the family. See Jeune Afrique, 2014.
6 Names have been modified.

References

Benradi, Malika. 2003. "Genre et Droit de la Famille: Les Droits des Femmes dans la Moudawana. De la Révision de 1993 à la Réforme de 2003." In *Féminin-Masculin, La Marche vers l'Égalité au Maroc-1993–2003*. http://library.fes.de/pdf-files/iez/03260.pdf 17–90.

Bilge, Sirma. 2009. "Théorisations Féministes de l'Intersectionnalité." *Diogène* no 225 (Janvier–Mars): 70–88.

Bouzidi, Zhour, Saker El Nour, and Wided Moumen. 2011. "Le Travail des Femmes dans le Secteur Agricole: Entre Précarité et Empowerment: Cas de Trois Régions en Egypte, au Maroc et en Tunisie." Gender and work in the MENA Region Working Paper Series, No. 22. Cairo: The Population Council. www.popcouncil.org/uploads/pdfs/wp/mena/22_fr.pdf.

Food and Agriculture Organization of the United Nations (FAO). Statistics Division. 2014. http://faostat3.fao.org/home/F.

hooks, bell. 1997. "Sisterhood: Political Solidarity between Women." In *Dangerous Liaisons: Gender, Nation, and Postcolonial Perspectives*, edited by Anne McClintock, Aamir Mufti, and Ella Shohat, 396–414. Minneapolis: University of Minnesota Press.

Huston, Nancy. 2010. *L'Espèce Fabulatrice*. Paris: Acte Sud.

Jeune Afrique. 2014. "Maroc: le Premier Ministre Préfère la Femme au Foyer." www.jeuneafrique.com/depeches/15301/politique/maroc-le-premier-ministre-prefere-la-femme-au-foyer/.

Lamrabet, Asma. 2010. "Le Code de la Famille est-il le Dernier Bastion Patriarcal dans les Pays Musulmans?" www.asma-lamrabet.com/articles/le-code-de-la-famille-cf-est-il-le-dernier-bastion-patriarcal-dans-les-pays-musulmans/.

———. 2015. *Les Femmes et l'Islam: une Vision Réformiste*. Paris: Fondation pour l'Innovation Politique.

Morocco. High Commissioner for Planning (HCP), Department of Statistics. 2014. *National Study on Labor Market for the 1st Quarter of 2014*. www.hcp. ma/La-Situation-du-marche-du-travail-au-premier-trimestre-de-l-annee-2014_a1392.html.

Morocco. Ministry of Labor and Social Affairs. 2013. *Social Balance Sheet*. www.emploi.gov.ma/ministre/attachments/article/158/livre%20franc%CC%A7ais.pdf.

Morocco. ORMAL (Office de Mise en Valeur Agricole du Loukkos/Regional Office of Agricultural Development of Loukkos). 2013. "Les Petits Fruits Rouges au Loukkos: Le Cas de la Fraise."

———. 2014. "Les Fruits Rouges dans les Périmètres du Loukkos et du Gharb." Official presentation at Oxfam's Seminaire Rabat, Rabat, Morocco. www.ormval. ma/index.php/fr/actuali/91-ha.

Mouaqit, Mohamed. 2003. "Genre, Développement et Égalité." *Dans Féminin-Masculin, La Marche vers l'Égalité au Maroc-1993–2003*, 277–95. http://library.fes.de/pdf-files/iez/03260.pdf.

Oxfam. 2010. *Etude sur les Producteurs de la Fraise dans la Région de Larache et Moulay Busselham au Maroc*. Rabat: Oxfam au Maroc.

———. 2012. *Etude Relative aux Intermédiaires dans le Secteur de la Fraise dans la Région de Larache et Moulay Boussaleham*. Rabat: Oxfam au Maroc.

———. 2014a. *Social Protection, Building Dignity!* Oxfam Intermon, http://policy-practice.oxfam.org.uk/publications/social-protection-building-dignity-improving-working-conditions-of-women-worker-560924.

———. 2014b. *Transformative Leadership for Women's Rights, An Oxfam Guide*. www.oxfam.org/sites/www.oxfam.org/files/transformative-leadership-womens-rights-oxfam-guide.pdf.

Puar, Jasbir Kaur, and Isabelle Barker. 2002. "Feminist Problematization of Rights Language and Universal Conceptualizations of Human Rights." *Concilium International Journal of Theology*. 608–16.

Sweetman, Caroline. 2012. "Introduction." *Gender & Development* 20 (3): 389–403.

Trade Map. 2013. "Trade Statistics for International Business Development." International Trade Center. www.trademap.org/Index.aspx.

Zeneidi, Djemila. 2013. *Femmes/Fraises Import/Export*. Paris: Presses Universitaires de France.

United States of America

15 Building power through community
Women creating and theorizing change

Angie Carter, Betty Wells, Ashley Hand, and Jessica Soulis

Introduction

The Women, Food and Agriculture Network (WFAN) originated in 1994 in Iowa, United States, in response to systemic problems in the food and agricultural sector, including the absence of women's voices. Since then, we have grown to become a nationally recognized non-profit organization serving women in sustainable agriculture while remaining rooted in an area of the United States dominated by mainstream, patriarchal agriculture. This chapter focuses on three core WFAN programs that engage creative, alternative methods of learning to build community among women and to build a new community-focused agricultural vision. Yet, the actualization of women's empowerment within agriculture remains challenged locally and unrealized culturally. As researchers and practitioners involved with WFAN, we have a unique contribution to make to the story of agriculture. In this chapter we draw from our experiences with WFAN programs and as members of the WFAN board to focus on these key questions: In what ways do incremental gains for women support or subvert existing power structures? How does WFAN continue to elevate women and remain gender-focused in efforts to achieve systemic change? We explore these questions in the context of three WFAN programs and hope to offer insight into efforts beyond the Midwestern United States.

WFAN's ecofeminist history

WFAN was founded in Iowa, United States, following the mobilization of women seeking to address concerns about systemic problems in agriculture and rural communities. While the negative consequences of industrial agriculture upon the environment, local knowledge, and local people (in particular, women and children) are well documented (Mies and Shiva 1993; Sachs 1996), the same patriarchal capitalist structures that privilege profit over environmental and social justice in industrial agriculture also exist in sustainable agriculture (Allen 2004; Sachs 1996). WFAN was born of a cultural context of male dominance and hegemony, and a cultural "conspiracy of courtesy" that also served to silence women. WFAN's mission, set in 1998 – "to link and amplify women's voices on issues of food systems, sustainable communities and environmental integrity" – conveyed breadth of focus and belief in the value of women's voices (Wells 2002, 142) and, in particular, women's voices in sustainable agriculture.

WFAN's seeds were planted in 1994 in processes leading to the United Nations Fourth World Women's Conference in Beijing. To prepare input for the Women's Conference, Julia Anderson and Betty Wells convened with other Iowa women in Grinnell, Iowa, to gather data on rural women's access to land, credit, and decision-making structures to inform a workshop for a conference in Iowa City. At this conference, Anderson and Wells were joined by presenters Pat Boddy, Denise O'Brien, and Cindy Fletcher, with Bev Everett recording and Dorothy Paul reporting. Despite a growing international literature on women in development and agriculture, we had discovered scant information on rural and agricultural women in the US in general, and Iowa in particular (although we did find data on women's ownership of farmland that was to fuel considerable future programming). Also in 1994, Iowa's Denise O'Brien and Kathy Lawrence of The National Campaign for Sustainable Agriculture formed a Women, Food and Agriculture working group in preparation for Beijing to remedy the neglect of food and agricultural issues. We would later append the word "network" to this name upon the founding of WFAN in 1997.

The organizational goals WFAN's feminist founding members adopted in March 1998 flew in the face of common conjecture at the time that there were no rural feminists, much less feminist farmers. A selection of these goals, germane to the focus of this paper, include:

- advocating change by exploring alternatives and challenging the globalization of economies, cultures of domination and institutionalized discrimination;
- insisting on social and ecological justice for current and future human and non-human communities;
- providing experiential education on economics and environment that articulates a holistic view of agriculture, instills a sense of place and draws forward useful experiences from the past;
- creating networks that support communities who strive for sustainability; providing safe places for self-expression; and respecting the spirituality of the land and people.

Challenging "cultures of domination" affirms that our task is not only about women (although we privilege women). Patriarchal domination cannot be eradicated while racism and other forms of group oppression stay intact, because these systems share an ideological foundation: "feminism must exist apart from and as part of the larger struggle to eradicate all forms of domination" (hooks 1989, 22). Ecofeminists further the complexity of the feminist notion of intersectionality by integrating nature "as a fourth category of analysis in an extended feminist theory which employs a race, class and gender analysis" (Plumwood 1993, 1–2). An ecofeminist framework helps us draw connections between systemic agriculture and rural problems and the patriarchal and corporate domination of rural and agricultural institutions and organizations. The need is urgent, so we insist on justice, while recognizing that we must work across organizations for both social justice and sustainability. WFAN is committed to holistic, experiential learning that is respectful of past and place, providing safe spaces, and valuing spirituality.

WFAN has evolved from an informal network to become a legally sanctioned 501(c)(3) non-profit organization (Code of Federal Regulations, title 10, sec 501.15) in 2011, with paid staff and funded projects. Our continued relevance is underscored by the persistence of gendered systemic problems in agriculture, and our vitality by the entry of a new generation of organizational leadership. Against this historical backdrop, we shift focus to three programs that align with the intent of the founders to challenge the status quo in agricultural institutions.

Building community: WFAN's programs

WFAN's programs emerged from the need to address intransigent problems associated with industrial agriculture and an institutional context that has largely excluded women. They include:

- Women Caring for the Land (WCL): reaching women farmland owners for increased conservation/land stewardship through peer-to-peer learning circles and field visits;
- Harvesting our Potential (HOP): supporting experienced, beginning, and aspiring women farmers through a mentor/mentee partnership program;
- Plate to Politics (P2P): increasing women's political participation in food systems through political advocacy and leadership training.

Our work with woman farmland owners started in 2001, with participatory research with a group of women farmland owners in Cass County, Iowa (Wells 2004). This pilot project gave birth to two successor programs: Women Caring for the Land (WCL), which we write about in this chapter, and Women, Land and Legacy, which also continues to this day in partnership with other organizations. The first of several projects matching experienced women farmers in mentoring relationships with aspiring and beginning women farmers began in 2000, predating what we now call Harvesting Our Potential (HOP). As the WCL and HOP programs are contemporaneous and longer standing, we describe, compare, and contrast them first. We then turn attention to the third and newest program, Plate to Politics (P2P). We will also analyze how these programs support or challenge existing power structures and conclude with a discussion of how our experience informs our elevation of women and gender-focused programs to achieve systemic change.

Program 1. Women Caring for the Land (WCL)

The magnitude of women's farmland ownership – women own or co-own 47 percent of farmland in Iowa and rent their farmland at higher rates than their counterparts (Duffy and Johanns 2014) – brought our efforts to the attention of state and national agricultural agencies and likely increased our funding opportunities. Women Caring for the Land (WCL) works to provide information and resources directly to women farmland owners. WCL operates from a respectful, asset-based (rather than a deficit or remedial) model to build on what women know instead of focusing on what they do not know. This approach focuses on respecting and reaching out to women where they are. We understand that while prescribed gender expectations have limited some women's involvement in mainstream production agriculture, these women acquired knowledge in socially acceptable realms and possess an abundant stock of tacit knowledge.

WCL features six-hour meetings called learning circles for women who own land but may or may not be actively involved in making farm management decisions, especially related to conservation. These learning circles are conversational, peer-to-peer gatherings facilitated by WFAN-affiliated women resource conservationists. Women from conservation agencies are invited to attend for part of the day as an antidote to the often male-dominated conservation offices. Women share their stories, learn about local conservation programs, and visit conservation sites on neighboring farms, shared experiences which enhance appreciation for ecological complexity and diversity. Women learn about programs/meetings offered by partnering organizations covering topics such as setting appropriate rent prices, getting leases (including with conservation provisions) in writing (preferably for multiple years), and estate planning for passing their land to heirs. Women are also encouraged to discuss their experiences with agricultural conservation with their legislators who could act to improve institutional effectiveness in helping women.

WCL features educational materials that show women in photos and use the bright colors that many women say that they prefer. Eells (2010) has tested WCL curriculum innovations[1] that draw on experiences that may be more familiar to women, such as the ingredients and processes used in cooking or the fabrics used in sewing or quilting, with the goal to determine how readily recognition of shapes, textures, and patterns from different contexts might be transferred to the landscape. One of the activities in the curriculum asks women to collaboratively create farmscapes of their dream farms (Figure 15.1), an activity that inspires conversations about both changes on the landscape and visions for the futures of their farms.

WCL is unique in the United States for its focus on agricultural conservation for women non-operator landowners. Evaluations of the outcomes of these single-day meetings show that women leave the learning circles and take action to improve conservation on their land. Surveys of women who have attended WCL learning circles show that 50–60 percent have taken

Figure 15.1 Farmscape from a WCL learning circle activity.

farmland-related conservation action. Eells and Soulis (2014) reviewed literature related to women landowners and found that the lack of differentiation between men and women operators and owners in census or survey studies leaves us knowing little about the interests and values of women farmland owners. By creating space for women farmland owners to connect and share experiences, WCL fosters future interaction and conservation actions, and increases their visibility to researchers, policy makers, and conservation professionals.

Program 2. Harvesting Our Potential (HOP)

WFAN programs to develop skills, confidence, and community among beginning or aspiring women farmers by matching them with experienced women farmers date to 2000. The current version of this program, Harvesting Our Potential (HOP), provides stipends to mentors and mentees in a variety of mentorship arrangements. The mentees and mentors in the HOP program are exclusively women engaged in non-industrial agriculture (e.g., fruit and vegetable farmers, CSA owners, or pasture-raised livestock farmers). An award of a United States Department of Agriculture (USDA) Beginning Farmer and Rancher Development Program grant in 2012 scaled up our efforts to reach the growing number of women exploring careers in small-scale, diversified agriculture in states dominated by conventional agriculture. HOP complements existing beginning farmer programming in the upper Midwest by adding on-farm mentoring and business planning designed and delivered by women, for women. Many women benefit from and prefer being mentored by another woman, yet few if any programs build explicitly on this preference. HOP does so, while also emphasizing methods and approaches congruent with our goals and feminist roots, such as peer-to-peer learning.

HOP consists of three program components – on-farm mentoring (with training), business training, and structured networking – consistent with an appreciative inquiry approach, which engages participants and partners in improving the program as it unfolds. At participants' request, we have adjusted our program to allow successful mentor–mentee matches to continue in a second year. Although a trade-off in terms of numbers of new women served, especially given that our target numbers are small compared to many other beginning farmer programs, this change reflects our growing appreciation that an eight-week experience does not a farmer make (although it may be adequate for learning that one does not want to be a farmer, which we count as a successful program outcome). A typical aspiring/beginning farmer may end her menteeship with more questions than when she started. A partnership that works, whether due to complementary skills, compatible personalities, or work ethic, is a solid foundation on which to build for the next season.

Mentor training has evolved to reflect increased appreciation of reciprocal learning, and blurred distinction between mentee and mentor. We continue to emphasize expectations, legalities, and goal setting and to use examples from the farms of participating mentors to ground the discussion of varied farm calendars and approaches to lesson planning. We have added a learning circles component for aspiring farmers, building on the success of this approach in WCL. For the business component, we have begun a new collaboration in Iowa with Iowa State University Extension's "Annie's Project,"[2] expanding their audience beyond women partners in more conventional agriculture operations.

What do these programs have in common? What generic issues cross the programs?

WCL and HOP are complementary, but the audiences are distinct. WCL participants are primarily women whose land is farmed using conventional agricultural practices and who do not identify as organic or sustainable farmers – in fact, many do not identify as farmers at all. They have often been excluded from or have not engaged in traditional agricultural knowledge-sharing networks. Further, while many are leaders within their families or communities, and identify many gender-based challenges in their relationships with tenants or in regards to their management of their farmland, few would identify as feminist. Although many of the women landowners depend upon income derived from renting land and are not necessarily wealthy, generally they would have assets that many beginning or aspiring farmers lack, notably land. WCL has garnered broad support and recognition, including the Governor's Environmental Excellence Award for WFAN's work with women farmland owners and conservation education.[3]

HOP participants align more with an ecological, Leopoldian land-as-community (as opposed to land-as-commodity) conception of agriculture.[4] The farms and farmers that affiliate with WFAN tend to be small-scale, diversified operations, sometimes organic or using largely organic practices. Many focus on fruits and vegetables or other niche products. Their agricultural enterprises are sometimes referred to as small market or value-added. HOP participants are more active in WFAN, attending conferences, serving on the board, serving as leaders in local and national level agricultural and food advocacy organizations, and are more likely to identify as feminist.

Consistent with WFAN goals, both programs employ alternative methods of outreach.[5] We feature learning circles in both WCL and HOP programming, an approach which gives voice to women by fostering safe or privileged spaces and by building their confidence to enter more public spaces.

We next turn attention to the P2P, the third program of focus, which is the most recent addition to WFAN's program portfolio.

Program 3. Plate to Politics (P2P)

Thirty women food-systems advocates from across the country convened at the Wingspread Center in Racine, Wisconsin, for the Cultivate 2012 summit focused on how the growth of women in farmers' markets, organic sales, community gardens, and the farm to school movement could launch a larger initiative to increase the number of women in politics. P2P emerged from this program as a joint effort among the now defunct White House Project, the MOSES Rural Women's Project, and WFAN, and is now a WFAN program.[6] Through our experiences with HOP and WCL, we saw a need for training to assist women interested in entering into political leadership within their communities. P2P originated from our identified need to elevate the unique challenges to women in agriculture, assist in changing systemic constraints, and create opportunities for social change. P2P, and its focus on training women to be leaders in their communities, is unique to WFAN.

Of the WFAN programs, only P2P is overtly "political," and that is only in terms of getting women to run for political office, not so much in terms of positions taken. P2P does not take positions on issues; rather, it prepares women to run for office in their communities with the idea that more women involved with politics will elevate women in agriculture and food systems work and help address the challenges they face.

This program is proving most challenging to fund. Small grants have funded webinars and trainings targeting rural women, but this funding has not been consistent. Engaging rural women in political leadership development is a challenge, and the P2P program has focused on building interactive opportunities through webinars to reach women where they are. Sessions at the annual WFAN conferences, the 2013 national Women in Sustainable Agriculture Conference, and meetings of allied organizations, such as the Minnesota Farmers Union, have provided opportunities to engage agricultural women in networking and trainings related to running for office. Webinars are available on our website resource library and are accessible to the public at no cost. We remain hopeful that we might obtain a larger grant to fund more in-person interactions for women interested in political leadership.

Theorizing systemic change in sustainable agriculture

Both our WCL and HOP programs address *practical* more than *strategic* gender needs. As Moser (1993, 40) explains: "Practical gender needs are those that women identify in their socially accepted roles in society ... [They] do not challenge the gender divisions of labour or women's subordinate position in society, although rising out of them. Practical gender needs are a response to immediate perceived necessity, identified within a specific context." Housing, water quantity and quality, health care, employment, and adequate food supply are examples of practical gender needs.

Moser (1993, 39) defines strategic gender needs as those

> women identify because of their subordinate position to men in their society. Strategic gender needs vary according to particular contexts. They relate to gender divisions of labor, power and control and may include such issues as legal rights, domestic violence, equal wages and women's control over their bodies. Meeting strategic gender needs helps women to achieve greater equality. It also changes existing roles and therefore challenges women's subordinate position.

While a useful distinction, in practice the line between practical and strategic gender needs is often blurred. WCL and HOP both provide a practical potential foothold for beginning to address strategic gender needs. WCL challenges the historical position of women in agricultural conservation and seeks to build confidence and knowledge of conservation practices by bringing them together in peer-to-peer women-only learning circles. Similarly, HOP challenges the historical position of women in agriculture by connecting them with peers and mentors to share knowledge and experiences that may not be valued in industrial agricultural systems. In conversational gatherings and through mentor–mentee relationships, women give voice to their dreams for their farms and farmland, learn about the existing "rules of the game" imposed by the policies of the institution of agriculture, and begin to deconstruct the social isolation associated with their historic roles in agriculture – all important for challenging current directions in agriculture and creating alternative paths.

These safe spaces give women the opportunity to discuss issues related to power – not an easy topic to broach in everyday conversation, but an important one, as gendered relations are often about power. As women reflect concretely on their unique contexts – where they live, the land they own, and their relationships to others – a window may open on how issues of land and gender play out on the ground. A safe group provides opportunities for more open discussion and to role-play conversations with tenants about conservation or with aging parents about transitioning the land.

Critique of such programs suggests that in creating space for the unique concerns and work of women in sustainable agriculture, these programs may remove discussion of these concerns from the mainstream (Shortall 2001). However, WFAN's experience and success in these programs suggests that this space is paramount for women in agriculture to find and create community. We know an important first step is inviting women to participate in a program that values their experiences as women, but it is not enough (Wells and Eells 2011). We must move into longer-term shifts in agriculture at cultural levels to address deeper structural change:

> [P]articipation without a change in power relations may simply reinforce the status quo, simply adding to the mobilization of bias the claim to a more 'democratic' face. The illusion of inclusion means not only that what emerges is treated as if it represents what 'the people' really want, but also that it gains a moral authority that becomes hard to challenge or question.
>
> (Gaventa and Cornwall 2001, 75)

Among the first steps in addressing gender issues in agriculture may be creating space to acknowledge and discuss inequalities, to create a network to assist women in confronting or navigating the challenges or violence they face as they challenge the boundaries of the agricultural status quo. Hassanein (1997), who has studied sustainable agricultural women's networks, reports that these spaces are important for exchanging informal and formal knowledge.

The women in the WCL program are the rightful decision makers for the land they own, and agricultural conservation services are meant to apply equally to all landowners, but an institutional ethnography (Smith 2004) conducted by Jean Eells (2008) uncovered gaps in services provided by the natural resource agency staff who form the conservation plans that qualify landowners for supplemental government funds for implementation. She concludes that the "institution" of agricultural conservation has, in a number of ways, systematically excluded women farmland owners from active participation in programs.

Eiman Zein-Elabdin (1996, 941) challenges us to identify and understand "the actual institutions and processes that lead to gender-specific actions toward the environment and use of natural resources within different historical and cultural confines as opposed to undertaking a theoretical dissection of development, gender, and the environment."[7] An institutional perspective on gender illuminates its path dependence, economic and political significance, and resistance to change (929). Because institutions are culture-specific, the ways in which gender specification plays out "can only be understood within specific temporal and spatial contexts" (939). Placing the relation of women to the environment in context also illuminates issues of power and policy, (Zein-Elabdin 1996), unmasking power structures that tend to privilege men over women and political interests that block "gender-based redefinition of power relations and wealth distribution" (942) – all germane to the project of sustainability. We gain insight about the glue that holds the current system together, the very system we would wish to dismantle.

We acknowledge that creating programs specifically for women is not alone enough to transform agriculture as an institution. Simply adding women to traditional groups or championing women's advances does not contest or overcome the challenges women face. One reason *add women and stir* (Bunch 1987, 140) rarely works is because it assumes that exclusion is the only issue. It does not question the dominant land-as-commodity view being presented or the information being conveyed, which come from a knowledge system that women had little to do with generating. It fails to question the size and fit of government-sponsored conservation programs and educational needs. If programs – educational and otherwise – adequately met women's needs, women would already be at the table. We can address content shortcomings and gender inequities at the same time by bringing women into programs designed with their input and needs in mind, programs with a more inclusive land-as-community approach that embraces diversity and differences.

Add women and stir is also flawed because it ignores context. Putting matters into context requires attending to often unseen background, looking behind the practices. To attend to context is to attend to relationships, such as the complex dynamics of tenant–landowner relations, the specific, embodied experience, and the claims of particular people in particular situations. There comes a time to move out of the comfort zone, and toward an ecological agriculture, as Leopold (1949) advocated, to take the standpoint of what he referred to collectively as "the land," to become citizen-members of the land community, to enlarge the ethical boundaries of community to include soils, waters, plants, and animals.

We applaud this position, but caution that *undifferentiated citizens* default to *male*. Elizabeth Ransom and Carmen Bain (2011), in an analysis of secondary data from international development projects, conclude that women lost ground when gender became the conceptual currency and projects came to focus on gender rather than women. "Gender mainstreaming" has produced diminished material gains for women. We might heed this cautionary tale.

Decrying the snail's pace of progress in conservation, Leopold (1949, 207) did not question the need for conservation education, but asked, "is it certain that only the volume of education needs stepping up? Is something lacking in the content as well?" Wells and Eells (2011) agree that education is not enough, and that things are also lacking in content, a related emphasis on land-as-community/community agriculture and ecological agricultural practices. They point out the obvious: that women have also been missing.

"Women need to be invited," said Bev Everett in 1983 (Everett 1983, 69). Her call to engage more women in conservation was based partly in equity for women and partly in needed human qualities, the need for people with good judgment and people who hold values about resource stewardship. Her belief was that "women, more so than men, hold such holistic views of agriculture and want to express them" (1983, 69). While the qualities in short supply are not exclusive to women, the values connected to all-out production have had a masculine bent, and more feminine leaning values – caring, community, and family – have gotten short shrift.

WFAN's quilt in the making

Karen Warren's (2000) articulation of ecofeminist theory as quilting shines light on how WFAN and these three programs have developed, as well as our way forward. Several features of quilts, not the least that quilting is historically identified with women (68), make this metaphor apt. More so, "quilts are highly contextual; they grow out of and reflect specific historical, social, economic, and political influences" (Warren 2000, 67). They are forms of discourse; quilts "tell stories, record people's lives, provide portraits of the quilters who make them, and often give shape and form to the experiences of those whose stories are not told in the literature discourse" (68). They preserve the histories of distinct cultural traditions.

Quilts can also raise issue awareness, as in the case of the AIDS Names Project quilts highlighted by Warren (2000, 66–67), and in our earlier example of the WCL program, in which farmland owners create quilt-like pieces from familiar materials and fabrics to portray their dream farmscapes, and which can be pieced together with those of their neighbors to inspire conversations about landscape-level changes. Quilts are aesthetic and increasingly appreciated as works of art: "exciting visually, with precise, varied, and vibrant designs, bold color combinations and exuberant displays of individual and community identities" (Warren 2000, 68). And, of course, quilts are quintessentially practical, as "comforters" (Warren 2000, 68) that provide warmth or even income for their makers.

We can see how the design of WFAN's quilt has emerged from the diverse perspectives and experiences of its makers. Warren (2000) understands theory as a set of necessary, but not sufficient, conditions. Our mission and goals form the border of WFAN's quilt, framing our commitment to women, agricultural sustainability, social justice, and healthy, accessible community food systems. "[N]othing that is knowingly, intentionally, or consciously naturist, sexist, racist, or classist – or which maintains *isms of domination* – belongs on the quilt. Nor does anything that is not, in some way, about nonhuman nature or human-nature relationships" (Warren 2000, 67). These border conditions would align with ecofeminist quilters in a variety of different settings.

The patches are a different matter. Quilters in different historical, material and cultural contexts will construct different pieces. For this reason, we cannot know beforehand what the interior of the quilt will look like; we do not know enough to specify all the sufficient conditions for a quilt piece. We may find a piece from one time or setting now fails to satisfy the border condition that denies any *ism* of domination a place on the quilt. Our task is then to repair, replace, remove, or alter to preserve the value and usefulness of the quilt, building on the work of previous quilters, but reflecting new insights and perspectives (Warren 2000, 67). The pattern of the quilt is in process, not preordained.

The interior of WFAN's quilt may also change in light of matters practical and strategic, such as funding streams, decisions about where to invest limited program resources, or evolving definitions of sustainable agriculture, diversity, inclusion and women's identity. Chiappe and Flora (1998, 374) point to elements that may need a more prominent place on our quilt when they ask: "To what degree does the male derived paradigm leave out elements essential for the effective development of technology, policy, and education capable of facilitating a movement toward a more sustainable food system?" Other questions may prompt soul searching (and quilt mending) as to the depth of our commitment to social change as we stumble into new unthought-of *isms* or experience the full implications of challenges such as climate change for our modes of being in the world. The quilting will continue.

Conclusion and lingering questions

Our goal in this chapter is empirical and analytical, to describe and theorize change, in order to inform practice. Borrowing from Chris Cuomo (2003, 41), we define theory as "a form of knowledge-making that creates order, reifies and challenges power, and informs particular practical decisions and interactions." Cuomo (2003, 53) reminds us also that:

> Theory is practice, and it informs and is shaped by myriad other practices, material conditions, and political realities ... theory is no distanced knower, gazing upon reality from above and attempting a perfect sketch. As a form of interactive reflection, theory does aim to capture and convey, but those aims are never pure, disinterested, or only intellectual.

As feminist theorists often remind, there is nothing so practical as a good theory, but they fully understand the complexity of the feminist theoretical project.

Our experience is working with primarily white women in a Midwestern agricultural landscape dominated by row crop agriculture. While the majority of the world's women farmers have very different experiences, the industrial agriculture of the Midwest is an important context in that it is used as a model for agricultural progress and exported to the developing world under the guise of agricultural development. Our hope is that sharing our lessons learned and continuing questions will inform agricultural systems intervention and change beyond this context. We draw upon our experience through these programs to ask: in what ways do our incremental gains as women support or subvert existing power structures? How do we continue to elevate women and remain gender-focused in our efforts to achieve systemic change?

We are not naïve about the challenges we face in both our larger ambitions of achieving sustainability or more modest realms of having a seat at the table. Resistance to change is deep; institutions do not give up power willingly. To achieve sustainability may require both the participation of women and the advancement of certain values. We can open and hold (learning) space, speak against patriarchal power in agriculture, call out and name hegemony, speak truth to power, and create community.

In participating in the creation of alternative spaces and exchanging needed skills and knowledge, participants in WFAN's programs may begin to construct new narratives for their landscapes. Through their participatory creation of local knowledge, WFAN's program participants engage in reflection and generation of strategies or interventions within the "structural relationships of power and the ways through which they are maintained by monopolies of knowledge," creating the potential to "challenge deep-rooted power inequities" (Gaventa and Cornwall 2001, 70).

WFAN's commitment to exploring alternatives, drawing from Noël Sturgeon (1995), is both critical and creative, oppositional and prefigurative. Working to end one system without providing a complete model for its replacement may to some extent be unavoidable. We make the road by walking, and our journey is an ongoing one. As Rebecca Solnit (2015, n.p.) reminds us:

> Our world is both better (more inclusive, less discriminatory) and worse (think corporate consolidation, ecological devastation, the surveillance state) than the world of fifty years ago. The ways in which it is better happened because people made demands and then acted to realize them. It was not inevitable that Native Americans, women, gays, lesbians, and transgender people would gain rights and respect. The better part of our present happened because of enormous efforts, sometimes over decades or, as with the vote for women, nearly a century of effort and social transformation.

Programs alone will not revolutionize agriculture; however their successes provide ideas for how to create local change through networks that support a more equitable system when opportunities arise. To transform and rebuild democratic power within our agricultural system, we must do more than contest inequities within industrial agriculture, but also work together to create alternative and new opportunities. Building power through women-specific programs creates new communities in which women are decision-makers, mentors, leaders, and, most importantly, change-makers.

Notes

1 See curriculum manual at http://womencaringfortheland.org/wfan-publications/.
2 Annie's Project is a national educational program for farm and ranch women facilitated by land grant universities in the United States. For more information: www.extension.iastate.edu/annie/.
3 See http://womencaringfortheland.org/blog/2013/06/05/women-caring-for-the-land-program-wins-governors-environmental-excellence-award/.
4 Here we contrast the dominant treatment of land with Aldo Leopold's (1949) land ethic, which views land as a biotic community of which we are a part, rather than land as something to be conquered and controlled.
5 Since our earliest days we have engaged in popular education and participatory research.
6 See http://platetopolitics.org/cultivate-2012-summit-at-wingspread/.
7 We find value in Zein-Elabdin's institutional approach, and note that her emphasis on *actual* work processes dovetails nicely with Dorothy Smith's (2004) institutional ethnography. However, her arguments against ecofeminism are less persuasive, given our view of ecofeminist theory expressed in these pages.

References

Allen, Patricia. 2004. *Together at the Table. Sustainability and Sustenance in the American Agrifood System.* University Park: Pennsylvania State University Press.

Bunch, Charlotte. 1987. *Passionate Politics, Essays 1968–1986: Feminist Theory in Action.* New York: St. Martin's Press.

Chiappe, Marta B., and C. Butler Flora. 1998. "Gendered Elements of the Alternative Agriculture Paradigm." *Rural Sociology* 63 (3): 372–93.

Cuomo, Chris. 2003. "Critical Theory and the Science of Complexity." In *The Philosopher Queen: Feminist Essays on War, Love, and Knowledge*, 41–56. Lanham: Rowman & Littlefield.

Duffy, Michael, and Ann Johanns. 2014. "Farmland Ownership and Tenure in Iowa 2012." Iowa State University Extension and Outreach. Revised 2014. www.extension.iastate.edu/Publications/PM1983.pdf.

Eells, Jean C. 2008. "The Land, It's Everything: Women Farmland Owners and the Institution of Agricultural Conservation in the U.S. Midwest." PhD diss., Iowa State University.

———. 2010. "Loving the Land is Not Enough: Empowering Women Landowners to Prevent Environmental Degradation." *Ecopsychology* 2 (3): 179–85.

Eells, Jean C., and Jessica Soulis. 2014. "Do Women Farmland Owners Count in Agricultural Conservation? A Review of Research on Women Farmland Owners in the United States." *Journal of Soil and Water Conservation* 68 (5): 121A–23A.

Everett, B.B. 1983. "Viewpoint: Soil Conservation; A Farm Woman's Perspective." *Journal of Soil and Water Conservation* 38 (2): 69.

Gaventa, John, and Andrea Cornwall. 2001. "Power and Knowledge." In *Handbook of Action Research: Participative Inquiry and Practice*, edited by Peter Reason and Hilary Bradbury, 70–80. London: Sage Publications.

Hassanein, Neva. 1997. "Networking Knowledge in the Sustainable Agriculture Movement: Some Implications of the Gender Dimension." *Society & Natural Resources: An International Journal* 10 (3): 251–57.

hooks, bell. 1989. *Talking back*. Boston: South End Press.

Leopold, Aldo. (1949) 1987. "The Land Ethic." In *Sand County Almanac and Sketches Here and There*, 201–226. New York: Oxford University Press.

Mies, Maria, and Vandana Shiva. 1993. *Ecofeminism*. London: Zed Books.

Moser, Caroline O.N. 1993. *Gender Planning and Development: Theory, Practice and Training*. New York: Routledge.

Plumwood, Val. 1993. *Feminism and the Mastery of Nature*. New York: Routledge.

Ransom, Elizabeth, and Carmen Bain. 2011. "Gendering Agricultural Aid: An Analysis of Whether International Development Assistance Targets Women and Gender." *Gender & Society* 25 (1): 48–74.

Sachs, Carolyn. 1996. *Gendered Fields: Rural Women, Agriculture, and Environment*. Boulder, CO: Westview Press.

Shortall, Sally. 2001. "Women in the Field: Women, Farming and Organizations." *Gender Work and Organization* 8 (2): 164–81.

Smith, Dorothy. 2004. *Institutional Ethnography: A Sociology for People*. New York: Alta Mira.

Solnit, Rebecca. 2015. "The Most Important Thing We Can Do to Fight Climate Change is Try." *The Nation*, March 31. www.thenation.com/article/198537/unpredictable-weather.

Sturgeon, Noël. 1995. "Theorizing Movements: Direct Action and Direct Theory." In *Cultural Politics and Social Movements*, edited by Marcy Darnovsky, Barbara Epstein, and Richard Flacks, 35–51. Philadelphia: Temple University Press.

US National Archives and Records Administration. 2015. Code of Federal Regulations. Title 26. Income Taxes.

Warren, Karen. 2000. *Ecofeminist Philosophy: A Western Perspective on What It Is and Why It Matters*. Lanham, MD: Rowman & Littlefield Publishers, Inc.

Wells, Betty. 2002. "Context, Strategy, Ground: Rural Women Organizing to Confront Local/Global Economic Issues." In *Women's Activism and Globalization: Linking Local Struggles and Global Politics*, edited by Nancy A. Naples and Manisha Desai, 143–55, New York: Routledge.

———. 2004. *Results of Survey of Cass County Women Farmland Owners*. Ames, IA: ISU Sociology Extension. www.soc.iastate.edu/extension/pub/Wells%202004%20Cass%20County%20Women%20Farmland%20Owners%20Survey%20Report.pdf.

Wells, Betty, and Jean Eells. 2011. "One Size Does Not Fit All: Customizing Conservation to a Changing Demographic." *Journal of Soil and Water Conservation* 66 (September – October): 136A – 39A.

Zein-Elabdin, Eiman. 1996. "Development, Gender, and the Environment: Theoretical or Contextual Link? Toward an Institutional Analysis of Gender." *Journal of Economic Issues* 30 (December): 929–47.

Canada

16 Ploughing new ground

A feminist interpretation of youth farm internships in Ontario, Canada

Jan Kainer

Introduction

This chapter discusses research findings on young and beginning farmer training programs in Ontario. It draws on interviews with a small sample of women farmers practicing sustainable or small-scale ecologically oriented farming who deliver farm youth training programs. Rather than focusing on the experiences of youth interns, the paper investigates the work contributions of those who provide the training – the women farmers – and discusses their backgrounds, their food politics, and their commitment to engaging youth in sustainable farming. Referring to feminist perspectives on gender and work, the chapter argues small-scale women farmers are important contributors to developing food alternatives and to offering innovative ways of delivering education and training in sustainable farming. However, the range of skills they bring to their role as trainers and educators are not fully recognized, and they often do not receive needed substantive supports for their diligent and creative efforts.

A note on methodology

The findings below are based on a research project that is part of a large, federally funded Social Science and Humanities Community University Research Alliance grant entitled Work in a Warming World (W3). The main purpose of W3 is to map the impact of climate change on job futures. Taking sustainable farming as its starting point, this research set out to investigate the experience of a new generation of farmers engaged in youth agricultural internships. A small sample of seven small-scale farmers in south western Ontario delivering training in ecological or sustainable farming to youth interns was contacted; of these, two farmers declined to be interviewed and a third did not answer our request for an interview. There could be any number of reasons for their refusal to participate, such as lack of time and busyness of the farming season or their unfamiliarity with academic research. However, at the time of the field research the media was widely reporting on the "unpaid intern debate." Numerous newspaper articles documented the plight of the estimated 100,000 student interns working in Ontario – many who work for long hours and at menial tasks for no pay. In response to this journalistic inquiry the Ontario Ministry of Labour carried out an investigation blitz shutting down internships in establishments it deemed illegal (Mandryk, Seaborn, and Langille 2014; McKnight 2014; Oved 2014). Given these circumstances it is quite possible farmers were nervous about discussing internships at their farms.

In the end four semi-structured interviews lasting about two hours were conducted with farmers and their interns in the summer of 2014 (see Table 16.1). An ethics review of the project was conducted and approved by the Office of Research Ethics at the author's university (certificate no. e2014-178). One of the interviewees refused to be tape-recorded; all of the other interviews were taped and transcribed. The farmers, all of whom were women, were selected based on their willingness to engage interns and young people on their farms; questions were asked about their reasons for practicing ecologically oriented farming, why they use interns and what they perceived to be most important in training their interns. This study did not begin with the question of why women predominate in this type of farming or why women participate in youth agricultural skills training, rather, the gender dimension emerged in the course of doing the research. Three interns were also interviewed; however, space does not allow for detailed discussion of these findings.

Background and literature review

Feminist researchers generally agree that the important work of food preparation and food production, often performed by women and crucial to social reproduction, is greatly undervalued. This finding particularly applies to women farmers, who remain invisible and subordinate within the agricultural sector. Traditionally, women on farms have been excluded from land ownership; historical convention ensured continuity of the "family name" by passing land possession intergenerationally to men.

In North America and Europe acquiring farmland was mostly achieved through family inheritance rather than through the market, a pattern that persists today despite the forces of economic globalization and other cultural changes in the Global North (Shortall 1999). As a result of this patrilineal and patriarchal system, women were largely relegated to performing non-wage reproductive labor.

In the current context the work of farmwomen has expanded to include a broad range of productive activities; however, their labor continues to be socially and economically devalued for ideological reasons tied to gender and because it is seen to be divorced from commercial activities of the farm (e.g., Desmarais 2005; Blum 2012). As Shortall explains, "[m]uch of the work which women do in sustaining the family household and the farm business is not recognized and rendered invisible" (1999, 117). Kubik uses the term "invisible women farmers" to convey their cultural devaluation while in reality, she argues, women contribute significantly to the farm enterprise, and indirectly to subsidizing the consumer price of food (2005, 87).

Table 16.1 Interview participants

Name*	Sarah	Marg	Kelly	Diana
Date of interview	August 19	August 20	August 12	August 12
Years farming	Since 2010	Since 2004	Since 2000	Since 2005
Type of farm enterprise	Garden (vegetables, berries, fruits)	Dairy cows, sheep and goats; owns restaurant and retails dairy	Garden (vegetables, berries, fruits); laying hens, goats; Honey	Garden (vegetables, berries, fruits); chickens, cows, goats, pigs
Self-described	Certified organic	Local and sustainable	Organic	Local and sustainable
CSA	yes	no	yes	yes
Other food initiatives, activities		Home farm	Children and mothers food program Permaculture	Proposed local commercial kitchen Community food handler advisor
Occupational Background	Actor; arts administrator; counsellor	Chef	Horticultural therapist	Human resources; business

* Pseudonyms.

Figure 16.1 Ontario farm woman marketing farm eggs.

The lack of recognition of the value of female farm labor and women's marginalization from the farm economy created the impetus for farmwomen to collectively organize to demand greater recognition for their labor. A key demand of farmwomen's organizations was access to women-only agricultural skills training, which they argued would help valorize and make visible their farm labor. In Canada the need for gender specific agricultural education was touted as one of the first objectives of the Canadian Farm Women's Network, founded in 1985 (Shortall 1999, 106, 131). Today, as my interviews below indicate, women farmers continue to observe the shortage of formal skills training, particularly in sustainable agriculture, and remain deeply committed to providing education in this field especially to young people. Indeed, the current focus on farm skills training has turned primarily to youth, due in large part to an aging farm population.

In Canada the average age of a farm operator is 54 and in the province of Ontario, the subject of this case study, the average age of a farmer is 55 (Statistics Canada 2011). Particularly worrisome is the severe decline of young farmer operators; in 2011 only 8 percent of farms were operated solely by young farmers (defined as under 40 years old), "whereas two decades earlier it was about one in four" (Beaulieu 2015). According to a federal government report, while 20 percent of Canadian farms involved young farmer operators in 2008, the remaining 80 percent had operators 40 years of age and older (Agriculture and Agri-Food Canada, 2011). To encourage youth engagement in farming, both the federal and provincial governments in Canada offer programs to facilitate skills training programs for young people aged 18 to 39, referred to as "young and beginning farmers" (YBF), who operate "young farmer enterprises" (YFE). YFEs tend to be small but perform better economically than other farms earning slightly higher profit margins, and rely less on off-farm sources of income (Agriculture and Agri-Food Canada 2011). These YBFs are increasingly being recognized as essential to alleviating the drastic decline of small farms and necessary to replacing aging farmers (e.g., FarmON Alliance Ontario 2012; Wiebe 2012; on the United States see Blum 2012).

A formal curriculum and a systematic approach to mentoring youth in ecological and agricultural practices in Canada have yet to be fully established (Bloom and Young 2012; FarmON Alliance Ontario 2012). Instead, various farm youth skills programs such as the Canadian Young Farmers Forum (CYFF) provide networking, informal mentorship (e.g., Step-Up) and workshops to educate and encourage young people to develop agricultural knowledge and skills and to become leaders in the farm community.

The most important and popular youth farmer skills training programs are internships delivered by farmers who typically use non-governmental food organizations' websites to access participants. These programs match volunteer youth with small-scale farmers offering training in organic or local, sustainable farming practices. Youth interest in these programs and in sustainable food has escalated in recent years, likely an outgrowth of their awareness and knowledge of, and activism in, the growing alternative food movement. Alternative food initiatives challenge corporate or industrial approaches to the food system, replacing them with ecological or sustainable practices of food production. As a social movement "alternatives" expands upon the notion of sustainability extending its meaning beyond ecological concerns to include fair and equitable systems of social relations such as support for food cooperatives and other non-profit or anti-capitalist arrangements that "sustain" and reproduce social life (Sumner and Llewelyn 2011, 102–03). This dual commitment to ecological and social sustainability seems to hold significant appeal to young people (Kane 2012; Lopez 2014).

In Ontario (as elsewhere) local and sustainable food enterprises have multiplied (Bain, 2015; Baker, Campsie, and Rabinowicz 2010). The *Local Food Act* was enacted in 2013 in Ontario to foster successful local food economies and systems, to raise awareness of local food and to encourage new markets of local food. Funding from the provincial government (Local Food Fund) is provided to individuals for community food initiatives and to organizations such as the Greenbelt Fund to connect institutions such as schools and hospitals to local food growers. Furthermore, various regional communities have pledged support of local food (e.g., Simcoe County; towns of Stratford, Kingston) which in turn supports restaurants serving local food, fair trade coffee/cafes, community share agriculture programs, and so on. Youth internship programs provide an important link to supporting such initiatives.

A number of programs offering youth skills in sustainable farming are available, including: FarmStart, FarmLINK, and Collaborative Regional Alliance for Farm Training (CRAFT/Ontario/Canada). Additionally, apprentices at various farms around the province such as Everdale Farm and Green Being Farm, and internationally, the World Wide Opportunities on Farms (WWOOF) program connects students and other youth (called WWOOFers) to Ontario farmers. Farm internships are structured on a volunteer basis and do not offer compensation such as an hourly wage although a small cash stipend is often paid; interns also receive room and board, and of course training and/or mentorship in sustainable farming practices. As discussed below, interns can create challenges for farm sponsors, particularly concerning issues surrounding living arrangements. However, many small-scale farmers are very dependent on this non-wage labor to support their enterprise. As Levkoe et al. (2015, 4) explain:

> Finding and maintaining dependable farm labour presents a challenge for farm operators due to the intensive labour required for small-scale farming (e.g. limited mechanization), and the nature of farm work (e.g. seasonal fluctuation, long hours, physical labour, specific skills and knowledge needs, and negative cultural attitudes [toward farming]. Further, the low profit margins from fresh produce and livestock (Qualman 2011; Wiebe 2012) can make it difficult to employ workers on a full-time basis.

Practically speaking, then, many small-scale sustainable farmers cannot survive economically without the assistance of volunteer labor and this is one of the major reasons for engaging youth interns.

Feminist scholars, as noted above, have identified the importance of women's non-wage work in agriculture – this is especially the case with labor intensive small-scale farm enterprises, many of which practice sustainable farming. Since non-wage work is essential to maintaining small diverse farms it is not surprising that many women operate these types of enterprises. Data from North America and Europe indicate that many women farmers practice ecological or organic agriculture, for example, "in the U.S. and U.K. women are 17 times more likely than men to adopt organic methods of horticulture production" (Sumner and Llewelyn 2011, 104). In Canada the Census of Agriculture data reveal an increasing number of women engaging in sustainable farming. Of all organic farmers, one-third of operators were women in 2001 (Sumner 2005). By 2011 45 percent of all organic farm operations involved women (Statistics Canada 2011). Evidence in Ontario also points to more women than men in farm internships (WWOOF 2015a, 4; FarmON Alliance Ontario 2012, 6). A 2014 survey specifically investigating small-scale ecologically oriented farmers' labor practices found a majority of female interns. According to this study "58% [were] female, 91% white, nearly 80%

were aged 16–30 years, and 54% had a university undergraduate or graduate degree" (Levkoe et al. 2015, 8). The program director of FarmSTART in Ontario, a trainee program for young or new farmers, also noticed a majority of female interns stating that the "most successful farms I know are run by young women" (Kane 2012, GT 4).

Women's connection to small-scale and sustainable farming has a long history. In the developed world women have been involved in "organic agriculture since its inception" (Sumner and Llewelyn 2011, 103). In the current context small-scale farming is linked to alternative food politics; according to McMahon, it "represents a form of cultural resistance as well as economic resistance" to the commodification of food within global capitalist agriculture (2013, 526). From this ecological feminist viewpoint food is not an object but rather embodies a complexity of social relationships operating within the food system so that "[a] potato is not just a potato, it carries in it, and into us when we eat it, a host of social relationships ... [hence] when we partake in food, we consume relationships" (McMahon 2013, 526). In this perspective food and the food system are gendered and small-scale farming is understood to be feminized, meaning that these farmers are both men and women who identify with alternative (female-like) politics that challenge existing industrial capitalist globalized agriculture.

While it is important to conceptualize the gender identity of farmers in non-essentialist terms, it is also evident that many women engage in small-scale farming and are active contributors to its alternative philosophy, its holistic values, and whole-system approach to farming. For some farm women sustainable agriculture is way of life, or calling, that expresses their spiritual connection to the land and nature (Roppel, Desmarais, and Martz 2006, 32–33). According to Blum, who investigated life stories of female sustainable farmers in the United States, the "labor of small-scale sustainable farming, with all its components, provides a livelihood, but it requires every bit of the farmer's selfhood; body, mind, heart, spirit and social network" (2012, 332). Canadian women farmers also express connections to farming in relational and idealistic ways feeling a responsibility to:

> maintain a healthy environment and produce food safely... [and they] also want others to discover and become connected to the land as they are. Many women see farming as contributing to continuing life, and ensuring that their children and grandchildren know the source of food they eat.
>
> (Roppel, Desmarais, and Martz 2006, 33)

Of particular significance to small-scale ecological farmers is contributing to the broader community economically, socially, and politically. Women farmers are very involved and widely represented in organic farm organizations and in the sustainable or ecological farm movement in Canada (Desmarais 2005; Sumner and Llewelyn 2011, 104). Their activism extends to a broad range of activities, many of which are local, that challenge capitalist

Figure 16.2 Ontario farm woman in her greenhouse.

commodification, not only of food, but capitalist market relations generally. The women I interviewed expressed strong sentiments and deep commitment to building alternatives distinct from market-based practices and articulated support for those that create greater human connection to the land, to animals, and to the broader community. Teaching a new generation of people how to farm using ecological and sustainable farming methods was, for these women, of paramount importance to imagining and building alternatives.

Findings

All of the farmers involved in this study spoke about their strong commitment to the agricultural community and of the importance of sustainable farming practices for the survival of the planet. As Sarah commented, "every organic seed that is planted makes a difference." Another commonality was their recent commitment to farming; all four women had had non-farming careers and began small-scale sustainable farming later in their lives. They were middle- to late middle-aged and brought considerable knowledge, skill, and life experience to their work as farmers. They were also very active locally within their agricultural communities, occupying a variety of roles related to their foodwork.

With respect to their relationship with youth and youth interns, their responses were mixed. Two of the respondents were intensely engaged in delivering and developing innovative training and educational programs and saw these as a commitment to envisioning sustainable food futures. The other two women interviewed, although supportive of internships, expressed certain frustrations associated with training young people in sustainable farming. As explained in greater detail below, these two kinds of responses reflect the contradictory position of women in small-scale sustainable farming. On the one hand, because their reproductive work as farmers is devalued (and invisible) they face certain taken-for-granted assumptions about their capacity to deliver youth training that can operate to their disadvantage. On the other hand, because they own their farms, are knowledgeable of the local food system, and are well connected within their communities, they are uniquely situated to imagine and create innovative or transformative food programs. The following discussion is divided into several themes. I begin by discussing the farmers' occupational backgrounds and how they came to take up farming. The second theme addresses their motives for hiring youth interns and their experiences with them. Lastly, I consider how their commitment to building community and food alternatives is related to their profound concern to ensure a sustainable food system for future generations.

The farmers

Only one of the women interviewed had grown up on a farm. Kelly was raised on a farm settled by her ancestor in 1806. She had learned some sustainable framing practices from her father who incorporated them alongside conventional farming. But after she grew up she left the farm to go to university and became a horticultural therapist in the hospital sector. "At the hospital, interestingly enough, I had to learn organic practices. Because, of course, we didn't want to expose people with compromised immune systems to any sort of sprays or any sort of toxins" (Kelly, August 12, 2014). Her job convinced her of the importance of accessing healthy food in healthy environments. In 2000 she and her husband returned to her family's farm, and after her parents' recent death they took over managing it, though her husband continued to do off-farm wage work (he was planning to quit his job in the fall of 2014). They rent most of the farm to a conventional farmer except for a small parcel of land where "everything we grow is organic and we are slowly transitioning small sections" (Kelly, August 12, 2014).

None of the other women had farm experience and all are self-taught sustainable farmers. Diana bought a farm because her daughter wanted a horse. She previously worked in business and was educated in human resource management. She explained that "thanks to her husband's pay cheque" she is able to run the farm (Diana, August 12, 2014). Marg also did not grow up on a farm but had worked as a chef for 25 years. Because she did not receive financial and moral support to attend university from her father, who was a medical doctor, she went to cooking school. At the time, she explains, "it was all about women into non-traditional occupations and there was lots of funding for that kind of stuff and I went into chef school and that was a great career for me" (Marg, August 20, 2014). While working as a chef she became fascinated with cheese making and eventually left her job to develop a dairy business, though this led to a huge drop in her income and ended her marriage. Marg explains her motive for going into dairy was to help change the food system; she describes her approach to sustainable farming as:

> Hard core. We don't allow any fermented seeds and no GMOs and only seasonal breeding and milking. So, [the cows] are only allowed to be milked for nine or ten months of the year and then they they're mandated to rest ... so that means our milk comes flooding in from March through the end of November – it can be quite intense.

Lastly, Sarah also had no farming in her background. She worked as an actor for 15 years, then as an administrator in the Arts for another eight, and finally ended up in addiction counselling where she continues to work, travelling to Burma (Myanmar) during the winters to teach others about counselling people with addictions. Her counselling work supplements her economically on the farm. Sarah had some experience gardening growing up because her mother, a high school teacher, grew a large half-acre garden during the summer. Her sister is also a horticulturalist but she is mainly self-taught and has learned about organic/sustainable farming from her mother, from reading, and by attending workshops.

To operate and maintain their farm enterprises successfully these women combine a variety of material or income sources, which is common on farms. As mentioned, two farmers relied on off-farm income from their spouse while another worked in the winter season to supplement her income. During the summer Sarah sells produce to local restaurants. Marg owns and operates a restaurant, as well as retailing dairy products (e.g., cheese, ice cream) at her own outlet.

All of the women sell at farmers' markets and participate in community supported agriculture (CSA) programs, a production and marketing model whereby customers buy shares in a farmer's proceeds in advance of the harvest. They all said that their primary source of farm income derives from their CSA. For instance, Kelly stated that "we have CSA on Wednesday" [for 50 bi-weekly shares] "and then Thursday to Monday is market stand." As discussed below, Marg pioneered the CSA model in new and innovative directions. Interestingly, two women commented that participants in both market gardens and CSAs are mostly women. After seven years of running a CSA Diana observed that "the CSA's are mostly women; this is the first year I have a guy. He contacted me." Kelly remarked that in her rural community "there's an interesting piece that popped into my awareness was that the majority of market gardeners ... not all but the majority of market gardeners are women."

Training interns

The women said their main reason for engaging interns was to acquire labor to help them manage their farms. As already mentioned, sustainable farming is very labor intensive and not highly profitable so the use of volunteer interns provides the necessary support to accomplish the wide array of labor consuming tasks on their farms. Sarah said she found it hard to farm by herself and could not afford to hire people. She hosted ten WWOOFers in 2013 alone. Kelly spoke highly of her relationship with interns, describing a particular WWOOFing volunteer in glowing terms:

> We joke that he's been adopted by our family. Last year, I was in a situation where my Dad was dying and my Mom with Alzheimer's and I just needed to be away a lot … you know he was able to maintain things enough that, you know, made our way through the summer and we fulfilled our commitment to the CSA, which of course, is our first goal.

Another practical incentive for engaging interns is to access benefits such as networking and workshops offered by the farm organization CRAFT. "If you want to join the CRAFT organization, you have to do it, you need to agree to have an intern, to have training days" (Diana).

Although interns were often invaluable to the farmers, they could also be demanding, gobbling up resources of time and money:

> Our interns we pay a stipend. I know some farmers who pay $400 a month. It's not easy to have an intern. You don't say: 'pick this row of beans.' You go: 'this is why I grew it, this is how you grow it, this how you pick it' … that's the difference. … Do you know how many tools they break? You can't take it out of their pay, they're not employees. It's not easy having an intern.
>
> (Diana)

Providing experiential learning is mentally taxing, requiring the farmer to explain seemingly simple things such as: "This is a hoe, what is a hoe? How is it different from a shovel? How do you shovel? Et cetera" (Sarah). If the intern is not motivated to learn then the training process is especially demanding, "You don't want to work with someone who goes … like this, 'oh, God it's *hot*! Ooh, my *back* hurts …' because, you know, this is hard work … farming." (Diana)

The greatest problems encountered relate to live-in and boarding of interns. For instance, meals must be provided and even some of the incidental costs such as providing toilet paper and laundering can add up. A variety of hidden costs are attached to "being hospitable," such as paying for transportation, wine or beer at dinner, or a movie ticket if the family decides to go out for the evening (Diana).

Socializing can become burdensome when international interns want to practice English or have high personal needs; according to Sarah, "interns can talk all day and all night." Cooking meals every evening is onerous and unavoidable because "a lot of people, especially men, cannot cook (Sarah)." Sarah remarked that inviting an intern on your farm "is a leap of faith" as they can have personal problems or mental problems including anxiety disorders, a mental disability, depression, and addictions. Internship organizations do not have a process for vetting interns and when they do not work out, the onus is solely on the farmer to sever the relationship, regardless of the severity of the problems (WWOOF 2015b, 23).

Educating and teaching about food: visioning food futures

Although there are certain drawbacks to hosting farm interns, the women in this study expressed strong enthusiasm about the importance of training youth in internship programs, stating that it is crucial to "give back." Kelly's comment is typical:

> The intern piece, certainly, that's a huge key to me, you know, to help anybody learn ... I do think that it's key that we have people engaged in our food system, and growing food and knowing how to grow food. And teaching another generation.

A commitment to educating people about food was shared by all of the women farmers and was stated as one of the major reasons they participate in CSAs. Diana offers training workshops to CSA participants:

> I put in one thousand tomato plants. I asked my CSA's. I have two or three that asked: 'is that a potato?' They are a reminder to me of where I came from and what I have learned. People don't know a carrot top. Or children [ask] 'is that where our chicken fingers come from?'

Three of the farmwomen developed innovative food programs specifically to teach people about growing food and food preparation and had applied for government funding to implement their ideas. Kelly received a grant from the Ministry of Health to "pilot test a series of classes on teaching children how to grow food." The activities invite mothers and their children to explore gardens and the outdoors:

> I really feel strongly that from a life skills point of view, from a psycho-social, from a spiritual point of view, children need to be outside. And they love being in the soil, right? Children are naturally drawn to soil. There's no reason that all children cannot grow some food. It's such a rewarding experience to plant a seed and to take care of it and see it grow. (Kelly)

Although Kelly created the children's program, under the terms of the funding agreement she is only allowed to hire a consultant to deliver the activities at her farm; all of the conceptual work and other labor she performs for the project is non-waged and volunteer. Still, she would like the program idea to be expanded to other communities to promote a "a healthy good sustainable environment for ourselves and our children."

Diana entered a competition soliciting entrepreneurs for a business proposal sponsored by the Local Food Fund "where you could win space" and she "got picked as the top 30 ideas."

> My business idea is to open up a commercial kitchen where we could promote local eating, where people can come and learn how to can, to ferment, to dehydrate, to pickle ... But we have yet to hear back ... I submitted it February 28th. I am still waiting – unbelievable. Six months later. I fit perfectly because they are promoting a local food hub.

Her concept of a commercial kitchen came from her customers at the farmer's market who said they lacked knowledge and skill in food preservation. A commercial kitchen would not only promote more local food purchasing, but would allow its users to prepare food and sell it according to public health standards.

Marg, who operates the dairy business, also has a strong commitment to teaching foodwork. Her goal is to open up an artisanal cheese school to run during the off-season months because: "there's no educational system set up for any of our artisanal food crafts at all and we really need to get back to that. So, we're running a school this spring." In her view, "it's the most important thing we can do because we don't have any history of it." The cheese school is part of Marg's bigger vision of an alternative farming model she calls the Home Farm.

In 2014 Marg purchased land with a house and barn nearby to her dairy. It is being paid for through a CSA scheme whereby customers contribute money of varying amounts ($500–1,000) in exchange for receiving vouchers for cheese and other products produced on the farm, otherwise known as "food futures." As Marg explains, "to repay those vouchers on a weekly basis was huge in terms of the pleasure that it gives. You know you have other debt. You have bank debt and credit card debt that you need to service and those are sometimes painful just because they're not based on relationships." The farm will offer bed and breakfast, cooking classes and the cheese school, and most importantly it will provide young people access to land. Purchasing the property was an extremely risky venture with tremendous financial pressure but she saw it as a commitment to the future of food security and necessary to promoting the next generation of farmers: "They [young people] have no access to land, right? So, the farm we bought is 40 acres and we paid a million dollars for it; we paid $25,000 an acre." Unexpectedly, Farm Credit Canada, a federal bank, agreed to back the mortgage and consolidate her debt at half the interest rate so that her "rates on a monthly basis are only a little less than $2,000 a month more than [her] existing payments." Marg has plans to experiment with various food initiatives but central to her vision is to:

> Set up gardens to grow produce for the restaurant and for sale at markets ... cook wonderful farm dinners, milk water buffalo, make raw milk cheese. My mission is to encourage an alternative farming model that helps young farmers have access to land – a place for people to come and stay and be part of the community.

Conclusion

Providing internship training requires affective labor, reproductive work, and work in production activities. The women not only demonstrate the necessary social skills to effectively relate to their interns; they also have the technical competencies to teach them everyday farm tasks and to educate them about sustainable farming practices. They support their interns' reproductive daily needs by doing cooking, laundering of linens, and other needed domestic labor. Moreover, they partake in the productive labor of physically tending to gardens, feeding and caring for livestock, doing the overall planning and budgeting, marketing their CSAs, and selling at farmers' markets. All of this work comprises the conventional labor assigned to farmwomen and much of the knowledge and specialized skill required to perform it is transmitted by farmwomen to interns.

Additionally, the farmers bring a diversity of skills and know-how to their farming based on their life experiences and years in the labor market that tends to go unrecognized by farm training organizations and funding agencies. For instance, Sarah said she learned from her "addiction counselling how to put up with adversity; from my administrative work I learned to make budgets, to learn how to plan, and how to raise money." Marg was able to finance her restaurant and dairy business based on her successful career as a chef. Kelly devised an educational food program that was informed by her experience in horticultural therapy and from her degree in psychology and physical education, and Diana relied on her business background to write a proposal to support a local food initiative. Interestingly, their knowledge and expertise is mostly unrelated to food and farming but their backgrounds provided them with the knowledge and expertise to develop innovative food projects.

While much of the work of these small-scale farmers is not acknowledged they are nonetheless dedicated to organic or sustainable food production, as is evident in their food politics and practices. All of the food initiatives the women participated in or devised themselves challenge industrial capitalist agriculture. Their participation in local food communities demonstrates their commitment to food sustainability that "resist[s] the commodification of life and farming under capitalism" (McMahon 2013, 526) and supports the claim that "rural women are at the forefront of environmental activism and social change" (Milne 2013, 242). Particularly challenging to the conventional food system is treating food production as part of a wider social space in which people, particularly young people, are mobilized and educated to engage in sustainable food practices, and alternative communities of producers are constructed. By creating and participating in educational food initiatives such as a commercial kitchen, the Home Farm, CSAs and youth farm internships it can be argued that the women are contributing to "new forms of sociality" that reconstruct the everyday life of reproduction (Federici 2012, 146). For instance, the CSAs, including the Home Farm, oppose capitalist values and market-based relationships through the creation of debt relationships founded on day-to-day personal connections and community ties that significantly depart from the impersonal and abstract money relations that underpin capitalist markets. In this sense, these food enterprises have wide connections and implications for forming alternatives to capitalism. Understanding food as a social relation – that healthy communities are built in the everyday activities of growing, preparing, and distributing sustainable food – creates alternatives within a feminine world of non-competition and social connectivity. As noted by Federici, "we cannot build an alternative society and a strong self-reproducing movement unless we redefine in more cooperative ways our reproduction and put an end to the separation between the personal and political, political activism and the reproduction of everyday life" (2012, 147).

To conclude, the narratives of the farmwomen in this study demonstrate their contradictory and complicated relationship to foodwork and the food system. While the women expressed frustration concerning the devaluation of their reproductive labor, they embraced positive food alternatives as a means of achieving greater personal and collective empowerment.

References

Agriculture and Agri-Food Canada. Research and Analysis Directorate, Strategic Policy Branch. 2011. *Agriculture 2020: Challenges and Opportunities*. Ottawa: Public Works and Government Services Canada.

Bain, Jennifer. 2015. "Stratford's Restaurant Shake Up." *Toronto Star*, May 1, L1, L3.

Baker, Laurel, Philippa Campsie, and Katie Rabinowicz. 2010. *Menu 2020 Ten Good Food Ideas for Ontario*. Toronto: Metcalf Foundation. http://metcalffoundation. com/publications-resources/view/menu-2020-ten-good-food-ideas-for-ontario/.

Beaulieu, Martin S. 2015. "Demographic Changes in Canadian Agriculture." *Canadian Agriculture at a Glance*. Statistics Canada Catalogue no. 96-325-XWE. www.statcan.gc.ca/pub/96-325-x/2014001/article/11905-eng.htm#a5.

Bloom, Shauna, and Christie Young, eds. 2012. "Supporting Success: Coaching, Mentorship and Advising for New Farmers in Ontario; How Farmers are Passing on Business Know–How, Technical Knowledge Production and Moral Support to a New Generation." Guelph, ON: FarmON Alliance Ontario. www.farmstart.ca/ wp-content/uploads/FINAL-CMA-doc_Sept2012-1.pdf.

Blum, Susan D. 2012. "Called By The Earth: Women In Sustainable Farming." *Journal of Workplace Rights* 16 (3/4): 315–36.

Desmarais, Annette. 2005. "You Are Mostly Promised You Will Not Be Alone." *Canadian Woman Studies* 24 (4): 7–11.

FarmON Alliance Ontario. 2012. "Learning to Become a Farmer: Findings From a FarmON Alliance Survey of New Farmers in Ontario." Guelph, ON: FarmON Alliance. www.farmstart.ca/wp-content/uploads/Learning-to-Become-a-Farmer-2012.pdf.

Federici, Silvia. 2012. *Revolution at Point Zero: Housework, Reproduction, and Feminist Struggle.* Brooklyn, NY: PM Press.

Kane, Laura. 2012. "Growing Passion for Farming." *Toronto Star*, August 13, GT3, GT4.

Kubik, Wendee. 2005. "Farm Women: The Hidden Subsidy in Our Food." *Canadian Woman Studies* 24 (4): 85–90.

Levkoe, Charles, Michael Ekers, Bryan Dale, and Samuel Walker. 2015. "Will Work for Food: The Local Food Movement and the New Face of Non-Wage Labour on Small-Scale Ecologically Oriented Farms." Paper presented at the 2015 American Association of Geographers Meeting, Chicago, Illinois, April 24.

Lopez, Ricardo. 2014. "Organic Agriculture Attracts a New Generation of Farmers." *Los Angeles Times*, June 7.

Mandryk, Josh, Claire Seaborn, and Andrew Langille. 2014. "Protect Co-op Students on the Job." *Toronto Star*, October 7, A17.

McKnight, Zoe. 2014. "Ottawa to Fund 3000 Paid Internships for New Grads." *Toronto Star*, May 4, A4.

McMahon, Martha. 2013. "Alternatives to Globalization: Women Small-Scale Farmers and Local Food Systems." In *Women in a Globalizing World: Transforming Equality, Development and Peace*, edited by Angela Miles, 525–32. Toronto: Inanna Publications and Education Inc.

Milne, Wendy. 2013. "Changing Climate, Uncertain Future: Considering Rural Women in Climate Change Policies and Strategies." In *Women in a Globalizing World: Transforming Equality, Development and Peace*, edited by Angela Miles, 236–45. Toronto: Inanna Publications and Education Inc.

Oved, Chown Marco. 2014. "Walrus Unpaid Interns are Back – with Pay." *Toronto Star*, May 4, A4.

Qualman, Darrin. 2011. "Advancing Agriculture by Destroying Farms? The State of Agriculture in Canada." In *Food Sovereignty in Canada: Creating Just and Sustainable Food Systems*, edited by Hannah Wittman, Annette Aurelie Desmarais, and Nettie Wiebe, 20–42. Halifax: Fernwood Publishing.

Roppel, Carla, Annette Aurelie Desmarais, and Diane Martz. 2006. *Farm Women and Canadian Agricultural Policy.* Ottawa: Status of Women Canada. www.aic.ca/gender/pdf/Farm_Women.pdf.

Shortall, Sally. 1999. *Women and Farming: Property and Power.* New York: St. Martin's Press.

Statistics Canada. 2011. *Census of Agriculture.* Ottawa, ON: Government of Canada.

Sumner, Jennifer. 2005. "'Small is Beautiful': The Responses of Women Organic Farmers to the Crisis in Agriculture." *Canadian Woman Studies* 24 (4): 78–84.

Sumner, Jennifer, and Sophie Llewelyn. 2011. "Organic Solutions? Gender and Organic Farming in the Age of Industrial Agriculture." *Capitalism Nature Socialism* 22 (1): 100–118.

Wiebe, Nettie. 2012. "Crisis in the Food System: The Farm Crisis." In *Critical Perspectives in Food Studies*, edited by Mustafa Koc, Jennifer Sumner, and Anthony Winson, 155–70. Don Mills, ON: Oxford University Press.

World Wide Opportunities on Farms (WWOOF). 2015a. "WWOOF Canada Guide to WWOOFing." *World Wide Opportunities on Organic Farms*. Procter, B.C. Last modified February 10. www.wwoof.ca/sites/default/files/wwooferfiles/WWOOFer%20Guidelines.pdf.

———. 2015b. "WWOOF Canada Host Guidelines." *World Wide Opportunities on Organic Farms*. Procter, B.C. Last modified April 17. www.wwoof.ca/sites/default/files/hostfiles/Host%20Guidelines.pdf.

Conclusion

17 What works for women in agriculture?

Amber J. Fletcher

Introduction

What works for women in agriculture? This question has been central to the chapters in this book. In this final chapter, I highlight and integrate some main insights from this collection, exploring its major themes in more depth. We opened this volume with the contention that practical solutions can ultimately inform our theorizing about women in agriculture more broadly while, at the same time, creating positive changes in women's everyday lives. In the following sections I identify some theoretical and practical implications of this collection of chapters from around the world. I examine two interconnected themes arising from the book: the transformative potential of everyday practice and agency, and the significance of gradual change. I explore the relevance of this collection within its broader global context and conclude with a summary overview of the practical solutions presented in this book.

Around the world, agricultural production continues to occur mostly on family farms (Food and Agriculture Organization of the United Nations 2014). Farm families from Tanzania to Australia are often conceptualized as cohesive units, but this notion masks the complexities that exist within households and farm operations, such as complex ownership patterns, gender roles, and inequalities. At the same time, however, it can be risky to reduce gender analysis only to the intra-household level; this approach fails to consider how macro-level structures, such as national and international agricultural policy, are also gendered.

The chapters in this collection examine power relationships within agricultural households, such as gendered divisions of labor and women's unequal access to land and agricultural inputs. But, many chapters also link their analysis to broader meso- and macro-level structures and systems. Individuals are integrated into households and households are integrated into broader systems such as communities and economies. As Crawford-Garrett et al. (Chapter 13, this volume) illustrate in their Theory of Change, transformation at one level can lead to transformation in another. Women's participation in organizations, communities, and economies can lead to household empowerment, but household empowerment enhances women's ability to participate at these broader levels. An integrated, multi-level approach is key.

Recognizing women in agriculture means recognizing how current structures and systems – whether formal or informal – continue to disadvantage farm women in relation to farm men. The chapters in this collection clearly illustrate the extent of this disadvantage while simultaneously emphasizing agency and the possibility of change. Altering social structures that hamper women's full participation and recognition in agriculture begins with the need to denaturalize these structures, to view them as impermanent and mutable (Apter and Garnsey 1994). As Mahoney and Thelen (2010) argued in their theory of institutional change, people's compliance with existing systems can be seen as a variable, not an inevitability. This observation can apply not only to formal institutional arrangements but also to the more informal aspects of gender orders. Positive change for women in agriculture means acknowledging women's agency to create this change.

Agents necessarily operate within the boundaries of pre-existing social structures not of their own design, such as gender orders, but such structures are not entirely deterministic. At the heart of this collection is the belief that action shapes future gender orders, either by reinforcing existing arrangements so that they continue or by reshaping these arrangements into something new. It is important to question how everyday practices can reinforce or challenge existing social relations. In Chapter 15, Carter and colleagues ask this question directly: "in what ways do our incremental gains as women support or subvert existing power structures?". Embedded in this important question are two interconnected themes from this book: first, the issue of how everyday practices can challenge the dominant gender order in agriculture, and second, the powerful potential of incremental and gradual change. I will explore each of these issues in turn.

Transformation through everyday life

Although several of these chapters show the importance of major macro-level and formal interventions such as policy changes, it is inaccurate to conclude that such interventions are the only mechanism for transforming gender relations. Indeed, many of the chapters show the importance of multifaceted intervention through multiple structures and levels. A useful example can be found in the issue of food security (see Part II of this book). The section moves from Alston and Whittenbury's call for effective gender mainstreaming to enhance food security at the national level (Chapter 5), to community- and household-level interventions in the form of urban agriculture (Chapter 6) and nutritional gardens (Chapters 7 and 8). Throughout the text, some authors suggest the need for far-reaching international and domestic policy changes (see for example Chapters 9 and 12), while others show the power of household activities for increasing women's visibility and empowerment in agriculture.

It is crucial to enhance women's control over agricultural production and their access to the necessary inputs for agriculture. Women's representation and voice – and, better yet, transformative *feminist* representation and voice – is essential to positively transform the political, economic, and ecological conditions of agriculture. At the same time, however, it is also important to recognize the power of women's everyday contributions, especially contributions that are less likely to be instantly recognized as "agriculture," but which are crucial to food and agricultural systems. Social reproduction – a concept that refers to both the "biological reproduction of the species (including its ecological framework) and ongoing reproduction of the commodity labour power" (Bakker and Gill 2008, 2) – can be seen as an important site of agency and change potential. Social reproduction involves the reproduction not just of farmers and farm workers, but also of agricultural systems more broadly. Women's socially determined responsibility for social reproduction means that they have the power to change those systems – for example, by using their existing agricultural activities as sites of power.

The power of everyday actions to change the status quo becomes clear through a morphogenetic perspective on structure and agency (Archer 2010). This approach suggests that human agency – conditioned but not determined by existing social structures – has the power to elaborate and alter structures over time, resulting in identifiably changed structures ("structural elaboration"). This perspective can help us understand how women's empowerment in agriculture can occur through their existing roles. Several chapters in this volume (see, for example, Chapters 7, 11, 14, 15, and 16) document women's involvement with activities conventionally associated with women (i.e., operating school nutritional gardens; quilting). These activities may seem to reinforce existing gender relations and ideologies that position women as primarily responsible for the household sphere of caregiving and social reproduction. However, these chapters show how women's involvement in such activities can lead to important social changes, such as increased education levels for children or training of young women to be environmentally sustainable farmers. Similar trends have been found in the literature on microcredit, for example, where women's access to microcredit is often linked to increased education for children, including girl children (see for example Holvoet 2004; Nader 2008). The chapters in this volume indicate that similar effects may occur from women's empowerment in agriculture. Existing structures and systems can be elaborated and changed. These changes hold the possibility for further transformation over time and generations.

Can gradual change be transformative change?

This book has focused on practical and concrete strategies that benefit women in agriculture. The second important issue raised here is the relevance and significance of gradual, incremental change. Archer (2010, 241) acknowledged "the slow work of structural elaboration," during which the actors have the ability (working within their given contexts) to alter circumstances and create new social structures over time. Indeed, "gradual changes can be of great significance in their own right; and gradually unfolding changes may be hugely consequential as causes of other outcomes" (Mahoney and Thelen 2010, 3). We need not focus exclusively on dramatic "focusing events" as the cause of social change, although such events certainly have the ability to provoke change. There is potency and potential in the everyday.

Several of the chapters in this book suggest that gradual change is sustainable change. Rapid and dramatic change may cause a reactionary or backlash effect that reinforces existing inequalities. For example, some literature has indicated that challenges to the existing gender order – such as women's increased financial empowerment or alterations to men's conventional roles, like unemployment – may be linked to increased violence against women in certain contexts (Jewkes 2002; Campbell et al. 2003; Rocca et al. 2009; Heath 2014; Crawford-Garrett et al., this volume). In Ghana, Carr (2008) found that the most accepted agricultural adaptation strategies were those that drew on already-accepted social structures; unfortunately, in Carr's study, those already-accepted social structures did not necessarily benefit women and therefore reinforced gender inequality.

Positive change in agriculture may occur most easily when change strategies align with familiar social structures, while simultaneously challenging negative ones. In other words, if concrete strategies for empowering women in agriculture correspond with existing social ideologies, routines, and norms that are *not* problematic from an equality or sustainability perspective, these strategies may be sufficiently accepted to move forward and challenge ones that *are* problematic. Several chapters discuss the importance of aligning interventions with the work women already do. For example, Moraes and Rocha (Chapter 12) illustrate how successful food procurement policies allow women to benefit economically from goods they already produce. However, the chapter also shows the other side of this relation: programs that required women to establish new organizations, which did not already exist and required additional time and effort to create, were not as successful as programs that drew on existing social networks and resources.

The issue of gradual, culturally safe change also raises the question of including men in women's projects. I have discussed the importance of looking within and beyond the household to examine gender inequalities. At the same time, many of these chapters remind us that most farm women are still part of agricultural households – households that often include men, and which are deeply intertwined with the farm operation and the community at large. Overly individualized approaches may negatively affect women's position in the family, the farm, and the community, rendering these approaches unsustainable.

Small adjustments to existing roles in family-based agriculture may also benefit men. In Chapter 13, Crawford-Garrett et al. describe household discussions in which gender equality was seen as economically beneficial for the entire household. In this way, a household-level focus can be strategically used to advance gender equality. Such approaches acknowledge "the relational character of gender" and avoid the overly simplistic treatment of women and men as "different market segments for some service" (Connell 2005, 1806).

Involvement of men may actually facilitate modifications more quickly by reducing resistance or mitigating undesirable fall-out that can occur from rapid change (e.g., violence against women). I recall here Talpade Mohanty's (1988) well-known admonition that women's inequality is the product of material and ideological structures and systems of power, not individual men-as-oppressors. Men can participate in women's empowerment in agriculture; indeed, in Chapter 8, Rengalakshmi Raj et al. found that involving men in the garden initiative eventually led to men's participation in work initially stereo-typed as "women's work."

These chapters illustrate that practical approaches to pressing issues have the power to transform gender relations over the longer term. Most of the chapters in this book do not advocate rapid and revolutionary change; rather, they offer concrete steps for provoking transformation through small inter-ventions that still benefit people's everyday lives. Often, so much emphasis is placed on major and rapid transformation that we forget the powerful poten-tial of micro-level and gradual change. Our goal in this book has been to collect important change strategies from diverse contexts around the world.

Global change, gendered solutions

Despite our emphasis on concrete, contextualized approaches, our book is situated on a global scale. Agriculture itself is increasingly globalized. Producers in many countries now operate within neoliberal policy paradigms that emphasize liberalized trade, privatization, and declining state support for food production (Lawrence, Richards, and Lyons 2013). Writing from my own location in Canada, I see how agriculture has increasingly shifted toward a large-scale, intensified model of production. New seed varieties produced by private companies promise climate resistance and high yields (especially when paired with particular agri-chemicals), yet these inputs can dramatically increase farmers' production costs (Fletcher 2013). Farms are growing larger and more mechanized as family farmers struggle to achieve economies of scale (Magnan 2012), and small-scale farmers are pushed out. The neoliberal political-economic context is creating new challenges for family farmers around the world.

Women worldwide are playing important roles in resistance movements to challenge the negative impacts of globalization and neoliberal policy. Working within and leading peasant movements like La Vía Campesina (Desmarais 2007) – a movement guided by principles of gender parity and equality (Martínez-Torres and Rosset 2010) – women are pushing for impor-tant causes like environmental sustainability and food sovereignty (Desmarais, Wittman, and Wiebe 2010). They are challenging the power of international governing bodies and corporations to shape the current state of agriculture, and in doing so, are demonstrating the power of collective agency for social change (Patel 2012a). A discussion about the important work of these organi-zations, and of women within them, could fill volumes of its own. Although our book has focused primarily on individual, household, and community level interventions, it is nonetheless important to recognize the important collective work being done by transnational grassroots organizations.

Several chapters in this volume do bring a gender analysis to macro-level political-economic changes. In Chapter 1, Clarke and Alston illustrate how agricultural restructuring in Australia has intensified the masculinization of farming, and Chapter 2 documents similar structural changes affecting women's work in Canadian agriculture. Neoliberal restructuring is often presented as a gender-neutral economic phenomenon; however, it is increasingly important to recognize the social and gendered impacts of structural adjustment in topic areas that, like agriculture, are more likely to be viewed through an economic than a social lens.

By applying a gender lens, the chapters in this volume explicitly acknowledge the everyday lives of agricultural producers, moving away from the neoliberal-individualist or *homo economicus* understanding of "producers" as solely economic actors. The authors challenge this dominant discourse by refocusing on farmers' humanity, their experiences, and their needs. It is through this social and gender lens that we can challenge the lived impacts of the neoliberal agricultural paradigm currently dominant in so many countries around the world.

Gender analysis can reveal much more than gender inequality. Some authors' gender analyses expose problems in agriculture more broadly – problems like institutionalized racism and human rights violations (Chapter 3), economic problems, and sustainability concerns. The solutions are also broadly applicable. As the chapters by Vent, Sabarmatee, and Uphoff (Chapter 4) and Vasseur (Chapter 7) show, technological advancement is not the sole domain of industrialized agriculture or large biotechnology corporations. Rather, relatively minor changes in methods of planting or fertilizing crops can reduce the use of agro-chemicals while empowering women and even improving their physical health. In Chapter 14, women in the Moroccan strawberry industry used international food chains strategically, convincing importers to support better working conditions in the strawberry fields. In Brazil (Chapter 12), domestic food procurement policies (designed with a gender lens) have resulted in more managed and localized food chains, thus challenging the dominant discourse that deregulation and liberalized food trade is the only way to feed a population. Simiarly, Meinzen-Dick et al. (2012) have also discussed the importance of a gender focus in policies that connect smallholders with markets; this insight can be pushed further to invigorate local, domestic markets instead of international ones.

The ideas in this book allow us to think outside of our localized contexts, to gain new ideas from innovations occurring around the world and bring those ideas home. In an international context, discussions about agricultural solutions often present these solutions as one-way transfer of beneficial knowledge and good ideas from the global North to the global South. Our goal in this book is to show how solutions from low- and middle-income countries can inform agricultural policy and practice in the North, as well as vice-versa.

In the next section, I highlight and summarize the important solutions offered throughout this book.

Practical solutions for women in agriculture

Visibility and data

Invisibility and lack of recognition for women's contributions is a longstanding problem in agriculture. Early feminist research on farm women sought to address this problem by documenting women's activities and the structural conditions affecting their work (e.g., Boserup 1970; Ireland 1983; Sachs 1983; Gasson 1992; Rosenfeld 1985; Shaver 1991). In our introduction to this volume, we noted the rapid pace of change in agriculture, which has prompted further information needs. Several chapters in this volume expose the ongoing invisibility problem associated with insufficient data collection: in Australia (Chapter 1), Brazil (Chapter 12), and Canada (Chapter 2), national data collection efforts fail to capture the diverse ways women contribute to agricultural economies, rendering these contributions invisible. As Alston and Whittenbury show in Chapter 5, women's invisibility is a barrier to necessary agricultural infrastructure and services. Significant efforts have been made recently to establish indicators and indices for data collection on women in agriculture (Alkire et al. 2013). These indicators can usefully inform data collection efforts by national governments and international organizations. These chapters collectively show the importance of such data collection tools and indicators created through a gender lens.

Policy and gender mainstreaming

Sex-disaggregated data is a crucial input for effective policymaking. Policy, in turn, is a crucial macro-level intervention to address gender inequality. Several chapters here indicate the need for gender mainstreaming (GM) in agricultural policy (see Chapters 1 and 5, for example). In light of strong international support for GM since the Fourth World Conference on Women in 1995, the approach holds promise if integrated effectively and properly into agricultural policy at domestic and international levels. GM in agricultural policy is important considering that agricultural policy is often portrayed as "gender neutral" in contrast to policy areas that are more readily "gendered," such as social policy.

Unfortunately, feminist political economists have documented a steady erosion of gender-based policy analysis in an era of neoliberal individualism. Paradoxically, as neoliberal policy changes have intensified inequality, the discourse that "we are all equal now" (Brodie 2008) has resulted in the erosion of gender as a legitimate basis for policy analysis (Bakker 2007). Despite these challenges, this book suggests that GM is an important approach for addressing gender issues in agriculture.

At the same time, some important caveats can be raised regarding GM. Carter et al. (Chapter 15) caution that GM can sometimes result in the erasure of women in favor of a more diluted and generalized gender focus. In some countries the "mainstreaming" of gender across government has been used as a pretext to dismantle policy machinery for gender analysis (Hankivsky 2008; Alston 2014). Shortall (2014) discussed how GM in European Union rural policy has been problematically based on a static essentialist category "rural women". New research suggests that GM should shift toward more intersectional policy analysis that considers how race, class, geopolitical location, and other axes of power and privilege intersect with gender (Hankivsky and Cormier 2011). It is possible that this type of highly contextualized and intersectional analysis will help identify issues affecting women in rural and agricultural contexts – as well as highlighting important differences between them – so long as its complexity does not provoke a retreat from equality-focused policy analysis altogether.

These issues indicate the overarching importance of *intentionality* in policy design. Many of the policies and programs described in this book were intentionally designed to include, benefit, and empower women in agriculture. From intentional inclusion of women in food procurement programs (Chapters 12 and 13) to intersectional analysis of how we can change legal frameworks that currently facilitate racist and sexist oppression (Chapter 3), an intentional focus on gender equality in policy is necessary.

Social capital and sustainability

Beyond the formal policy sphere, informal social networks and social capital are important structural supports for women in agriculture (see Chapters 10 and 11). Rural social infrastructures are being affected by the industrialization of agriculture (see Chapters 1, 2, and 5). In North America, farms have grown larger, neighbors have grown apart, and rural communities are being lost. In South Asia, families and communities are affected as loved ones migrate away for paid employment. Past experience shows that the uncritical export of industrial, "Green Revolution" technologies from their headquarters in rich countries has had damaging impacts on social sustainability in the global South (Sweetman 1999; Patel 2012b).

In contrast, carefully designed policies and programs can help to build social capital and sustainable agricultural communities. Social capital can reduce vulnerability and help actors adapt to adverse conditions – whether political, economic, or climatic. In Chapter 14, for example, Théroux-Séguin describes how women workers in the Moroccan strawberry sector rely on each other for safety and to avoid charges of "dishonor." But, social capital can go beyond reducing vulnerability. Adler and Kwon (2002, 17) described social capital as "the goodwill that is engendered by the fabric of social relations and that can be *mobilized to facilitate action*" (emphasis added). Social capital can facilitate sustainable structural change over the longer term. The educational programs described in Chapters 15 and 16 illustrate that farmer-to-farmer programs are useful not only for increasing women's involvement in agriculture generally, but also for positioning young female farmers as leaders in more environmentally and socially sustainable forms of agriculture. Chapter 14 shows us that formal organizations can play a role in supporting these endeavors, but that to be sustainable, change must be led by women, families, and communities themselves.

Intersectionality: a future focus

This book has examined key issues affecting women in agriculture with an emphasis on practical approaches for addressing these issues. The chapters show that ongoing gender ideologies and material inequalities continue to disadvantage women in the agricultural sector, but that differences like geopolitical location have a major impact on women's experiences and daily lives. Life is very different for a female subsistence farmer in Zimbabwe, who grows food for her family's consumption on a small plot of land, than for a farm woman in Canada who relies on store-bought food to cook large meals for hired workers on a 20,000-acre industrialized farm. Although both lives are shaped by gender in distinct ways, other axes of social difference and privilege are important. Through this book, our main entry point into the discussion is the intersection of gender and geopolitical location; accordingly, the chapters in this book examine a common topic but in very different geopolitical contexts. Yet, a number of chapters go even further in showing how "women" is a diverse and heterogenous social category. Although gendered inequality is very real, other social systems of power and oppression intersect with gender, creating very different experiences *between* those in the social category "women" (Crenshaw 1991). Our focus on context, then, necessarily leads to intersectional insights. Writing from South Africa, Vettori (Chapter 3) documents how histories of racial segregation, exploitation, and dispossession have led to ongoing oppression of people of color, who are disproportionately represented as farm workers and not farm owners. Vettori shows how race-based and gender-based oppressions intersect to create specific conditions of marginalization and exploitation for female farm workers of color. These women's experiences are different than the experiences of *male* farm workers of color, and are also very different from the experiences of *white* female farm owners.

In their chapter on urban agriculture (Chapter 6), Chiweshe and Muzanago question the idea that potato sack farming is primarily a practice of the poor. Examining the practice at the intersection of gender and class, the authors draw attention to the potential exclusion of poor women from potato farming due to the cost of inputs. In Chapter 4, authors Vent, Sabarmatee, and Uphoff note that although mechanized weeding can reduce physical impact on female rice farmers, mechanization has also resulted in loss of jobs for Dalit women.

It is crucial, then, to examine the broader implications of any intervention for different groups of people, particularly the most marginalized. The best solutions are those that empower women while reducing their time-poverty and stress, are culturally sensitive and done with the participation and support of men and communities broadly, and which do not cause ripple effects of hardship elsewhere. These issues are made visible through an intersectionality lens. An intersectionality focus, then, is necessary for future research on women in agriculture.

What principles should guide the future research and action agenda for women in agriculture? This international team of authors has shown that powerful change potential can be found in everyday life. They show that gradual change can be powerful. The common themes across their contributions – visibility and data; policy and gender mainstreaming; social capital and sustainability; and intersectionality – are avenues for linking the insights of everyday experience with broader social, political, and economic structures. Increased visibility and recognition of women's contributions to agriculture, including their contributions to agricultural households and social capital in agricultural communities, is crucial to build more effective (gender-aware) solutions. Effective solutions require recognition of both the diversity and agency of women in agriculture. Women are the key to the sustainability and the security of agriculture around the world. By recognizing and integrating the knowledge of women farmers from around the globe we can ensure that food production is healthy, sustainable, and available to all.

References

Adler, Paul S., and Seok-Woo Kwon. 2002. "Social Capital: Prospects for a New Concept." *Academy of Management Review* 27 (1): 17–40.

Alkire, Sabina, Ruth Meinzen-Dick, Amber Peterman, Agnes Quisumbing, Greg Seymour, and Ana Vaz. 2013. "The Women's Empowerment in Agriculture Index." *World Development* 52: 71–91. doi:10.1016/j.worlddev.2013.06.007.

Alston, Margaret. 2014. "Gender Mainstreaming and Climate Change." *Women's Studies International Forum* 47 (November): 287–94. doi:10.1016/j.wsif.2013.01.016.

Apter, Terri, and Elizabeth Garnsey. 1994. "Enacting Inequality: Structure, Agency, and Gender." *Women's Studies International Forum* 17 (1): 19–31.

Archer, Margaret S. 2010. "Morphogenesis versus Structuration: On Combining Structure and Action." *The British Journal of Sociology* 61: 225–52. doi:10.1111/j.1468-4446.2009.01245.x.

Bakker, Isabella. 2007. "Social Reproduction and the Constitution of a Gendered Political Economy." *New Political Economy* 12 (4): 541–56. doi:10.1080/135634 60701661561.

Bakker, Isabella, and Stephen Gill. 2008. "New Constitutionalism and Social Reproduction." In *Beyond States and Markets: The Challenges of Social Reproduction*, edited by Isabella Bakker and Rachel Silvey, 19–33. RIPE Series in Global Political Economy. New York, N.Y.: Routledge.

Boserup, Ester. 1970. *Woman's Role in Economic Development*. Crows Nest, NSW: Allen & Unwin.

Brodie, Janine. 2008. "We Are All Equal Now: Contemporary Gender Politics in Canada." *Feminist Theory* 9 (2): 145–64. doi:10.1177/1464700108090408.

Campbell, Jacquelyn C., Daniel Webster, Jane Koziol-McLain, Carolyn Block, Doris Campbell, Mary Ann Curry, Faye Gary, et al. 2003. "Risk Factors for Femicide in Abusive Relationships: Results From a Multisite Case Control Study." *American Journal of Public Health* 93 (7): 1089–97.

Carr, Edward R. 2008. "Between Structure and Agency: Livelihoods and Adaptation in Ghana's Central Region." *Global Environmental Change* 18 (4): 689–99. doi:10.1016/j.gloenvcha.2008.06.004.

Connell, R. W. 2005. "Change Among the Gatekeepers: Men, Masculinities, and Gender Equality in the Global Arena." *Signs: Journal of Women in Culture and Society* 30 (3): 1801–25. doi:10.1086/427525.

Crenshaw, Kimberle. 1991. "Mapping the Margins: Intersectionality, Identity Politics, and Violence against Women of Color." *Stanford Law Review* 43 (6): 1241. doi:10.2307/1229039.

Desmarais, Annette Aurelie. 2007. *La Vía Campesina: Globalization and the Power of Peasants*. Halifax, NS: Fernwood.

Desmarais, Annette Aurelie, Hannah Wittman, and Nettie Wiebe. 2010. *Food Sovereignty: Reconnecting Food, Nature & Community*. Halifax, N.S.: Fernwood.

Fletcher, Amber J. 2013. "The View From Here: Agricultural Policy, Climate Change, and the Future of Farm Women in Saskatchewan." Regina, SK: University of Regina.

Food and Agriculture Organization of the United Nations. 2014. *The State of Food and Agriculture 2014: Innovation in Family Farming*. Rome: Food and Agriculture Organization of the United Nations.

Gasson, Ruth. 1992. "Farmers' Wives – Their Contribution to the Farm Business." *Journal of Agricultural Economics* 43 (1): 74–87.

Hankivsky, Olena. 2008. "Gender Mainstreaming in Canada and Australia: A Comparative Analysis." *Policy and Society* 27 (1): 69–81. doi:10.1016/j.polsoc.2008.07.006.

Hankivsky, Olena, and Renee Cormier. 2011. "Intersectionality and Public Policy: Some Lessons from Existing Models." *Political Research Quarterly* 64 (1): 217–29. doi:10.1177/1065912910376385.

Heath, Rachel. 2014. "Women's Access to Labor Market Opportunities, Control of Household Resources, and Domestic Violence: Evidence from Bangladesh." *World Development* 57: 32–46.

Holvoet, Nathalie. 2004. "Impact of Microfinance Programs on Children's Education: Do the Gender of the Borrower and the Delivery Model Matter?" *Journal of Microfinance/ESR Review* 6 (2): 27–50.

Ireland, Gisele. 1983. *The Farmer Takes a Wife*. Chesley, ON: Concerned Farm Women.

Jewkes, Rachel. 2002. "Intimate Partner Violence: Causes and Prevention." *The Lancet* 359: 1423–29.

Lawrence, Geoffrey, Carol Richards, and Kristen Lyons. 2013. "Food Security in Australia in an Era of Neoliberalism, Productivism and Climate Change." *Journal of Rural Studies*, Food Security, 29: 30–39. doi:10.1016/j.jrurstud.2011.12.005.

Magnan, André. 2012. "New Avenues of Farm Corporatization in the Prairie Grains Sector: Farm Family Entrepreneurs and the Case of One Earth Farms." *Agriculture and Human Values* 29 (2): 161–75.

Mahoney, James, and Kathleen Thelen. 2010. "A Theory of Gradual Institutional Change." In *Explaining Institutional Change: Ambiguity, Agency, and Power,* edited by James Mahoney and Kathleen Thelen, 1–37. New York: Cambridge University Press.

Martínez-Torres, María Elena, and Peter M. Rosset. 2010. "La Vía Campesina: The Birth and Evolution of a Transnational Social Movement." *Journal of Peasant Studies* 37 (1): 149–75. doi:10.1080/03066150903498804.

Meinzen-Dick, Ruth, Julia Behrman, Purnima Menon, and Agnes Quisumbing. 2012. "Gender: A Key Dimension Linking Agricultural Programs to Improved Nutrition and Health." In *Reshaping Agriculture for Nutrition and Health*, edited by Shenggen Fan and Rajul Pandya-Lorch, 135–44. Washington, DC: International Food Policy Research Institute.

Mohanty, Chandra Talpade. 1988. "Under Western Eyes: Feminist Scholarship and Colonial Discourses." *Feminist Review* 30: 61–88.

Nader, Yasmine F. 2008. "Microcredit and the Socio-Economic Wellbeing of Women and Their Families in Cairo." *The Journal of Socio-Economics* 37 (2): 644–56. doi:10.1016/j.socec.2007.10.008.

Patel, Raj. 2012a. "Food Sovereignty: Power, Gender, and the Right to Food." *PLoS Med* 9 (6): e1001223. doi:10.1371/journal.pmed.1001223.

———. 2012b. *Stuffed and Starved: The Hidden Battle for the World Food System*. 2nd ed. Brooklyn: Melville House.

Rocca, Corinne H., Sujit Rathod, Tina Falle, Rohini P. Pande, and Suneeta Krishnan. 2009. "Challenging Assumptions about Women's Empowerment: Social and Economic Resources and Domestic Violence among Young Married Women in Urban South India." *International Journal of Epidemiology* 38 (2): 577–85. doi:10.1093/ije/dyn226.

Rosenfeld, Rachel. 1985. *Farm Women: Work, Farm, and Family in the United States*. Chapel Hill: University of North Carolina Press.

Sachs, Carolyn E. 1983. *The Invisible Farmers: Women in Agricultural Production*. Totowa: Rowman & Allanheld.

Shaver, Frances. 1991. "Women, Work and the Evolution of Agriculture." *Journal of Rural Studies* 7 (1–2): 37–42.

Shortall, Sally. 2014. "Gender Mainstreaming or Strategic Essentialism?: How to Achieve Rural Gender Equality." In *Feminisms and Ruralities*, edited by Barbara Pini, Berit Brandth, and Jo Little, 69–80. Lanham, MD: Lexington Books.

Sweetman, Caroline. 1999. "Editorial." In *Women, Land and Agriculture*, edited by Caroline Sweetman, 2–8. Oxford, UK: Oxfam.

Index

For Product Safety Concerns and Information please contact our EU
representative GPSR@taylorandfrancis.com Taylor & Francis Verlag GmbH,
Kaufingerstraße 24, 80331 München, Germany

Printed and bound by CPI Group (UK) Ltd, Croydon, CR0 4YY

01/05/2025

01858357-0003